Last in the List

Last in the List –

The Life and Times of an English Barrister

by Eric Crowther, O.B.E.
West London Stipendiary Magistrate

Basset Publications
Plymouth

Published April 1988

No part of this publication may be reproduced, stored in a retrieval system or transmitted, in any form or by any means, electronic, mechanical, photocopying, recording or otherwise, without the prior permission in writing of Basset Publications.

ISBN 0 946873 11 9

Published by Basset Publications, North Hill, Plymouth

Printed by The Western Litho Company of Plymouth

Foreword

I was brought up in a legal household. My grandfather was a solicitor and my father a QC and then a High Court Judge. He had a great sense of humour and his children much enjoyed his legal stories.

Eric Crowther has shown an equal ability in this book. He is also to be congratulated on his criticisms (not many) of some members of the Judiciary.

He and I were opponents (in a very friendly way) for nearly 20 years after we first met at Ipswich Quarter Sessions. He has shown in this book the sense of humour and commonsense which made him so successful at the Bar.

Michael Havers

Contents

Introduction

I started off my first (and, so far, my only other) book by quoting a Chinese philosopher who said that there were three things that a man had to do in his life: to have a son, to write a book, and to plant a tree. I remarked that on writing "Advocacy for the Advocate" I had achieved two goals out of three; but I hardly expected ever to complete the hat-trick.

At the beginning of August 1987 I received a most pressing invitation from a schoolmaster and a Justice of the Peace, Bernard Widdowson, to attend a party at his home in Cumbria: "You will come, won't you?" he urged: "It's most important". I could not understand why he was so insistent on my presence, until, upon my arrival, I found him with a small tree for me to plant. I did it, but frankly I don't want to plant any more trees. It was too much like hard work: in fact it **was** hard work! I only hope that my little incompetently planted tree survived the dreadful gales of the following October.

But if I am averse to hard work, – and I am, – why write another book? I cannot always quote my sources – a bad fault in a lawyer (I did not and do not remember the name of the Chinese philosopher) – but someone else said that one has to be an odd or eccentric person to want to write one's autobiography, and probably I am an odd person. But let me tell you how it came about. "Advocacy for the Advocate" had a modest success – more than either Barry Rose, the publisher, or I had expected; so, one day, Barry came to me and asked: "Why don't you write another book? I'll publish it if it is as good as the last one. What subject interests you most?" I paused a moment. "Well, me, actually". I eventually replied with candour, if not with too much honesty.

"Then write about yourself", said Barry encouragingly.

"You've led quite an interesting life".

I was not too pleased about the use of the perfect tense, but agreed with the proposition.

Part of the book having been written, Barry wrote to me a few months later a letter that began:

"Dear Eric,

"This is going to come as something of a shock to you . . ."

and he went on to say how he had sold the book side of his publishing interests (though not the "Justice of the Peace") to a firm called Kluwer based in Holland, and that Kluwer was not in the least interested in my autobiography. Barry, being Barry, offered to compensate me for the work I had already done; but one does not quantify in monetary terms the effort that one makes on behalf of one's friends.

During the ensuing stage of despondency I ran a course called "Crime and the Citizen" at the Earnley Concourse near Chichester. One of the "students" was a highly successful writer of detective novels who was most sympathetic to my problem. "I'll put you in touch with my publishing agent", she promised.

My advice to any would-be writer, based on a single experience of one publisher's agent, is to avoid them like the plague. If I may presume to paraphrase Bunyan's famous hymn (which we sang in the standard version at my wedding):-

"There's all discouragement
To make him at one relent
His first avowed intent
To be an author".

The typing, by various lady-friends who had worked hard for me, was below the required standard and badly spaced; the pagination was all wrong; the three chapters about life (if that be the right word) in the British Council, and the subsequent chapter on "Dotheboys Hall", would hold not the slightest interest for lawyers and very little for the general public and should be deleted, and the book bristled with libels. (I as a lawyer must appreciate that an action lay to the personal representatives of a deceased person against whom derogatory remarks were made). Such were the strictures of the publishers' agent. If I would cut out those four chapters in the middle and delete the spicy bits he would be pleased to try to find a publisher – for an uninteresting book, omitting a vitally important element in my life.

Disconsolate once again, I turned for advice to my old friend Cliff Moiser, the ebullient and ever-entertaining Clerk to the Plymouth Justices.

"My son's in publishing", said Cliff: "Send it down to Chris and if he likes it, he'll publish it".

Chris Moiser provided no trouble, no hassle. He agreed with the agent that the British Council chapters and that on the strange educational establishment in Suffolk might not be of much interest to readers from the legal profession, but he added: "However, they are a part of your life, and your autobiography would be incomplete without them, so warn the "legal reader" in the preface that he may wish to skip from the end of Chapter Three to the beginning of Chapter Seven. Those who work or have worked for the British Council will probably only want to read Chapters Four to Six, anyway!"

So I promised to do this, which is the main reason for my writing this preface.

As to the suggestion regarding possible libels, Chris, coming from a legal background, shared my view on the law. You do not libel anyone civilly when you tell the truth about him, and all that I have said in the book is true – "to the best of my knowledge and belief"; I have added that very legal caveat because most of what I have written relates to what happened twenty or more years ago, and memory can play tricks.

I am writing this preface in the West Indies, where, to my great joy I met again, after thirty-six years, my good friend from student days Allan Rae, the great West Indian cricketer. I showed him Chapter 2, relating to the case of *Rex v. the Equity Examiners,* and invited his comments on it. It was, he said, completely accurate, except that according to his recollection the Judge, Mr. Cleveland Stevens, K.C., simply said *"Curia ad vult"* – "The Court will advise" – before getting up and walking out of the amazed Old Hall. Allan could be right, although it makes no difference to the final result – and the *"Curia"* never in fact *"vulted"*. Megarry and Kahn won, but the Examiners had a Pyrrhic victory. The maxim: "The greater the truth the greater the libel" applies to criminal libel prosecutions, of which there have been only about a couple this century. I doubt if this book would merit a third, as it is unlikely to provoke a breach of the peace!

I believe that the maxim *"actio personalis moritur cum persona"* –

a personal action dies with the person – still obtains as a principle of our law. Possibly it should not, but I think it does. However, the object of this book is not to hurt anyone. We are all as God made us, although one has to be more full of Christian charity than I am to see everyone as fashioned in God's image. In common, I suspect, with the experience of most people, there have been those whom I have met whom I have like immensely, and others whom I have disliked intensely. I see no reason to water down these sentiments if I am to write a truthful book. But whereas people whom I have liked and to whom I have reason to be grateful – people like M.A.S.A. Kahn who Allan Rae told me, to my great sorrow, is dead, and Robert, my second clerk, and "V", are referred to by their true identities, I have adopted pseudonyms for those I disliked or who seemed determined to hold me back in my career. Will Byford was not Will Byford; Mr. Strong was certainly not Strong – both these characters so far as I am aware are still alive and can challenge what I say if they choose to reveal themselves, but there is another useful legal maxim: *"Volenti non fit injuria"*, which is apposite but difficult briefly to translate. "Roy" my first clerk was not called Roy and he died young, leaving a charming and extremely kind wife: I should not like her to be needlessly hurt by what I say concerning her late (in every sense of the word) husband.

The sole exception to the "pseudonymity rule" lies with the lawyers. Barristers, and especially Judges, have got to be tough, and, by tradition, they do not complain of what is said of them. As a magistrate I have had hurtful things said about me without, in my opinion, any justification by reporters (or more likely sub-editors) wishing, in the interest of sensationalism, to stir up trouble over my decisions, in "The Sun", "The Sunday Express", "The News on Sunday", "The Law Society Gazette" and even on BBC 2 Television; but I have learned to accept this as a hazard of minor judicial office. What as a barrister I found unforgivable in Judges or magistrates was bullying, boorishness, intolerance, impatience, undue fussiness and especially inhumanity. This last quality was evident to me in Judge Mervyn Griffith-Jones, who is dead, and in Mr. Justice Gerald Thesiger, of whose present whereabouts – in this world or one of the next – I am uncertain. But I draw comfort from the fact that nothing that I have said about those two distinguished (in the bad sense) former Judges is as harsh as the criticisms by that great Judge Lord Devlin of the former and late Attorney-General, Sir Reginald Manningham-Buller, Q.C., (to whose "parody name" of "Sir Bullying-Manner" he calls attention) in his recently-published book on the trial of Dr. Bodkin Adams, "Easing the Passing". The main difference is that I have criticised those before whom I appeared; Lord Devlin castigated one who appeared before him (and who subsequently was made Lord Chancellor).

The Bar is a fair profession and if others found Thesiger (who was a good Judge in civil cases) or Griffith-Jones (who probably never did a civil case in his life) understanding and merciful when dealing with those who had transgressed the criminal law they will, I am sure, rush forward to say so and be heard with respect. But the Judges themselves, like Her Majesty the Queen whom they represent, submit uncomplainingly to

"the whips and scorns of time,
The oppressor's wrong, the proud man's contumely . . .
The law's delays, the insolence of office,
And the spurns that patient merit of the unworthy takes."
Tradition makes them bear their fardels quietly.

Can there be any other motive except odd eccentricity and self-aggrandisement for writing one's autobiography? I would like to think that in my case there is. I started out poor. My mother, who had received nothing but debts under my father's intestacy, left me £25 under her will, proved a few days before my Call to the Bar. This sum represented my total savings in 1951. When I came into the legal profession, I knew no-one in it. Many (very many as it seemed) years later I was a reasonably successful barrister and was to achieve my life-long ambition of becoming a Metropolitan Stipendiary Magistrate, and now I know nearly everyone at the London Bar and on the Bench. If the recital of those simple facts gives encouragement to carry on to any young man or woman about to embark on a career in the law – and recently I met a miner rendered redundant by the antics of Arthur Scargill who is just taking up the legal profession (the redundant miner I mean; not, I am glad to say, Arthur Scargill) – that will be worth infinitely more than the amour propre derived from the publication of this first part of my autobiography. Let such young people take courage from the words to me of a bus inspector friend in those early days when everything seemed to be going

wrong and I was particularly depressed:
"Always keep a stout heart".

They may derive even more succour from the story of Gandee, who made the portrait of me that appears at the beginning of this book (an extremely flattering one, my none too flattering friends insist). I first met Gandee in Malaysia in 1977, when he was thirteen years old, and accompanying his father Krishnan Vaikunthavasan – an ex-British Council student, then a magistrate in Zambia – to the Commonwealth Magistrates' Association Conference in Kuala Lumpur. Gandee had just taken up painting, and Krishnan asked me to try to persuade Lord Denning, who was attending the conference, to sit for a portrait by Gandee. In this I succeeded, but the portrait itself was not an unqualified success. Executed in a hurry, the paint was still wet when it was handed over to the Master of the Rolls at the Farewell Dinner, and Lord Denning's hands got smeared with it. Gandee had tried to put too much into the picture, and Joan, the subject's wife, commented: "I'm glad the artist managed to squeeze Tom's head in". But Lord Denning accepted it graciously and said that it would hang on the wall of his flat in Lincoln's Inn, and it was then left to me to persuade a reluctant British Council representative to package and despatch this curious picture; reluctant because, as he put it: "I don't think this portrait would ever have been commissioned by our Fine Arts Department."

But a few years later Gandee was in London to pursue his artistic talent. When Harold MacMillan was approaching his ninetieth birthday a City Livery Company asked him if he would sit for a portrait to mark this great occasion. The former Prime Minister agreed, subject to two conditions:- the artist must be under thirty and must never have had a picture hung in a public exhibition. The Livery Company announced a competition, for which Gandee entered. What the Company thought were the hundred best entries were hung in a gallery in Piccadilly and it was Gandee's that was chosen by the selectors. In due course he was making visits to MacMillan's country home to complete the portrait, which I saw in Gandee's little garret in Paddington a week before the official presentation. This was made to MacMillan by the Duke of Edinburgh and a memorable photograph appeared next day in "The Times" of Prince Philip shaking hands with Gandee, the artist.

Now I was never a great admirer of Supermac as a politician. I thought that his slogan to the British people: "You've never had it so good", lacked correct syntax and savoured of materialism. Butler would, in my view at the time of Suez, have been a better choice by the Queen for Prime Minister. But Mac's two "conditions" made me take a different view of the man. We all know the extent to which the young can and do help the old – more so perhaps in Eastern countries than in our "civilised" Western society – but how marvellous it is when a nonagenarian, without much longer to live, ensures that an unknown young artist achieves well-deserved fame. Old and Young can indeed help each other.

Mac was, after all, Super!

Chapter 1

The Bishop and The Sister

They come in all shapes and sizes: tall ones, short ones; thin ones, fat ones; black ones, white ones; young and old, they come tumbling out of the tube at the Temple around ten in the morning. The only similarity lies in their dress. Some wear the uniform of black jacket, waistcoat and pinstripe trousers, while the more daring sport a dark double-breasted suit concealing the lack of a waistcoat. Many wear bowler hats and carry rolled umbrellas, even on hot, fine days. And in August and September almost all change into light-coloured suits, for, during the vacation, unconventionality is the convention.

But there is no prototype of the British barrister. The stage image of him or her is for the most part inaccurate. Rumpole on television comes nearer the mark, a sort of cross between his creator, John Mortimer, and a taxi-driver who had sued for damages in the High Court following personal injuries in an accident, and been so impressed with his first experience of legal proceedings that with his spoils he studied law in middle age and the Middle Temple and became an advocate, and a good one at that. It would be difficult for him to do so now. When he (and I) studied for the Bar all that one had to do was to attend some rather tedious lectures, pass some fairly easy examinations (and those in Part I could be taken one at a time) and eat one's way through seventy-two rather unappetising but fortunately very cheap dinners in three years. Without any practice in public speaking one could become – a barrister! But now the aspiring advocate has to go to University and obtain a very good degree (not necessarily in law) before he or she can be admitted to the Inns of Court, to the exclusion of many like the taxi-driver – and me.

Another misconception about the profession is that admission to it is the prerogative of the privileged rich and that on Call to the Bar one enters an Ivory Tower (or Temple) remote from ordinary folk. This is not so. Many barristers come from humble backgrounds. My parents were poor, but my father was the most honest man I have ever met. I got a scholarship from my state school ("Council School" as it was called in those days) to University College School in Hampstead, but the local authority insisted that parents of scholarship boys paid a contribution to the school fees, based on the father's earnings. The fees themselves were £39 a year, and my parents' annual contribution was assessed at twenty-five shillings (£1.25) but unfortunately they were too impecunious to pay that sum, and eventually they were told that I was not to return next day to the school where I was so happy. My mother – always good in a crisis – took me that night to the cinema (sixpence each) to console me. I am not sure that her choice of films was wise, though. They were called "The Ghost Goes West" and "The Last Journey".

Then a miracle happened. My father's boss at that time was a brusque ex-Army officer, Colonel Bartram. Next morning, while I remained away from school, he enquired of my father: "You look very depressed this morning, Crowther. What's the matter?" My father told him, and the Colonel opened his wallet and gave my father a large white five pound note, saying: "There, that will keep the boy at school for another four years". The following day I returned to U.C.S.

I was ten when I got my scholarship and the second youngest boy ever to go to the senior branch of U.C.S. My only close relative apart from my parents was my sister, twelve years older than I. She got a crush on the Bishop of Willesden, Dr Guy Vernon-Smith. This does rather date me, doesn't it? What girl in her early twenties gets a crush on the clergy now? – on a pop star or football player or television idol perhaps, but the young cleric is safe. When the good Bishop, who fortunately was a bachelor, was translated to the Diocese of Leicester my sister wrote to him a valedictory letter couched in modestly adulatory terms. He responded with an invitation to tea. My parents for some reason thought it right that I should go along as an unwilling and inappropriate chaperon.

"And what are you going to be when you grow up, little boy?" the Bishop asked, with a condescending pat on the head. Without hesitation I replied "I'm going to be a metropolitan stipendiary magistrate." All three persons present – the Bishop, my sister and myself – were astonished, for I had revealed this secret ambition to no-one before. On reflection I think it derived from a rather mundane source. My father always worked very hard and at that time got home at about nine o'clock at night. We had no radio – and certainly no television – so we awaited eagerly his arrival with the London "Evening News". For my part I turned immediately to James A Jones's entertaining and graphic nightly column "Courts Day by Day" to see how "Old Vera" was progressing in her determination to drink London dry. Unlike present-day columnists James A Jones was never malicious but always warm and kind –and very humorous. The London beaks of those days he really brought to life in our sitting-room: the leonine Sir Laurence Dunne sadly shaking his mane; the enigmatic and taciturn little figure of Harold McKenna; John Brown Sandbach, the country squire of Marlborough Street, beloved of the barrow boys who gave him an inscribed gold watch on retirement; and the genial and smiling Daniel Hopkin, father of the present Chief Magistrate. Yes I wanted to be one of these. There were only twenty-eight of them in those days (now that figure has almost doubled) but I had to be of their number.

But there was one slight obstacle: I would have to get Called to the Bar and practise there for a couple of decades before I could be considered for this most human of all legal appointments. With this my mother helped a lot. My father had died during my last week at school. The war was on, and for nearly three years he had worked fourteen hours a day, six days a week, in a factory. The job started at 6.30 a.m. and he had to travel by a bus and two trolley-buses to get there, leaving home at 5.00 a.m. and usually returning after 10.00 p.m. He was sixty-five and it was too much for him and suddenly he succumbed to a heart attack. The Headmaster called me out of class and told me to go home. It was my first experience of the death of someone really near and dear to me, and it was terrible. The breadwinner of the family gone in those pre-Beveridge days of little or no Social Security, my mother displayed that resilience of which she was so capable in times of crisis, and found a full-time job. This was no mean achievement, for she herself was in her early sixties: I was a late child and probably a mistake – a view with which certain of my present clients would almost certainly concur, judging by their occasional references to my parentage. The nightly "Evening News" came no more, but my mother called in at the public library on her way to work to glance through the daily papers.

In my last term at school I had volunteered for the Royal Air Force. We had been bombed twice in our homes in 1941, my grandmother being killed and my mother rendered partially deaf in the first explosion, and I saw myself as a fighter pilot gallantly shooting down the Focke-Wulfs as they came to kill and wound my relations and my friends. I failed the medical because of poor sight –and I am still short-sighted. "Never mind", said the doctor sympathetically. "You can still serve your country. You will soon be called up for the Army". I viewed this prospect with no great enthusiasm, and awaited the arrival of my call-up papers with resignation.

In due course the dreaded buff envelope arrived. "You will report next Monday at H.M.S. Royal Arthur, Skegness". Eventually it sank in – if that be the right verb. An administrative error had been made by the bureaucracy – not for either the first or the last time – and I was to join the Navy. The shock was not really alleviated by the insistence of a schoolfriend, himself already in the "Andrew", on accompanying me on the long and dreary train journey to Skegness, regaling me all the way with descriptions of "Jankers" and "Number Nines" and other forms of naval punishment. But once he had gone, and I had survived the first three days of naval torture, and got used to listening to modes of expression that I had never heard at U.C.S. (although I quite often hear them on television now) I came to enjoy the Navy. After about five months of training I was drafted to Trincomalee in Ceylon (now Sri Lanka). I fell ill and missed my draft, I was re-drafted and found myself sailing around the Mediterranean. I developed a love of my enemy, the Italians, which has never left me.

Meanwhile I rather forgot about being a metropolitan stipendiary magistrate. Not so my mother. On one of her daily visits to the library she noticed in either the *Times* or the *Telegraph* an announcement of the Christopher Tancred Studentship in Common Law. Christopher Tancred lived a rather wild life as a bachelor about a couple of centuries ago. He drank, he went with women, but above all he gambled. He had several sisters, who disapproved of his life-style, and he did not enjoy their constant rebukes. He was that rarity, a successful gambler, and he determined that his sisters should have nothing of his ill-gotten gains. So he set up a trust fund under which each year six scholarships of £100 per annum for each of six years would be given: two in medicine, two in divinity and two in the Law. The beneficiaries of this bounty had to be "indigent members of the Church of England", and I qualified on both counts. Those accepting the legal student-ships had to join Lincoln's Inn and undertake to practise at the Common Law Bar – a slightly perverse requirement, as Lincoln's Inn is traditionally the home of the Chancery barrister. When my mother saw this I was moving about between Gibraltar and Malta and Taranto and was difficult to contact, so she applied on my behalf. She made numerous visits to Lincoln's Inn Fields to see the trustees' solicitors, Frère Cholmeley and Co., and the Under-Treasurer and Deputy Under-Treasurer of Lincoln's Inn, Messrs. Fairchild and Coles. Her importuning was greeted with great consideration and kindness, and I am pleased to say that the tradition of the staff of Lincoln's Inn of looking after its students has been maintained up to the present day. My mother's not very secret desire was that I should come back to a "safe" job in a bank or "in the executive branch of the Civil Service", but fortunately Mr. Fairchild and Mr. Coles talked her out of condemning me to a fate worse than death. My mother had great charm as well as terrible determination, and I got the studentship.

Not that all was plain sailing when, after three and a half years, I left the Navy. I was entitled to, and claimed, a Further Education and Training Scheme Grant. Bureaucracy got to work again and the Ministry of Education lost my papers. I still believed in the efficiency of the Civil Service in those days, so I thought they were processing my application and I did not worry them. Instead I thought that I would acquire a little legal knowledge and experience and I took employment with a firm of solicitors in Lincoln's Inn Fields. They assigned to me the job of "assistant costs clerk" and I found myself authorising the payment of fees to counsel for cases which they had completed five years earlier. From time to time the solicitor for whom I worked got me to take along one of his innumerable cats to the P.D.S.A. to get it "doctored". My life in that office was nearly as dreary and uninteresting as that of the cats after they had been so treated. After nearly a year of unutterable boredom I got in touch with the Ministry of Education who miraculously found my papers hidden away somewhere and offered me £43. 15s. 0d. per quarter, and joyously I went to the Inn to impart the good news. Mr. Fairchild asked me what I had been doing for the last year, and I told him. "I think you had better see the Treasurer", he said. "He happens to be here at the moment"; and I was introduced to my first High Court Judge, whom, in my ignorance, I addressed as "Sir". "This is very serious", he said. "Some people might suspect you of touting for work". In vain did I protest that I had made no friends in the solicitors' office, apart from the cats – and they probably did not like me very much after what I had had done to them – and that I had learned nothing except that barristers had to wait a long time for their fees. "You will have to purge your contempt" he said gravely, "but we will allow you to be admitted a year from today". (Nowadays one can switch from solicitor to barrister and vice versa with the utmost facility, and there is even in contemplation a scheme for joint education of the two branches of the profession.)

So I went and worked for the next year in a Building Society. The office was large and open-plan and I liked the people, and five years later they were to ask me to lecture to them on Real Property Law, and about five years after that, when I married, they let me have a mortgage in circumstances which I am sure my "Status Enquiry Report" did not justify.

Chapter 2

From Yearning to Learning

Studying did not come easily at first. The Navy, the inefficiency of the Ministry of Education and my "punishment" by Lincoln's Inn had taken up five years, and by the time the Inn allowed me to be admitted it was 1948 (and half way through the academic year). Under the terms of my Tancred studentship I had every six months to visit a Lord Justice of Appeal to satisfy him that I was "pursuing a diligent course of studies". Lord Justice Jenkins looked very serious and very learned, and I was surprised when he confessed to me that he knew nothing about Roman Law: in those days I thought that High Court Judges (and especially Lords Justice of Appeal) would know everything about the law. It soon became clear to me that the only way I could satisfy Lord Justice Jenkins was by passing an examination each time the exams came round (which was three times a year), but in those five "lost" years I had got completely out of the habit of study. It was true that I attended all the lectures on Roman Law given by Professor Lee. The Professor appeared to have been a contemporary of Justinian, and his lectures consisted of reading his book on the subject to us. He was an octogenarian, and one day I observed his method of boarding a bus in Chancery Lane. As the number 67 approached at full speed – there was no bus stop near – the Professor strode out into the centre of the road, raised his rolled umbrella high in the air, and, rather like the Ancient Mariner, he held with his glittering eye the bus driver, who, duly terrified, stopped for the Professor to board and commence his journey.

Although he seemed so capable of taking care of himself, I did feel sorry for Professor Lee. There was no communication, no rapport between him and the students. I determined to make him feel happy and wanted in the classroom. I would ask him a question. I spent the week-end thinking about it, and then, on the Monday morning, I put up my hand. A shiver of anticipation went through the rest of the class. It was rather like one of those Bateman cartoons of the guest who sneezed at the Royal Garden Party (or was it at Lords?) Eventually the Professor observed my out-stretched limb and he stopped reading and glared at me. "Yes?", he demanded, with the same fierce look in his eye that he had employed so effectively on the bus driver, and I asked my question. There was a long and icy silence, until at last the Great Man replied: "Well, one expects people who come here to have at least a modicum of intelligence"; and then he resumed his reading of his book. Nobody ever asked a question of Professor Lee again ...

With or despite the aid of Professor Lee I awakened one Friday to realise that my first Bar examination was to take place the following Monday morning and I had learned absolutely nothing. A month later, when the results came out, I should have to revisit Lord Justice Jenkins. I decided not to go to bed again until after the exam. I worked solidly for seventy-two hours with only a few short breaks for meals. The result was that I got one of the highest marks awarded that time for Roman Law, and the best mark that I was to achieve in any Bar examination; and I nearly had a nervous breakdown. I resolved to work more systematically for all future examinations. After all, most people worked a regular eight-hour day, so perhaps I should follow this pattern. I did, and although I never failed any of the examinations, I never repeated my success in Roman Law.

Another of our elderly lecturers who read from his book – a much more interesting book, however – was Professor Winfield who taught us tort (if the reader will forgive the tautology). One Saturday morning (for there were Bar lectures six days a week then, as there still are) when the Professor was "lecturing", a large Nigerian in a duffel-coat walked up to the dais and laid upon it a copy of the early edition of the London "Evening Standard", thereafter resuming his place at the back of the classroom. Professor Winfield looked puzzled. He picked it up, put it down and then said, slightly testily: "I haven't got time to read the paper". The Nigerian student then walked up to the front of the classroom again, and, pointing to the main item, declared determinedly: "I was involved, sir" "Oh, well," remarked the Professor soothingly, "if you were involved I'll read it. I'll read it to the class. This will be interesting".

The main news item was headed: "Big Delay on the Underground". It occupied two columns on the front page and one on the back. The Professor read it out carefully to us. When he had finished, he looked even more perplexed. "I can't see your name here", he demanded of the Nigerian, who was standing proudly beside him. "I was one of thousands, sir" replied the student. "Oh," said the Professor sadly, and resumed reading his book.

But Professor Winfield was to spring a pleasant surprise on us. One day he asked us all to stay behind after his lecture and he produced about a dozen bottles of sherry. "It's my eightieth birthday", he said, "and I want to celebrate it with you, my fellow-students. We're all students of the law. You're all students and I'm a student. Never forget that no-one ever knows all about the law". It was a disconcerting statement, but one demonstrating that quality of humility that I have found in all the truly great lawyers that I have met, including, later on, Lord Denning; and it made me more understanding of Lord Justice Jenkins' ignorance of Roman Law.

In fact the first law lecture of all that I attended was given by a much younger man, Professor Henry Salt, Q.C. He had a finely chiselled keen legal face, but he was a pure academic. His subject was "Incorporeal Hereditaments" and to this day I should not recognise an incorporeal hereditament if I met one in the pub or at the corner of the street – but probably such an encounter is unlikely. During that first highly technical, completely incomprehensible lecture a little Indian sitting next to me asked me nervously: "Do you understand what he's talking about?" "Not a word", I replied. "I'm so glad" he murmured, "May I invite you for an Indian curry?" "I don't know", I answered, "I've never had Indian food"; but then I realised that it could not possibly be more indigestible than the diet being churned out to us in the lecture hall and I agreed and we crept out, I believe unnoticed. That day at the Taj Mahal began a firm friendship with P.T. Patel which was to last throughout our student days. P.T. was indeed the first of many friends from different parts of the Commonwealth who were to enrich my life in the ensuing years, but unfortunately we lost touch after we had both been Called and gone our respective ways. A lecture tour of India, organised for me by the British Council in 1981, included a few days in Bombay and I asked the Council to try to trace him, as he had originated from that city. They brought me the news that he was dead, and I grieved greatly for the loss of an old friend. I need not

9

have done so, as last year he rang me up, in London, to which he had returned (not from the dead) as his wife was to have an operation here, and our joy at meeting again was great – especially on my part, as I had never expected to see him again in this world.

Meanwhile Henry Salt continued to drone on about incorporeal hereditaments. P.T. gave up attending his lectures and I joined a group of English ex-service students, all of whom believed that non-attendance could involve the withdrawal of our Further Education and Training Scheme grants. But we paid no attention to Mr. Salt, preferring to do crosswords and play "boxes" and chat quietly at the back of the Old Hall in Lincoln's Inn. Although Mr. Salt did not read his lecture, which he appeared to give extempore, we all felt that, lost in his world of incorporeal hereditaments, he was quite oblivious to all that was going on around him. It came as a great shock therefore, when one afternoon he suddenly stopped his address and, pointing directly at me, requested piercingly: "You, there. Would you kindly give your attention? I find it most distracting to try to lecture while you are chattering away and jumping about like a Jack-in-a-box". His rebuke stunned me and all I managed to murmur was: "I'm so sorry". "That's quite all right", he rejoined with a flashing smile, and returned to his incorporeal hereditaments, leaving me to ponder how very civilised the law could be.

But not all the lectures were dull. It was a privilege to attend the main discourses on Real Property – of which Incorporeal Hereditaments formed a special part – given with great clarity by Professor Cheshire, who reminded me a lot of my father; or to listen to the witty dissection of the law of contract by Professor Fifoot (those two formed a wonderful team in their famous book on Contract, Cheshire and Fifoot) or to hear the explicit exposition of Equity of R.E. Megarry, who, later, was to become Vice-Chancellor. "Ted" Megarry, as I now dare to call him, had great charm. One of our "group" was a delightful, if somewhat talkative and indiscreet, girl called Vicky. Her father was Irish, her mother Russian – a volatile combination; a sort of Molotov cocktail. She adored Megarry. Once, in the canteen queue, just after one of his lectures, Vicky remarked to the slightly older lady in front of her: "Don't you think Megarry is marvellous?" "Yes" the other woman replied rather coldly, "that's why I married him".

But Megarry was a sport. The Inns were multi-racial in those days

– much more so than now. As alternatives to Real Property in Part I, students could take Roman-Dutch Law or Hindu and Mohammedan Law. There were not many South Africans around, but some students chose Roman-Dutch Law because it was easy. It was based, of course, on Roman Law, which we had all had to take (and was not, it was said, very different). The law in South Africa had not changed a lot since Roman times. (Some might say that the way of life has not changed much either). But those who took Hindu and Mohammedan Law instead of Real Property had a good reason for doing so. They wished to practise in India or Pakistan or other countries in which England land law was irrelevant. But they were suffering a high failure rate in Finals, and many were bitterly disappointed about this.

I became an active member of the Students' Union and decided to investigate the cause of these failures among the bright students from the Indian sub-continent. In almost all cases they came down in Equity, a vitally important subject in the Finals carrying about thirty per cent of the total marks. Perusal of examination papers over the previous few years revealed a possible (nay, a likely) cause. Equity papers were including an average of four questions out of the fourteen on Real Property, a subject that these students had never taken, and had not been recommended to study. For example, one question in an Equity Paper began "What is a building scheme?" and went on with a detailed problem on this topic. Snell's "Equity" contained just five lines on building schemes; the other recommended Equity book did not refer to them at all. But there was a lot about building schemes in Cheshire's "Manual of Real Property". Students who had not sat for Real Property in Part I – mainly Indians and Pakistanis – were being asked questions in the Finals on a subject that they had never studied, or been told to study. To me it seemed most unfair.

I approached the Secretary to the Council of Legal Education, and the Director, but failed to arouse their interests. I took it up with the then Chairman of the Students' Union, a West Indian, but he was cautious. He seemed to think that any of us who made a fuss would be bound to fail our Finals, and he did not wish to risk this. Nowadays I suppose there would be a student strike to fight this "blatant racialism" – although I am quite certain that racial discrimination never entered the examiners' minds. (I believe they just did not realise what they were doing). But eventually my

11

murmurings reached the ears of R.E. Megarry, our distinguished lecturer in Equity, and he asked to see me. I was rather alarmed as I came before him. "Why don't you sue the Equity examiners?" he asked me. I did not reply: "You must be joking" – that contemptuous retort was not yet current, but he clearly saw from my expression that this was what I was thinking. "No, I'm serious", he went on. "If you think the students, through their Union, have a grievance, bring an action. It can be heard in the Old Hall. The Director of Studies will try the case. You can appear for the prosecution, and I shall defend the examiners".

And so it was that the case of *Rex v. the Equity Examiners ex parte the Inns of Court Students' Union* came to be heard at 10 o'clock one Friday morning in the Old Hall, Lincoln's Inn. The case did not last as long as *Jarndice v. Jarndice*, but it did occupy most of the morning. Those taking part were as follows:– I led for the prosecution, my "junior" being the well-known West Indian cricketer Allan Rae, now in practice at the Bar of Jamaica, still a delightful friend. Leading for the defence was Ted Megarry, who took silk about then (not as a result of this case), and with him M.A.S.A. Kahn, of whom more – much more – later. Some of the students regarded Masa as a latter-day Judas Iscariot for appearing against them, but he had been won over by Megarry's "cabbie on the rank" argument and quoted against them Lord Atkin's dictum that "the advocate must take on any case, however unsavoury, whatever his personal feelings about the matter". And Masa was right.

The Judge was William Cleveland-Stevens, K.C., Director of Studies at the Council of Legal Education. He was the most Victorian gentleman I have ever met. Tall, slim, dapper and almost as old as Professor Lee, he always wore a waistcoat (summer and winter) and a wing-collar. Once a year he gave us a talk (always the same talk) on Etiquette at the Bar. Most of the hour was devoted to how male barristers (and male Bar students) should dress. At the end, directing his gaze at the very few women students of those days (now nearly half of those gaining admission to the Inns of Court are on the distaff side) he said: "I propose to say nothing about how female members of the Bar and girl students should dress. This is because I have never met a lady who was not beautifully and immaculately dressed". Had he been Director of Studies thirty, or even twenty years later, he would have had a nasty shock ...

The "Court reporter" was Edward O. Jackson, quite the most

brilliant student of my day. This scintillating "Ted" was called shortly before me, but our careers were to proceed along parallel lines for the first few years – which means that in those lean times of virtually no criminal legal aid (and comparatively little crime) we each made very slow progress. I had just my sister to keep, but Ted was married with, I think, four children, and eventually he had to give up the uneven economic struggle and go into the Inland Revenue, where his efforts were ultimately rewarded with the C.B.E. – but at what a cost to the Bar! Meanwhile another of our contemporaries, who had a large private income, soldiered on, and after losing many cases which ought to have been won, eventually, after ten years or more, by dint of experience became a competent advocate –just about! Such was the way of the legal world: it is different now.

The Students' Union had a quarterly magazine called "GLIM" – the mnemonics indicating the initial letters of the four Inns of Court. Anyone who has the time to search out the copy of Glim containing Ted Jackson's report of *R v. the Equity Examiners* will find his diligence well rewarded. It is a most marvellous piece of literature – a combination of a serious treatise by a member of the Incorporated Society of Law Reporters and an essay from A P Herbert's "Uncommon Law". Superficially it looks like a Law Report, except for occasional unusual words in brackets ("cheers") ("prolonged cheers") ("boos"). The boos were reserved for poor old Masa. Megarry's arguments were listened to in polite silence: in those days it was the custom of students to listen to experts presenting their cases, even if they did not wish to agree with what was being said. The cheers and the prolonged cheers were reserved for Allan Rae and me. With the right of reply to Megarry and Kahn I had the last word, and I finished: "These unidentified and unidentifiable Equity examiners, with their misguided machinations, have managed to create a thirteenth maxim of Equity: "He who seeks Equity must do Real Property." "(Loud acclaim)".

The packed Hall (I had never seen it so crowded) then silently awaited the judgment. Eventually Cleveland-Stevens spoke for the first and only time in the trial:– "Having heard all the arguments I have no hesitation in finding for the defendants in this case". He rose, and left rapidly.

There were no shouts, whistles or catcalls. All that we experienced was a feeling of complete desolation. Allan and I looked at each other in stunned disbelief. Then Megarry came over to us: "Come on boys, let's go and have some lunch".

We did not have our meal in Lincoln's Inn; somehow that would have seemed inappropriate. He took us (the three "advocates") to a hostelry in Chancery Lane. It was a somewhat gloomy repast. At last, over the sweet, I plucked up my courage. "What went wrong, sir?" I asked apprehensively. "Why did we lose?" "Nothing" replied Megarry, "except that you were on a case you couldn't win. Didn't you realise the implications of what you were doing? If you had won you would have invalidated many examination results going back over several years. We would have had claims from disappointed students from all over the Indian sub-continent. No, there was no way you could win. But I can promise you this. There will be no purely Real Property questions in the Equity exams in future. The Equity examiners have learned their lesson. Be content with that". I was; and, revealing all this now, I do not think that I shall be subjecting the Council of Legal Education to lots of belated lawsuits. I cannot imagine that there are hundreds of sixty year old "Bar-at-law (Failed)" in Bombay who will be rushing into international litigation.

I learned three things that day: firstly that you should always fight for what you believe to be right. Usuaully you will win; occasionally you will lose, sometimes at great personal cost (this has happened to me on at least two occasions) but at least you can live with your conscience; or perhaps you may appear to lose, but in a strange way you will win, as in *R v. the Equity Examiners*.

The second was that those who sit in judgment should always give reasons for their judgments. That Friday the students were not so much dismayed at losing, as at being given no reason for losing. Lord Jowett, when Lord Chancellor, gave this advice to magistrates:– "Give your judgment but never your reasons, for while your judgment will invariably be right, your reasons will always make it seem wrong".

I do not know of any dictum uttered by any Judge with which I more profoundly disagree. I will not even say "respectfully disagree", for I feel no respect for this advice. "Your judgment will invariably be right!" Whose judgment is *invariably* right? If on a busy morning in my Magistrates' Court with perhaps fifty people appearing before me, I get it somewhere near right in ninety per cent of the cases, I feel I have done a good morning's work. The other ten per cent ought to know my reasons so that they are encouraged to appeal if I have clearly gone wrong. County Court Judges, dealing with civil claims which by their very nature are usually less important (to the litigant and to society) than criminal cases, are required by law to give reasons. Magistrates should do the same: otherwise some of those appearing before them will feel the same sense of desolation that the students felt that black Friday morning.

The third was a feeling of elation, that a great advocate like Megarry could be such a good sort and such a good sport. But these are qualities that I was to find in all the truly great men of the law that I was to meet as I moved from learning to earning.

Chapter 3

The Influence of Masa

Apart from *Rex v. the Equity Examiners* there were no practical exercises in those days. A deaf mute could have qualified for and been called to practise at the English Bar. It was left to the Students' Union to organize any activities in any way connected with the art of advocacy, and the Students' Union was dominated by a group of West Indians, although the President was Donald Keating, now a very distinguished Queen's Counsel. I do not know why, but I was a bit afraid of those West Indians at first. (It seems ridiculous now, as some of them became among my closest friends.) They were large men, exuding self-confidence, and they appeared to hunt in a pack; and they had taken over most of the social side of life at the Inn. One of these was M.A.S.A. Kahn (hereinafter referred to as Masa). Masa was an extraordinary character. Years later, when we had both been called to the Bar (together), I was walking along the Strand with my brief case in my hand and I saw Masa walking towards me with a beautiful girl in his hand. "Ah, Crowther" he exclaimed (he has always called me by my surname, and always mispronounced it, making the "th" soft as in "think") "I should like you to meet my wife".

I affected indignation. "You didn't invite me to the wedding", I complained.

"Crowther", he said solemnly, "we were married in a state of nature".

I managed to mutter something about not having been invited to the "state of nature," but somehow it did not sound appropriate, so I hurried on.

But my first personal encounter with Masa had occurred many years earlier, and quite a long time before *Rex v. the Equity Examiners.* I had always tried to avoid him – he looked so big and intimidating –

but this time he came and stood right in front of me. He was the chairman of the debating society, which he had re-christened the "Literary and Debating Society" (Masa considered himself a great expert in literature) and he was holding two pieces of paper in his hands. "Crowther", he demanded, pen at the ready. "Am I to put you down for a debate or for the Contest in Advocacy?" (It was a cleverly planned question, permitting of no complete escape). I have always been by nature rather lazy, so I asked: "Which involves the less work?" "If you take part in a debate", Masa announced solemnly, "you will be expected to prepare your subject, whereas in the Contest in Advocacy you will speak ex tempore".

"Better put me down for the Contest in Advocacy", I said, perhaps not realising then quite what "ex tempore" meant. It was too late when I discovered that I, who had never spoken in public in my life before, would have to address an audience for ten minutes on a subject handed to me as I rose to speak. In vain did I plead with Masa to allow me to withdraw. "Your name is written down here," he said firmly. "It cannot be deleted".

So, one Tuesday morning I spoke – and I won. I went through three or four other rounds before finding myself in the Finals against H.E. Walter – afterwards to become Sir Harold Walter, a leading politician of Mauritius, who had come second the previous year. Publicity (by Masa) for the Final Round had been good, and the lecture theatre was crowded with about two hundred students, each marking the contestants out of ten. When the votes were counted "H.E." and I were exactly even. Masa insisted we should speak again, on new subjects that he had prepared against just such a contingency. The result was the same. Masa insisted on a third go. The strain was telling on both H.E. and me, and we secretly agreed that if there were no outright winner this time we would toss a coin to see whose name should appear on the shield. But this time one of us was victorious. I beat H.E. by half a mark. Masa was disinclined to accept this – he had forbidden fractions in the marking as he thought them vulgar – but H.E., then as now a most generous man, graciously conceded defeat. (A few weeks ago the telephone rang and the person at the other end said: "You'll never guess who this is" "Yes I will", I replied. "It's H.E. Walter". How could I forget the voice that had given me so much trouble thirty six years before?) But I went away from the Contest in Advocacy feeling that perhaps after all I had a career ahead of me as an advocate; perhaps one day I would be a metropolitan stipendiary magistrate. And what a lot of my new-found confidence in my future I owed to Masa! When in 1972, I was to visit Trinidad I lunched with the Chief Justice, and I stayed with the Ombudsman who showed me great kindness and hospitality, but one of the most pleasant evenings I had was with Masa, a junior barrister carrying on a happy and satisfying practice mainly in the Magistrates' Courts, and living with his natural wife and their large family in a modest little house in Carenage. How sad I was therefore, on visiting Allan Rae in Jamaica in 1987, to learn from him that Masa had died during the previous year.

There was a problem though about the Contest in Advocacy. Masa wanted to give certificates to H.E. and me, in addition to having my name inscribed upon the shield. The Council of Legal Education, which had bought the shield and some medals the previous year, refused to pay for the certificates. My mother had the most beautiful handwriting that I had ever seen, and I suggested that she might design and prepare the certificates, a suggestion which Masa accepted with enthusiasm. I am very pleased about this. From my point of view, I have my mother's caligraphy on the certificate that hangs on my wall. From her standpoint she could have believed then that I would after all become a successful barrister, that all her sacrifices on my behalf might not be in vain. It was the only real sign; she was not to be present at my Call to the Bar. Soon after she had made the certificates she called me into her room one morning and asked me to look at her back. I was astounded by the request, and horrified at what I saw. Around her shoulder there was a large red lump, looking like a virulent blood-orange. I immediately telephoned our doctor. He was on holiday but a young locum came. He was inexperienced and tactless. "Your mother has a terrible and deadly form of cancer", he diagnosed, "and we must get her immediately into hospital". Then he turned on me, accusingly: "Why have you let her get into this state and done nothing about it?" Later that day she was in the cancer ward of the Middlesex Hospital, which looked after her well for the rest of her life. But I realized from the young doctor's rebuke that I had been so pre-occupied with my studies and my success in the Contest in Advocacy that I had not noticed that my mother had been getting thinner and weaker – and had tried to hide her suffering because she did not want to interfere with my studies for Bar Finals. She would have liked me to have qualified, and for her then quietly to have died.

But that was not to be. The last months of 1950 and the first of 1951 were the worst of my life, so far. Most of the time my mother was in hospital, although she did have a week's "convalescence" in Folkestone, and she came home for a couple of weeks when surgery and radiation seemed to have improved her condition. Hospitals were very strict in those days about visiting hours, so I had to creep away part-way through the last lecture each day to be with her for half an hour; and to leave my studies each Saturday and Sunday to travel by bus from Hendon up to Oxford Circus for more liberal visits of an hour. Just before Christmas 1950 my mother relapsed into a coma, in which she remained until early in the New Year. Frequently the hospital telephoned, requesting my sister and me to go there to be with our mother in her last hours, but her strong spirit and constitution survived the disease's attack upon her. By the end of January 1951 she had recovered sufficiently for me to bring her home again – I shall always be grateful to the kindly bus crew who stopped between stops outside our flat for us to alight when I explained her predicament – but she was soon to relapse again and be taken back to the Middlesex Hospital. They telephoned us to come one evening when she was in a coma, and my sister and I spent the night at her bedside, but by morning she appeared a little better and we returned home on the first bus. However, that afternoon the hospital 'phoned again to say that her brave struggle for life was over. My sister had since birth suffered from a form of polio which was constantly getting worse. I was now effectively the head of what remained of the family, and I started going from door to door trying to sell brushes.

I was not very fit for the task, and not very good at it. (I am not by nature a salesman). The combined strain of studying for Bar Finals, which was to involve sitting for thirteen subjects in two and a half days, of my mother's illness, and responsibility for keeping the household going on just over £5 a week, had produced in me a duodenal ulcer, which at times was very painful. For about three years I was to live, on medical advice, on a diet of milk and boiled fish with no alcohol – a treatment soon thereafter to be rejected as wholly inappropriate in favour of underdone steaks and whisky. Even when I was Best Man at the wedding of my greatest naval friend I toasted the happy couple in orange juice – which may explain why their marriage ended in divorce. But I knew that before

19

her death my mother had given up the absurd idea of my having a safe career in a bank or in the Civil Service, and was reconciled to my embarking on the precarious life of a barrister, so I knew that, whatever the grief in my heart, I had to pass those examinations – and I did, about two and a half months after my mother left us. From a personal point of view I was disappointed that I did not do very well in Criminal Law, in which I have practised most of the time since 1951, and in Evidence, which I think is the most important of all legal topics, on which I give a lot of lectures – but at least I was able to tell Lord Justice Jenkins that I had passed.

And I was able to put my name down for Call to the Bar. The ceremony of Call at Lincoln's Inn has not changed much over the centuries. Those newly qualified are lined up on one side of the Great Hall, rather like a group of nervous chorus girls awaiting an audition. The actual ceremony of Call is performed by the Treasurer – usually a senior Judge, occasionally a member of the Royal Family – a Bencher of the Inn who holds that high office for a year. Behind him, in a semi-circle, sit all the other Benchers, normally playing no part in the ceremony. When his name is called out by the Under-Treasurer, the individual about to undergo the metamorphosis from law student to lawyer walks as fast as his palpitations will allow to take up a position in front of the Treasurer, and bows. The Treasurer then adapts some time-honoured words: "Eric Crowther, by the authority of and on behalf of the Benchers of this Honourable Society I now admit you to the Outer Bar." The Treasurer then extends his hand, which the newly called barrister seizes perhaps a little too eagerly before walking off to the other side of the Hall in a blaze of glory which he will afterwards be quite unable to recollect.

At least, that's the way it should be. Masa was immediately before me in the line of those awaiting Call, shambling his way casually along the first wall, as though he had been through all this many times before. When he reached the front of the queue he turned to me and said gravely: "Ah Crowther" (still mispronoucing my name) "we are twin poetic souls, are we not?" "Yes I expect you're right Masa", I managed to murmur, "but for goodness sake go over there. They've called your name".

Masa walked slowly and solemnly to take up his position before the Treasurer, Lord Simmonds, the Lord Chancellor. Masa seemed to bow more deeply than any of his predecessors had done, and the Treasurer responded by intoning those time-honoured words.

When the Treasurer proffered the handshake, Masa clasped the Treasurer's right hand in both of his hands and briefly engaged the Lord Chancellor in a conversation which I could not hear. After releasing the Treasurer from his grip Masa was expected to turn to the right, like everybody else, but instead he moved left. "No, no" I heard the Treasurer say, firmly. "Go that way". But Masa brushed him aside: he might be the Lord Chancellor, but Masa was a barrister now, and we are all equal at the Bar. Masa then moved behind the apparently rather astonished Lord Chancellor to visit the arc of Benchers half surrounding him, each of whose hands he shook warmly in turn. (One elderly Judge who had fallen asleep seemed profoundly shocked to be awakened by the massive figure of Masa in front of him). His task of promoting friendship between Bar and Bench completed, Masa took up a position in front of the Lord Chancellor, and proceeded to recite a lengthy passage from Fitzgerald's translation of the "Omar Khayam" – the passage that includes the part about "a piece of bread, a glass of wine and thou" (doubtless in anticipation of the excellent dinner with which we were to be regaled shortly afterwards). The divertissement over, Masa walked majestically over to the opposite wall.

Meanwhile, I was in a state of panic. I was convinced that all my attendance at lectures and hard work in the Library had been in vain: nobody would ever be Called to the Bar of England and Wales again. But I under-estimated the stoicism of the profession that I was joining. When he was quite certain that Masa had finally settled down the Lord Chancellor gave a signal to the Under-Treasurer, the latter pronounced my name, and I was Called to the Bar just as though the events of the previous ten minutes had never happened. So, as a newly qualified barrister, I was let loose on society, with almost no knowledge of the practical workings of the law.

Chapter 4

Financial Crisis:

The British Council to the Rescue

I have been lucky: I have had only three quarters of an hour of unemployment in my life. Most of those forty-five minutes were spent on a number 13 bus travelling between Aldwych and Oxford Street. I finished my last Bar examination at 5.15 on a Friday afternoon and started to work at the British Council at 6.00 p.m. that same evening.

This is probably the reason why I do not feel sympathy (in the Greek sense of the term) for all the millions of people now registered as unemployed. Of course I feel deeply sorry for those who by reason of age, infirmity or mental incapacity are unable to get jobs, but so far as London is concerned I do not believe that they comprise the majority on the dole. (I think that the position may be quite different in certain of the regions of Britain, especially the North-East of England.) In London much unemployment is selective or self-induced, and many young people will not take on what they regard as menial jobs or jobs not offering remuneration very substantially above what they can draw from social security. I think they make a big mistake. The price they pay in terms of apathy, boredom and discontent is a heavy one. They do not recognise that there are dignity and joy in serving others: The Indians and the Italians know this and rejoice in it, but we, perhaps because of our colonial heritage, ignore it – to our cost.

During my under-employed years at the Bar – the first seven – I worked for short periods as an insurance agent, brush salesman, gardener, butcher, farm labourer, newsvendor and factory worker – without telling my Inn, after the disaster over my being a solicitor's clerk. I think the Inn would have disapproved, but I wanted to stay at the Bar and could see no other way to support my sister, myself and my clerk. The worst of these jobs was in a factory in Chiswick, packing hampers daily from 8.00 a.m. to 8.00 p.m. for four weeks before Christmas. Conditions were terrible. The "gooses" (to use the foreman's form of plural) hung head downwards in a loft, and their blood dripped through the ceiling on to the heads of the workers in the warehouse below. A daily shampoo was the order of the night. But still, my sister and I did have an excellent dinner that Christmas.

My comparative cynicism on unemployment in London is based on several further factors. As a magistrate I often have to deal with the terribly serious offence of foreigners working without a permit. Frequently they have got their humble jobs speaking little or no English, within a few days of arriving in this country. Would not the employer prefer to have a British worker, with whom he could communicate?

The lists on Saturday afternoons at London Magistrates' Courts usually include a large number of fine and maintenance defaulters, the latter men who have not been paying Court orders in respect of their wives and children. The ultimate sanction for such non-payment is imprisonment, immediate or suspended, if the Court finds that there has been wilful refusal or culpable neglect to pay. Many reformers would withdraw this power from the magistrates: if their proposal comes to pass, Courts might as well give up imposing fines and making maintenance orders.

Any clerk who has sat with me at West London Court during the eleven years that I was there will recognise the following scene from the Saturday matinee, for it was played so often:–

The clerk: "You have paid nothing off this fine/maintenance order for nearly four years. Would you care to tell the magistrate why?"

Defendant: "I've been unemployed for three and a half years. Can't get a job anywhere. You must know that there's over three million unemployed."

Magistrate: "You look very fit and strong. Have you tried London Transport?"

Defendant: "Er, no."

Magistrate: "Well, I would like to come here to work by public transport but I can't because so many buses and trains are cancelled, and the reason given is usually lack of staff. Why don't you apply to their recruiting office?"

Defendant: "Well, you see, I don't do shift work."

Magistrate: "What does that mean?"

Defendant: "Well, I don't work Saturdays."

Magistrate: "Why not? I do."

Defendant: "Yes, I know, but I go to football on Saturdays."

Magistrate: "And is your commitment to football more important to you than your obligation to your children?"

Defendant: "No, not when you put it like that."

Magistrate: "Very well, I shall adjourn this case for exactly four weeks. When you come back to Court I shall expect you to be in the uniform of London Transport or British Rail or I shall probably send you to prison for six weeks."

Whilst my success rate was nothing like one hundred per cent, London Transport and British Rail do owe me a debt of gratitude, up to now unacknowledged, for my work as a recruitment officer. The majority would return, however, four weeks later, in mufti, looking rather apprehensive.

"I hope it's all right guv'nor, but the night after I was in front of you last time I happened to meet my brother-in-law in the pub and he offered me a job painting and decorating for his building business. It pays better than London Transport, so I can pay more off my kids' arrears than if I'd gone to work on the buses or the tubes. I can offer the maintenance and a tenner off the arrears; will that be all right?"

So the defendant continues to do the job he has been doing all the time while drawing his social security, but now is forced to pay his fine, or maintenance for his wife and children, by the order being sustained by a suspended committal order to take effect if, without good reason (such as genuine illness or redundancy) he stops paying again. I can see nothing oppressive or unjust in that, but many would disagree with me.

One February morning about five years ago I awakened after a night of heavy gales to find most of my front garden wall broken down. A firm of local builders enjoys a good reputation, so I asked them for an estimate. This came to £1600, but the principal of the firm advised me: "I must tell you that we shan't be able to do the work for at least eighteen months." "Why ever not?" I asked. "Shortage of labour," he replied. "Every legitimate builder will tell you the same. We pay well over the union rates but we can't get workers."

"What am I to do?", I demanded. "The children from the nearby school come and sit on my wall twice a day. I don't exactly welcome them, but if now one of them does himself a nasty injury I suppose I'll be responsible under the Occupiers' Liability Act. Can you advise anything?"

"Yes," he replied. "Put up a notice about your requirements in the local supermarket. You'll be inundated with offers."

He exaggerated slightly, but within a week six people came to offer their services. All for some reason insisted on payment in cash, and eventually I chose three strong-looking Irishmen who offered to do the work for £1500 and promised to complete it within a week. They started the following Monday and worked that day, and the Tuesday, Wednesday and Friday. I got home on the Friday night just as they were finishing the job – hard work, and a labour well executed within the time stipulated. I asked them in for a drink, while I paid them what amounted to £500 each for four day's work, less of course the cost of the materials. When they had consumed a fair amount of my whisky I enquired of their leader why they had chosen Thursday for their day off. He looked at me with the kind of tolerant sympathy that is normally reserved for really rather backward children and with a wink he explained: "That's the day we go to draw our unemployment benefit." I suppose I should have reported the matter, but I did not want to have to start seeking the services of a glazier.

I must admit though that my job with the British Council came to me: I did not have to go searching for it. The Government of the early 1950s believed, rightly in my opinion, that this country's relations with other nations would be improved if we did more to ensure the happiness and welfare of overseas students in our midst (not a very popular idea nowadays) and decided that the best non-political organ for this would be the British Council. In return for increased funds the Council was required to expand its facilities for student visitors from overseas, and this in turn, required an increase in staff. Most of the leisure-time activities to be provided would have to take place at weekends, a time when most Council staff preferred to be at home with their families and friends, so two part-timers were to be recruited. The Inns of Court had a Students' Advisory Officer who sat on a general committee for the welfare of overseas students in London on which the British Council was

25

represented by Muriel Ethel Whitehorn (hereinafter referred to as "Mew"). A formidable lady, who looked like a cross between Queen Mary and Margaret Rutherford, Mew put out feelers for the new part-timers at one of these committee meetings. She drew a blank, but the legal Students' Advisory Officer said that he would ask his secretary, as she knew all the students and he did not.

The secretary, Jean Sellers, was an amazing woman, absolutely dedicated to student welfare. Up to the time of my father's death my mother used to say that overwork had never killed anyone, but it killed him and it killed Jean Sellers. Often she would still be in her little office at 11.00 p.m., trying to solve students' problems. She knew us all (the many hundreds of us) by name and smile and she organised free theatre tickets for us. Once a month we were able to go to see a new, and usually very fine, production at the Arts Theatre, as Alec Clunes, the director, liked to have a large and appreciative audience for his first nights. So every month I followed the same routine:– The Arts Theatre, followed by a visit to Chez Auguste Restaurant where a meal for two including a glass of wine cost £1 in those halcyon days. (In the law of Criminal Evidence they call it "system".) Only the girl would change (except when Epi was around) – and the play, of course. It was my monthly outing, and I greatly enjoyed it – thanks to Alec Clunes and Jean Sellers.

And it was to Jean that I owe my invitation to do two "Introduction Courses" for the British Council during my last summer as a student, and my subsequent more permanent employment by that august body.

As a result of her efforts on my behalf Mew wrote to me to ask me if I would be interested in participating in two week-long introduction courses during that summer of 1951. Upon my replying in the affirmative, I was sent a form to fill up regarding my achievements up to then (this did not take long to complete) and was told that I needed four references, one of whom had to be a clergyman.

This last requirement (not altogether easy in my case) must soon thereafter have been dispensed with, judging by some of the subsequent recruits to the British Council staff.

When a person applies to become a Justice of the Peace, he or she is almost invariably asked the obvious, but pointed, question: "Why do you want to become a magistrate?" – and most suitable candidates have a suitable answer ready. A more difficult question for the uninitiated would be: "What is a magistrate?" or "What does a magistrate do?" If at my interview I had been asked: "What does the British Council do?", I should have been quite unable to answer, for the Council in those days persisted in hiding its light under a bushel. It did so with such success that no light at all shone forth and an analogy with an ostrich burying its head in the sand would perhaps be more appropriate. The "Press Officer's" job was a sinecure, and he meant to keep it that way. When, after what proved to be my solitary introduction course, I wrote an article praising the Council for its initiative in running these courses for lonely and bewildered overseas students newly arrived in Britain, I was called for and rebuked by no fewer than three high-ranking British Council officers, although my account of the course was entirely eulogic, and it was published only in "Glim", the law students' magazine, having a circulation of no more than a thousand. "We don't want publicity," the misnamed Press Officer told me, "because all publicity is bad publicity."

Certainly nearly all the publicity that the Council was getting at that time was bad publicity, because almost all of it came from Lord Beaverbrook, who was waging a vendetta against the Council. Beaverbrook was a Canadian, who had come to Great Britain with the idea of becoming her Prime Minister. Fortunately he did not achieve his ambition – Churchill was a far more suitable candidate – but he did become Minister of Aircraft Production in the war-time Coalition Government, where he invented the slogan: "Bigger bombs, better bombs, to blow up the Germans". The German people – not just the Nazis – were among his pathological hates. Others included the Duke of Edinburgh, Pandit Nehru and the Arts Council. Although he professed profound contempt for Field-Marshal Goering he had much in common with that bloated villain, whose catch-phrases included "Guns before butter", and "When I hear the word "culture" I reach for my gun". But foremost among Beaverbook's hates was the British Council.

The reason for this requires a little more research than the origins of the objects of his other loathings. Long before the second World War began Beaverbrook realised that the British people would not have him as Prime Minister, but he was power-hungry and created the "Beaverbrook Empire":– the "Daily Express", "Sunday Express", "Scottish Daily Express", the "London Evening Standard" and many provincial papers, a lot of which bore a sort of

27

symbol or mascot rather resembling Beaverbrook himself in a pose reminiscent of Queen Boadicia, and the slogan "For King" – or later "For Queen" – "and Empire". Beaverbrook chose to ignore the decision of the Conference of Commonwealth Prime Ministers in 1926 and the post-war emergence of "third world" colonies into dominions. Each edition of each newspaper must be "studded with stardust" he instructed his editors, and to make a paper sell you must make the readers happy. So for many years each edition of the "Daily Express" bore the encouraging promise from no less a prophet than Beaverbrook: "There will be no war this year or any year" – until Germany invaded Poland on 1st September 1939 when miraculously and without explanation it disappeared.

In 1934 the Government of the day decided to set up and finance the British Council with the object of strengthening Great Britain's ties with other countries through the medium of culture and the English language. The Council was to be a-political, although most of the Council officers I have met have been sincere socialists, and one or two convinced communists. Beaverbrook fancied himself as the head of such a potentially influential organisation: fortunately for the future of the Council others did not, and he was not appointed. So this newspaper baron bore a grudge against the British Council for the rest of his life, and waged a one-sided war against his "effete" (his word) and supine (mine) enemy. This continued, though less vigorously, after the little man died and his son took over as proprietor, but the fury has all been spent now, and last year I saw an item in the "London Standard" which could, with the exercise of a little imagination, even be construed favourably from the Council's point of view. But certainly while Beaverbrook was the overlord of his Empire seldom a day went by without an attack in at least one of his journals on some aspect of Council policy or activity, and no reporter or feature-writer who dared to suggest that the Council did anything worth while could expect to last long.

The official Council response to this was pusillanimous in the extreme. Apart from sending to the newspapers concerned corrections of their mis-statements, which corrections were almost never published, they did nothing. The feebleness of the response so angered members of the British Council Staff Association that at their own expense they printed and published in April 1954 a booklet entitled "The Beaverbrook Press and the British Council". This publication began:

"This pamphlet has been prepared to draw attention to the nature of the campaign waged against the British Council and its staff by the Beaverbrook newspapers. Their inaccurate and misleading attacks, often persisted in after the facts had been made known to them, and their frequent refusal to publish corrections of mis-statements, damage the reputation of the British Press among those who know the truth, particularly overseas, warp the judgment of those who accept the statements at their face value, and are harmful to British interests."

There followed what were called "Examples of Misrepresentation". I quote one from the pamphlet – because it enabled Beaverbrook to state his hatred of the Council and the German people at the same time:–"On October 16th 1952 the Daily Express had a two column-width headline on its front page, "British Serenade the Germans", with a report that British madrigal singers had arrived in Stuttgart to give a concert during "British Week" and that the British Council had provided them "as the highlight of the fun".

"The Daily Express was at once informed that the British Council had *not* provided these singers, who had been privately engaged by a German concert agency entirely at German expense.

"Ignoring this information the Daily Express published the following in a leading article:–

"With a fa-la-la! Observe what the British people get for their money. "British Serenade the Germans," said a Page One headline yesterday, announcing that the Council's carollers are to woo the beefy, beer-drinking Bavarians with Elizabethan madrigals."

Another report followed:– "With to-day's story of the steps that have led to something like £50,000,000 for ex-arms King Krupps comes news that "Weep no more, thou sorry boy" is one of the madrigals British Council singers are providing in Stuttgart."

This lying dog was too good to allow to sleep, so the Evening Standard revived it nearly a year later with: "The message of the British Council is a message of a collection of culture cranks –They disseminate it by ... having Elizabethan madrigals sung to Bavarians." This is just one of twelve instances given in the booklet which describes them as "a few illustrative examples .... selected from a very great number of careless, ignorant or deliberate mis-statements and misleading comments."

The publication of this Staff Association pamphlet offered great delight to all the other newspaper barons and to the BBC and achieved wide and immediate coverage throughout the media – except in the Beaverbrook Press, which remained silent for a while. Eventually, though, the storm of protest at these unjust lies became so strident that Beaverbrook himself had to answer it. His response was astonishing. In the previous few years, he asserted, his newspapers had attacked the British Council on over three hundred occasions. The British Council had been able to point out only twelve instances of inaccurate reporting. Therefore ninety-six per cent of the reports were true. What a waste of the tax-payers' money that such a booklet should be printed! This reply ignored of course the facts that the dozen instances had been stated to be "selected from a very great number of careless, ignorant, or deliberate mis-statements and misleading comments" and that the publication had been produced at the expense of the staff themselves.

Little wonder perhaps, that at about this time the Duke of Edinburgh while in Argentina referred to the Daily Express as a "bloody awful newspaper", thereby earning for himself the obliquy of Lord Beaverbrook and a barrage of personal attacks almost as great as that directed to the British Council.

I myself had been brought up to trust what was in the newspapers. More than once I had heard my mother utter the hackneyed phrase: "It must be true. I read it in the paper," and I used to believe this. I ceased to do so after reading "The Beaverbrook Press and the British Council", and I certainly do not believe it after reading some press reports of what is alleged to have gone on in my Court!

But, whatever Beaverbrook might have written (or caused to be written) I was pleased to know that I might be considered for those two Introduction Courses just before Bar Finals in the summer of 1951. After I had rounded up my four referees (including a reluctant clergyman) I was asked to attend the strangest interview of my life, conducted by Mr Strong of Personnel (now Recruitment) Department of the British Council. At about that time there was showing in London a most delightful musical called "Salad Days". It ran for years and I saw it several times – it was to be the first theatrical performance that I saw with my wife, and I still have the record of the music – and one of the minor characters in it was an "effete" and very affected couturier who spent much of his time on stage reclining on a chaise-longue, a cigarette in a lengthy holder dangling from his elegant lips, uttering such expressions as "I am a husk. I am drained of all emotion." Dorothy Reynolds and Julius Slade, the authors, must have based this part on Mr Strong.

As I entered his room in the British Council Headquarters he was lying on a settee, a cigarette in his artistic hand, and he greeted me wearily with: "Forgive me for not rising. I'm exhausted. The work here is so tiring. Do you think you're up to it? Have you the necessary stamina? These overseas students, they ask questions all the time, unanswerable questions. They run you into the ground."

I must have reassured Mr Strong that I was "up to it" and had the requisite "stamina", for before long I was to be dismissed without much further interrogation as to my qualifications for such a demanding job, when he extended in my direction a dainty hand, which I was not sure whether to shake or to kiss. A few days later I received my letter of appointment for that fortnight.

Weeks of hard study followed. Bar Finals were due in late September. My mother had died in February, and I had not been able to concentrate at all well during her long illness. Then one morning the bombshell arrived in the post, if Mr Strong were capable of creating anything as potent as a bombshell. It ran something like this:–

"Dear Mr Crowther,

I am instructed to inform you that due to a reorganisation of our internal staff we shall no longer require your services for the two Introduction Courses for which we provisionally booked you last month.

Nevertheless, I am instructed to thank you for your interest in this aspect of the Council's work.

Yours sincerely
J M Strong"

I was furious. All those references – including three visits to the clergyman to assure him that I was a bona-fide Anglo-Saxon Protestant – and that extraordinary interview with the recumbent Mr Strong; and now this! I began to pen my reply. It included the phrases: "Lord Beaverbrook is right. You are an effete and inefficient organisation which has wasted not only a lot of the taxpayers' money, but also a great deal of my time, during a period when I can ill-afford it ..."

Fortunately – most fortunately – the letter never got sent. As I sat writing it, I was smitten with the most intense internal pain and I fell writhing to the floor, where my sister Eileen found me lying in a pool of blood. The strain of my mother's illness and death, coupled with Bar Finals, and now possibly this letter as the last straw, had caused the duodenal ulcer which had afflicted me so painfully for the last year to burst, and I was rushed to the Edgware General Hospital, where I was to spend the next month. As I began to recover I forgot completely about the British Council and Mr Strong and the Introduction Courses, but asked Eileen to bring along my law books so that I could resume from my bed my studies for the examination at the end of September, for which I had paid the fees. She also brought my mail, and one day it contained a further letter from Mr Strong, who must have been completely worn out by the effort of so much correspondence:–

"Dear Mr Crowther,

I am instructed to inform you that due to a further reorganisation of our internal staff and the incidence of staff holidays the Council is now pleased to appoint you to assist on one introduction course of a week's duration commencing at 9.00 a.m. at Knutsford House on Monday September ...."

Should I do it? I discussed it with my sister who, like our mother, was full of wise proverbs and good common sense. "You wanted to do those two courses before, so why not do one now? It's no good cutting off your nose to spite your face. After all, half a loaf is better than no bread." So I left the hospital, feeling much better, on a Friday, and the following Monday morning at 9.00 a.m. I turned up at Knutsford House to begin my thirty year love-hate relationship with the British Council. My brief approbation of Lord Beaverbrook was confined to the wastepaper basket where it belonged. Mr Strong was right about one thing, however. Those overseas students did ask some unanswerable questions. On my first day a heavily-built Jordanian doctor, the holder of a British Council scholarship, came up to me with an air of one under great strain, and, taking me into a corner, asked urgently, "Tell me, where can I get a woman?" The next day Lawrence Lacey, of whom more – much more –later, gave an illuminating talk on "The Regions of Britain". Afterwards an unsophisticated young Nigerian, a private student of the kind no longer looked after by the Council (the Jordanian doctor would still be favoured, however) who up to then had not uttered a word, asked this question: "You said in your lecture that the people of Wales are short and dark. Are they as black as I am?" The third member of the staff team, a young blonde girl called Mair James, (who I afterwards learned had already been approached by the Jordanian doctor with his problem) remarked mildly, "I'm Welsh." It was encouraging to see that the näive Nigerian joined in the general laughter; he was beginning to feel at home in what was to be his new country. I was to write in my condemned article for "Glim" (the law students' magazine): "Differences of colour become laughable when the light of friendship is made to shine upon them." And the friendship of that first introduction course still remains. About a quarter of the students on it are still in touch with me –though not, I am glad to say, the disappointed Jordanian doctor. (I wrote the article for "Glim" because they offered a first prize of £10 for the best article, and I needed the money. I won the second prize – a life subscription to that rather dreary magazine).

Lawrence Lacey was in charge of the course: "Eric, will you do transport? You know, getting around London and all that sort of thing. Leave out taxis, they can't afford them."

It was a fortunate choice. Transport has always been one of my special interests, buses a passion. I advised the students who were staying in London always to travel by bus as London Transport buses were cheap, frequent and reliable, and, as Dr Johnson said: "The best way to see London is from the top of a bus" – even if it were a horse-bus in his day. I would not give the same advice in the late 1980s that I gave in the early 1950s.

Mew turned up to listen to my address. It was a bit disconcerting to have sitting at the back this immensely tall and impressive-looking lady. But it was clear that she approved. "My dear," she said encouragingly, "you must join us. We need young men like you. The British Council is a hen-ridden, hag-ridden organisation. It is run by a lot of bitches – of both sexes. We need new blood. Can it be yours?"

"Well, yes," I murmured. (As a child I had suffered from anaemia, but I was over that now, and felt that I had some blood to spare.)

"Good," she said. "The Government wants us to expand our

activities for overseas students, and I want us to produce a good programme for them every week-end. Most of our staff are too tired to work at week-ends" – I thought of Mr Strong and realised just what she meant – "but you will help us, won't you, my dear?"

"Well, yes." I replied (I have always had a tendency to say "Yes" rather than "No", and it has got me into a lot of trouble, but on the whole I do not regret that proclivity and would advise others to follow my example in that behalf, if they want an interesting, rather than a safe, life.) "Good," said Mew decisively. "I'll get Mr Strong to write to you." I hoped that the strain of all this correspondence would not be too much for him, but within a few days I got yet another letter from that eager beaver, offering me employment as a "Centre Assistant" as follows:–

Fridays   6.00 – 10.00p.m.
Saturdays   3.00 – 10.00p.m.
Sundays   2.30 – 10.00p.m.

The remuneration was to be at the rate of five shillings per hour on Fridays and six shillings per hour on Saturdays and Sundays. (Even in those days the concept of extra reward for "unsocial hours" was recognised). Mr Strong's letter warned me that my engagement was for a period of one year only and that I was not to be entitled to any of the emoluments, privileges or pension rights of "normal" British Council officers – whoever they might be.

Mew also gave me one further piece of advice before parting from me that day – wonderful advice that I would commend to anyone who has to deal with people from overseas, especially students: "Never forget that when you are talking to foreign students you are an ambassador for your own country. If you love your country, remember and respect your role." Unfortunately Mew was not to survive the mayhem of the Council for more than another year, and her admonition does not seem to have been passed down by or to all her successors; but I have never forgotten it. It is, moreover, a maxim for the most part ignored by some of the grim-faced officials of the Home Office Immigration Department.

And so it came about that for thirty years, except when I went on holiday, I was to give up all my week-ends; and one Friday night at the end of September 1951 I completed the last of the Bar Final Exams and rushed down to Fleet Street to catch a number 13 bus, hoping most anxiously that I should not be late for this exciting new employment at the Council's headquarters in Davies Street, off

Oxford Street. I arrived just on six o'clock and approached an elderly man in a slightly stained black suit. "My name is Crowther," I announced," and I am to start working here at six o'clock – that is, now."

He leered at me in a manner that was not altogether friendly and said: "Oh, you must be the new chairman."

I was surprised. I had not expected promotion to be quite so fast, even in an organisation that included officers as world-weary as Mr Strong. But Lamarque, the head porter, quickly made things clear to me.

"Yes, the new Chairman," he repeated. "Your job is to move the chairs and get things ready for the evening activity. Start with that pile over there." So, under Lamarque's supervision I did his work for the next twenty minutes and when he had finished ordering me about, hot and dirty, I went upstairs and reported to my real supervisor, Mrs Nina Cooper.

"Why are you so late?" she asked me. I was in that special world which is still known as the British Council. But it was that night that I met and fell in love with Epi.

Chapter 5

"A Venture into the Entertainment World"

"You should write a book about your experiences with the Council," many of my friends in the British Council have told me. If I did, it would be a best-seller among British Council staff, both past and present – a most introspective body of people – but I doubt whether there would be much of a demand for it outside, even though the work of the Council is far better known now than it was a few years ago, thanks to the efforts of Sir John Burgh, the last Director General, who completely reversed the policy of all his predecessors and courted publicity for all worth-while Council activities. This change would have come as a shock to the Press Officer of my early days! In fairness to him, and to Sir John's predecessors, nearly all of the five Chief Metropolitan Magistrates under whom I have served have also wished their colleagues to maintain a low profile, but that very great Chief Magistrate Sir Frank Milton never eschewed publicity or urged his colleagues to do so. To do the right thing for the right reason; and to demonstrate that this was what one was trying one's best to do, was, in his words, "good for our image." I am unaware of the views of Sir David Hopkin, the present Chief Magistrate, on this issue. He has never broached the subject with me. I am not sure if this is because he agrees with my view that in important cases it is useful to make pronouncements on public policy, or just that he regards me as beyond redemption. But certainly Sir John Burgh shared Sir Frank Milton's view. This must have come as a great disappointment to those who selected him for the post of Director-General from a wide field of candidates for this prestigious and well-paid appointment – including myself. I was not even short-listed, but simply received a "Strong-type" letter, thanking me for my interest in the Council's work; frankly, that was all I expected – I knew far too much about the Council to become its Director-General even if I were qualified in other respects, which is open to doubt! So they chose a top-ranking civil servant, believing that he would be "safe" and "quiet". They had had an outspoken Director-General in Sir John Henneker, former British Ambassador to Belgium, and they did not want to repeat that experience. They were in for a considerable shock! Sir John was nobody's fool, but he did make one very great mistake, in my opinion. He submitted to the spiteful pressures that were brought to bear on him in his early days to close down by far and away the most useful part of the whole organisation, the London Overseas Student Centre. After delaying his decision for a year he finally signed its death warrant, and the execution took place on 31st July 1981, on which date I left for good the Centre of which I had been an integral part for the previous thirty years. Or had I?

For the first year the people I worked for were Mew, whom I admired immensely, who held the key position of Deputy Director of what was then called Student Welfare Department (the Director was a remote individual, whom we seldom met; his main task seemed to be appeasing Mr Strong and others of his ilk at Headquarters); Nina Cooper, who was in charge of the rather select "British Council Scholars' Dances" on Fridays, and was a perfect lady; Lawrence Lacey, whom I have already mentioned, who was in charge of the more general Saturday dances (which were later to be called discos, to Lawrence's pained horror) and of Scottish Dancing and the Everyday English Classes on Wednesdays, both of which I was to inherit; and Vera Adamson, whose underlings always referred to her as "V", who was in charge of all the English classes except Lawrence's Everyday English (which, despite its name, took place only once a week) and of the cultural aspects of the programme, which manifested themselves on Sundays. Lawrence and V could not stand one another, and cleverly arranged to pursue their separate interests on different nights, but Mew loved and was loyal to them both. Lawrence and V were, in their different ways, difficult to work for, but Lawrence started me on Scottish Dancing and V on English Language Teaching and so I have reason to be grateful to both.

Lawrence was strange: a man at once most admirable and most irritating, much like Woody Allen in both appearance and mannerisms. I never saw him without a cigarette dangling from his lips. On my introduction course he gave a talk on "Romeo and Juliet" – which the students were to see at the Old Vic – in most cases the first Shakespeare play that they had ever seen. It was a most illuminating talk, literally as well as metaphorically. He advised the students to look out for all the references to light in Shakespeare's play – to the sun, the stars, the moon, the dawn; and to try to understand the inner meaning. It was the best talk on Shakespeare that I have ever heard – and I have listened since to many, mainly during V's cultural evenings. It was a surprise later on to learn that Lawrence had started life as a miner, won a scholarship to Sheffield University, and been a naval Commander in the Second World War. An even greater surprise in respect of a man in his position was his many prejudices, especially French girls (whom he referred to as "Frog bitches") and Nigerians, his description of whom I will not quote in deference to the Race Relations Act. On the other hand he loved all Italians without exception and nearly all Spaniards and South Americans. He had six weeks holiday a year, and on each occasion on the first evening he took the train from Victoria to Florence, returning on a Monday morning just in time to take the 25 bus from Victoria to his office. As Gerry Lloyd Evans, the funniest man I have ever met, who worked with me in the Council for only a year (alas) once asked me: "Can you imagine Lawrence in Florence?"

"Where do you stay when you go to Florence?" I asked him once, in a bold moment.

"Well, actually in a brothel," replied Lawrence, who loved to shock, "but it's a very respectable brothel."

In fact I do not think Lawrence would have had much effect on the life there, as he was a practised and practising homosexual.

He had a delightful term of phrase, however. I recall one Saturday in my first term when he called me over and said confidentially: "Eric. Three holy nuns have just come flapping in. I expect they want money. They usually do. Get rid of them, there's a dear. I can't stand holy nuns." He was right, the good ladies were collecting for a religious charity, and flapped off when I gave them sixpence each.

But, unlike V, Lawrence was not a fair person. (V, had no prejudices, except against those who were idle.) He was all over new people.

When I started to work at the Council the evening's activities terminated at 9.30 (just when life is beginning in the more civilised

Latin countries) and on my first Saturday Lawrence said: "Would you like to come to the flat?" "Well, yes," I replied rather nervously, and we adjourned to his home in Ebury Street for a party that was attended, apart from him and me, only by Italians. (It was a slight cultural shock for me, a few days ago, to be greeted in London by a buxom Italian woman approaching middle-age who introduced herself by saying: "I am Gino's daughter. You used to go to parties with my father in Lawrence Lacey's flat.")

I went every Saturday that autumn and the procedure was always the same. We had cheese and sherry and then we played "The Game". "The Game" was always the same game, but I am not sure if it should be called Charades or "In the Manner of the Word" (as in Noël Coward's "Hay Fever".) Anyway, there were two teams, one led by Lawrence and the other by me, and it was Lawrence who made up and enforced the rules and awarded the marks, and it was his team that invariably won. I am not, I hope, a bad loser, but after three months of this I got rather fed up, and one Saturday night at such a party just before Christmas 1951 I suggested: "Let's play another game. I know a good one called "Alibi"".

"No," said Lawrence coldly and firmly, "we'll play my game in my house." Not only was I never invited again, but it was many years before he spoke to me again. (I mentioned to Gerry Lloyd Evans that Lawrence had ceased to invite me after three months and Gerry replied, imitating Lawrence magnificently: "You're so lucky. He got tired of me after three days.")

By the time that Lawrence deigned to speak to me again I was beginning to build up my practice as a barrister. "Eric, do you do divorce cases?" he suddenly asked me, during the Saturday dance. "Well, yes," I replied, wondering what was coming next. "Then would you handle mine?" he enquired. I could not have been more surprised. I put him in touch with Norman Farmar's London partner Jimmy Miller (now a County Court Registrar) and in due course appeared for him before Judge Blagden.

Like most divorces, it was a sad little story of incompetence, incomprehension and intolerance. Lawrence had got married just after the war and almost immediately the British Council, for which he had worked (with a break during the war years) since its inception, sent him to Argentina. He and his wife of a few weeks arrived by ship in Buenos Aires; their luggage did not. Lawrence went daily to the dock to enquire about it but, it being South

America, he was invariably told to go away and return "mañana." Normally a meek person, he did as he was bidden. After several weeks of this his wife, fed up with not having most of her clothes and other personal belongings, packed her bags (or, more accurately, her one remaining bag) and left for England, and they never lived together again. The undefended divorce suit was based on her desertion.

Judge Blagden was a punctilious and rather difficult Judge. Woe betide the witness – or, worse still, the advocate – who arrived a minute late at his Court! When he was not sitting as a Special Commissioner of Divorce he was the Senior Judge at Westminster County Court, the most prestigious of the lower civil Courts. On one occasion there we were all punctually assembled at 2.00 p.m. after the luncheon adjournment; but surprisingly nothing happened, and five minutes ticked by. Then the usher appeared, got up on a chair in front of the Court room clock, which he proceeded to retard by six minutes. Descending from his perch he explained to his astonished audience: "This judge is a stickler for punctuality," and went and brought the Judge in.

Arriving at Court Lawrence was incredibly nervous. For a man of culture and education he knew remarkably little of the ways of the law. Outside the Courtroom he produced a wad of pound notes, asking, "Do I pay you now or after it's over?" When I had got him to put them away his next question was: "What do I call the Judge? Your Honour?" "No," I replied, " "Judge Blagden is sitting as a Special Commissioner of Divorce in the High Court, and is therefore addressed as "My Lord"."

"Why do I have to call him "My Lord" if he's only a commissionaire?" asked Lawrence. I still do not know if that question was based on ignorance or mischievous humour.

"And what about you?" Lawrence went on. "Do I call you "Eric" or "Mr Crowther"?"

"You will have to address me as "sir", "I replied with some satisfaction.

The case went reasonably well, for a time. We got to the point where Lawrence was giving evidence that in Buenos Aires his wife was continually complaining that he was not doing enough about the missing luggage. At that point the Judge intervened, looking sharply over his gold-rimmed spectacles.

"And were you doing enough? What exactly were you doing?"

His tone was unsympathetic, and put Lawrence off completely.

"Oh Your Honour," he stumbled. "Oh, Mr Blagden" – then, looking at me in desperation: "Oh, Eric."

Clearly, despite his wartime service as a naval Commander, poor Lawrence was out of his depth, and had to be rescued. "You did everything humanly possible in the difficult circumstances, didn't you?" I intervened.

"Oh yes, I did, I did, my Lord. Thank you, sir. Thank you very much."

"Then it's a pity you didn't say so when I asked you," remarked the Judge severely. "It would have saved your counsel from asking a grossly improper leading question."

After that little contretemps the rest of the case ran smoothly and a decree nisi was granted and Jimmy and I took a trembling Lawrence to the crypt of the Law Courts to revive him with a stimulating cup of tea.

I worked with Lawrence every Saturday for eight years, during about half of which he did not speak to me. In 1959 the Council transferred him from the Student Centre to Madrid, and he was replaced by George Mellors. This did not please me, at first, as I had recommended my own nominee, and he had been rejected.

In fact the Council was wise about this. My spondee was subsequently imprisoned for fraud, and the Council job involved handling a lot of small sums of money. My spondee turned out to be a really brilliant "con man". Among other things he had played the organ at my wedding. Afterwards I entrusted him to return my top hat and morning dress to Moss Brothers. I never got the deposit back ....

But as time went on I came to like and admire George Mellors very much, and the nine years that I worked with him were undoubtedly for me (and I think for the Council) the best years of my (Council) life.

When Lawrence left, George asked me to take over his very popular "Everyday English" class and I did. Learning that this had happened Lawrence very generously (and quite gratuitously) sent me all his notes from Madrid, and I use them to this day. (What a contrast to what happened when I succeeded an elderly barrister as Director of Studies of the Council of Legal Education's Post-Final Course! I asked my predecessor if I might use his practical exercises and he replied bluntly and bitterly: "No. If the School of Law doesn't want me, it can't have my exercises. Make up your own exercises!'")

I heard from Lawrence twice more. In about 1963 the British Council transferred him from Madrid to his beloved Italy, and soon thereafter he wrote to me in these terms:–

"Dear Eric,

I have adopted two Neapolitan orphans, aged five and four. Under the Deed of Adoption I had to appoint someone to look after them in case of my death until they reach the age of majority. Naturally, I could not think of anyone more suitable than you. I have told them, and the Adoption Society, that, should I die, they are to pack their bags and come to you and you will look after them.

As ever
L."

I could not think what to do except to pray for Lawrence to have a long and happy life, which I believe he did. The scunizzi have never arrived on my doorstep, so far, and I refused to believe the advice given to me by a jocular Italian lawyer friend that in Naples one does not attain majority until the age of fifty!

Lawrence retired from his service with the Council while in Italy and to everybody's surprise went to spend his remaining years not in Florence but in Madrid. It was from the Spanish capital that I received a telephone call in 1980.

"Eric, it's Lawrence here. I think I might die soon – I smoke too much – so I want to make a will. I want you to do it for me. I've arranged for you to stay three days and three nights in a nice little hotel in the centre of Madrid. I'll pay for your air ticket. Tell me when you'll arrive and I'll be there to meet you."

"But Lawrence," I protested, "I'm not a probate lawyer, I've never made a will in my life – not even my own – and I know nothing about Spanish law. I don't even speak Spanish." What I said was not entirely accurate. I hade once prepared a will for a bus driver friend who wanted to leave all his property to his mistress and had been too embarrassed, as he explained to me, to go to "a proper lawyer," and I was just beginning to go to evening classes in Spanish: but it was not until 1985 that I got my "O" Levels (Oral and Written) in that rich and rewarding language.

"But me no buts," insisted Lawrence. "It's all arranged with the hotel. And besides, you're the only lawyer in the world I trust. I shall never forget how you saved me from that dragon of a Judge when he turned on me during my divorce. You took all his wrath on to yourself. I was so relieved. If you won't come I won't make a will and then I shall die without testicles."

This last prospect was so horrifying that, as with the scunizzi, I felt that I had to accept the situation, so I asked a solicitor friend of mine in London who has international legal connections to recommend a Madrileño lawyer who knew about wills; and in due course I made my way to the Spanish capital.

Lawrence seemed almost as nervous at 9.00 a.m. outside the Spanish lawyer's office as he had been later in the day in front of Judge Blagden, and perhaps with more reason. We were ushered into a big, lavishly furnished room, in which we were introduced to no fewer than three very affluent-looking Spanish lawyers, a secretary and an interpreter. Lawrence proposed his modest dispositions:– a few small bequests to personal friends and to charities, mainly in Spain and Italy, and the residue, including all his beautiful furniture and pictures to his Spanish friend with whom he was living and whom I had met the previous evening and did not like at all.

There was no mention of the scunizzi. Either they had reached the age of majority or Lawrence had got tired of them. "Oh, and just one more thing," Lawrence added, almost as an after-thought: "I want to leave £100 to Eric Crowther here for all his hard work and friendship for me over the last thirty years."

In vain did I protest that I was not sure it was legal, with my being present here – shades of duress, perhaps; although the duress was all the other way. The consultation was over, and Lawrence produced a wallet full of pesetas. "Can I pay you now?" he asked. "No," replied the senior partner meaningfully, "we shall have a bill prepared and sent to you." I was glad that I should not be there when it arrived.

So we emerged into the hot sun of a city that is said to have six months of winter and six months of hell (seis meses di inverno y seis di infierno – it sounds better in Spanish) to have a modest lunch (everything about Lawrence was modest) at 11.00 a.m. when most Spaniards were just getting up or having breakfast; and that was the last time that I ever saw Lawrence.

Two or three years later I was back in Madrid, however, and I phoned him. The conversation went as follows:–

"Lawrence?"

"Si."

"I'm Eric."

"Si."

"Eric Crowther."

"Si."

"From London."

"Si."

"I'm in Madrid for a few days."

"Si."

"Do you want to see me?"

"No. Adios."

I have pondered many times this abrupt and sad ending to our long association. Could it have been the size of the bill of the Spanish lawyers, which I had inadvertently let Lawrence in for? But he was never a mercenary man. Surely he was not still resenting my reluctance to take part in "the Game" more than thirty years earlier?

In the summer of 1986 I received a letter from a mutual friend saying: "You will be sad to learn that Lawrence Lacey has died in Madrid as gently and as graciously as he always lived."

A few weeks after that I received a letter from solicitors in his native Sheffield informing me that Lawrence had made another will after the ill-fated Spanish one, and that under it I was to receive a legacy of £100 "in recognition of all your hard work and friendship for him."

From Saturday to Sunday, I had to undergo a complete metamorphosis, as I changed from working for Lawrence to working for Vera. With Lawrence, after the first friendly term, I knew that my main task was to keep out of his way; with Vera it was always to be around, ready to do more work. Lawrence was small, neat and dapper. "To be a gentleman," he used to tell the Introduction Course students (incorrectly in my opinion) "you need to have a clean shirt and clean shoes, and you must own a dressing gown. I always change my shirt twice a day." V was tall, thin and angular with a crop of untidy red hair and something of the manner of the late Joyce Grenfell. She did not worry at all about her appearance, but she was a natural intellectual, and what nowadays would be called a "workaholic." Unlike Lawrence, whose desk was as neat and uncluttered as himself, Vera had an incredibly untidy desk on which it took ages to find anything – but what she wanted was always there. On the other hand, she was immensely precise in her dealings with others, and all the many "Sunday Duty Officers" had their tasks clearly defined, down to the minute. I recall one occasion when there was a particularly distinguished speaker and my "duty roster" included the directions:–

"7.15 Escort speaker to lavatory."

"7.17 Bring speaker to Room 311."

I could not resist asking: "But Vera, supposing he wants to spend more than two minutes in the lavatory?"

This rigid regimentation V attempted to bring to the students, who did not accept it very well – especially the South Americans. To attend the Sunday lecture at six – and the Sunday lecture really was the big event of the week – one had to obtain a ticket (free of charge) by five. And students who had forgotten to bring their membership cards were sent home to Hampstead or Hounslow to get them, however well-known to staff they might be. "Rules are rules," I heard V declare many times, "and are made to be obeyed, not broken." This unyielding attitude made her unpopular with many students, whereas Lawrence, who appeared casual and easy-going and operated a very different regime on Saturdays, was popular. He was a character, and was regarded by many students (incorrectly in my view) as a "typical English gentleman." V's unpopularity was unfortunate, because in reality she did a great deal for the students in an utterly devoted and selfless way, and many of the thousands of students who came to 3 Hanover Street in the first half of the 1950s – a crucial time for the growth of the Commonwealth – went back with glowing memories largely on account of V's untiring efforts to put on a programme worthy of them. For me, it was quite difficult. A student member would bring a friend to the Saturday dance and I would let him or her in; the next day I would find myself refusing to admit the same person in the same circumstances. I was more popular on Saturdays than on Sundays!

But V was much loved by her staff – those who were prepared to work hard – because they could always depend on her support and her loyalty. It was a two-way process, however. We were required to give ourselves wholly and unreservedly to her – or rather to her programme. The other part-timer appointed with me was a handsome young Cambridge graduate and barrister called Michael

Catliff. One fine Sunday afternoon in June 1952 he and I found ourselves playing tennis with two beautiful Austrian nurses at Isleworth. We had no car and arrived an hour late at the Centre to a very chilly reception from V, who next day wrote to each of us a long and extremely pained letter about our dereliction of duty. Michael, who was not accustomed to being "ticked off", went into V's office one afternoon and said: "I say, Vera, this was intended as a joke, wasn't it?" and tore the letter up in front of her. He was no longer in that employment after the end of the month and soon thereafter, conditions at the Bar being as they were, he emigrated to Canada. I, on the other hand, saw that V had been right and wrote a letter of apology and promised to try to be a better boy in future. I was to be the only salaried part-timer thereafter.

But if V sought to command respect (for her work rather than herself) she also afforded it. Apart from Mew and Nina Cooper she was the only member of staff to treat me well in those early days –and, when you are young, you think a lot of respect is due to you. (As you get older, you are not quite so sure.) To V I was an equal member of the staff with the others, and the work – hard and cushy – was shared out fairly. Most others did not regard me as an equal: to them I was the hired man, hired at six shillings an hour. I was not "Council", not one of the elite. "It's a pity you're not one of us," they used to say to me, and one even remarked – I think intending to be kind: "It's a pity you're not Council. You're quite nice really." Obviously I would not have been allowed to marry a Council officer!

Not only did V treat me equally, she treated me well, and, looking back I think I have more to thank her for in my life than almost anyone else. She knew that I was poor, that I was struggling to survive at the Bar, and she cared – just as she cared for all the students, although she did not show it. After I had been in the Council for a year she started me on English classes, which paid well (£1 an hour – a far better rate than the Greater London Council was paying). I did three of these: British Life and Institutions, for which V thought my lawyer's training would suit me well – and I still use those notes, brought up to date, for a lot of lectures today; dictation and English conversation. This last class I found difficult to get going, and I used to struggle along with some contemporary theme week after week, trying vainly to imbue some interest, until one evening a very bright French girl said with disarming frankness:

"Sir, this class is very boring. Let's talk about something interesting. Let's talk about – sex." And so we did – for the rest of the term; and the class became more and more crowded and more and more lively.

Unfortunately it took place in the room next to V's Grammar Class, also very crowded, for V was an excellent teacher, and she apparently found the raucous laughter disturbing. I was told by one of her students that she had to stop her lessons occasionally because of our noise and would say wistfully: "I wonder what on earth is happening in Mr Crowther's class. But still, he's got them communicating ...."

Not only did V help me to do more work in the Student Centre, which I was now attending at least four nights a week, but she introduced me to a number of students requiring private lessons –some of them Ambassadors – and found me a holiday job for the next seven years.

However, even if to a great extent I was favoured by V ' I still had to obey the rules and be fair. One evening towards the end of her regime she called me into her office and said sternly:–

"Eric. During the tea-dance this afternoon you danced twice with Miss Winkelmann. We must not have favourites among the students, Eric."

"But V, I think that Elke and I are going to get married."

"Perhaps when you are married it may be permissible to dance twice with her, but until that happens you must not have favourites."

I wish in retrospect that these rather strict standards had been maintained throughout my Council (or pseudo-Council) career.

During my first few weeks I discovered that by tradition the staff put on a show for the students on the last Sunday of each term, and I was roped into the spectacle for Christmas 1951. I have very little recollection of it except for crawling about under a carpet half-naked wearing a kind of tiger-skin and getting extremely hot and dirty. After this ordeal was over the cast assembled upstairs in a self-congratulatory mood. I was afraid that they would ask me what I thought of it and I was reminded of Mr Winkle in "Pickwick Papers" when everyone was congratulating an after-dinner singer and he said: "I didn't like it." As the "new boy" I was eventually asked my opinion and I said: "I thought it was awful, and, what is more important, so did most of the students. There weren't many of them left at the end."

The lady who had produced the show, a sharp-faced and rather humourless acolyte of V, did not look pleased. "Well, if you think you could do better, perhaps you'd like to put on the next one."

The gauntlet was down, the gloves were on, and I accepted the challenge. "I should be ashamed if my show were any worse," I replied, "and I think I can promise it will be better."

As I thought of what I had taken on, I realised what an inexhaustable source of untapped international talent we had there in – the students! I was singularly lucky in that one of these was a young man of extraordinary charm, John Akar from Sierra Leone. The son of an African father and a French mother, he had absorbed the best of both cultures and was an excellent actor, singer, dancer and raconteur. Later he became his country's Ambassador to the United States (but he was a "private student" and would not be looked after by the British Council now) and, after being deposed in a coup, led the African Dance Group around the USA, my meeting him again quite by chance at the World's Fair in New York in, I think, 1960. Thereafter he settled in Wimbledon with his delightful American wife, who bore him five beautiful daughters, but he died in England at a tragically early age from a heart attack. With John as my assistant the show could hardly fail, and it was a tremendous success and the new tradition of the Students' Concert (the name being changed to the more accurate Students' Cabaret when the Council became less afraid of the Lord's Day Observance Society) was created. I was to put on a hundred of these shows before retiring from them, giving as my excuse a misquotation from the Chinese philosopher: "Confucius he say that no man should put on more than one hundred international cabarets."

When John Akar left England I had to look to other sources to strengthen the sometimes brilliant but often ragged student performances. I found it in the professional theatre. Greatly to my surprise V said one day that she would like to take me out, and I could choose any show in London. There were good revues in those days, and I chose one called "One Over the Eight." A brilliant but relatively unknown artist in that show was Ron Moody. His antics were so hilarious that a fat man sitting in the seat in front of V rocked back so much that his seat broke and he finished up with his head in V's lap. Even V herself was constrained to say to me: "That Mr Moody is rather amusing." I discovered that "Mr Moody" had been a student at the London School of Economics at the same time that I had been at Lincoln's Inn, and we might even have debated against each other. I wrote him a letter asking to see him and he invited me round one night after the show, and I succeeded in persuading him to appear as the star of my next concert. Aided by his able accompanist Eric Gilder, Ron was marvellous! "Marvellous" is by no means an adequate word to describe his performance but I do not like the expression: "He brought the house down", because it is never really true. V was impressed with my "catch" but said: "I think we ought to include a little more culture in your shows, Eric. After all, life is not all song and dance, and the shows do take place on Sundays." So I decided to set my sights elsewhere for the next performance.

The sister of a schoolfriend of mine, Elizabeth Butterfield, was at that time Assistant Stage Manager at the Old Vic – the precursor of the National Theatre – and sometimes got me free tickets for the classical performances there, so I decided to enlist her aid, and she introduced me to an actress whom I had seen and admired, and I asked her if she would be prepared to do a scene called "Women in Shakespeare." Claire Bloom proved to be a remarkably shy and diffident person for an up-and-coming actress and at first she seemed none too keen. "Shakespeare wasn't terribly interested in women and didn't write very good soliloquies for them," she informed me. "It would really be better if you had two people taking part. There's a young man who's just joined the company and I think he's very good. May I bring him along?"

I asked his name, and, as I had never heard of him, I agreed with some reluctance. And so it came to pass that Claire Bloom and Richard Burton gave one of the most powerful performances ever seen on the stage at the British Council Student Centre in Hanover Street. V agreed that it was good, but afterwards, as we sought to entertain the actors and she saw the Council's monthly ration of whisky diminishing with remarkable rapidity, she commented prophetically: "That young man drinks too much."

And so I had as stars of my shows such distinguished artists –and I am putting them more or less in alphabetical order – as Shirley Abicair, Maria Teresa Aracena, Felicity Baldwin, John Crocker, Leslie Crowther (no relation, although I traded on the name in writing to invite him!), George Browne (a most wonderful folk singer from Trinidad), Eranga and her husband Prianga from Sri

Lanka – these last three I visited recently in the United States –Derek Griffiths, Rolf Harris, Oscar James, David Kossoff, Isabel Lucas, Teresa Moreno, Carolyn Moody (who was generous enough to act opposite me in many sketches that I wrote), Nicholas Parsons, Paco Pena, Roger Whittaker, Danny Williams and Joanne Zorian – and I am sure I have forgotten some other great performers. All of these artists gave of their time and energy freely, some several times, without any form of payment; and I cannot pay too high a tribute to the generosity of the theatrical profession as I found it.

Not that all the performances were easy. V's main preoccupation was that they went on too long, and never finished by the magic hour of 9.30. She made her point rather effectively when once she said to me: "Eric, it would be nice if you could give me some assurance that the performance will finish on the same day that it starts." She was usually hovering in the wings, ordering me to "Get him off" if an item were too extended or the audience were shouting for too many encores. The process of removing artists who appeared to be outstaying their welcome could be quite dramatic in itself. There was one occasion when I was prevailed upon to have "the greatest living sitar player" in my show. Now I do not claim to a great appreciation of Indian music. I believe that "East is East and West is West" where this particular art-form is concerned. But we had a lot of Indian and Pakistani students at the Centre, and it seemed only fair to have their culture represented. So this beautifully attired artist settled down in a squatting position before his instrument which he proceeded to strum. Noises continued to emanate from the instrument for about twenty-five minutes and when at last there was a pause I went on stage, clapping my hands encouragingly, and saying: "Well, thank you very much for that fine performance on the sitar. The next item will be ...."

He turned on me angrily: "What is the matter with you?" he asked. "Up to now I have only been tuning up."

He did not, however, have to be physically removed from the stage like an Italian artist who came on to exercise the mouth-organ (or should I say the ocarina?). Having played tolerably well for a rather long time he kept producing from different pockets smaller and smaller instruments of the same kind on which he played the same tunes all over again, completely ignoring my admonitions that he should leave the stage.

Eventually V said to me determinedly: "Come along, Eric.

Enough is enough," and we each seized one end of him to carry him off bodily, he still defiantly playing "O Sole Mio" on the smallest mouth-organ that can be imagined. I was never sure whether the audience's loud cheers were directed to him or to us.

As producer of all these shows I did sometimes have to deal with displays of temperament. Edric Connor was a West Indian singer with a most wonderful voice. I frankly thought it more beautiful even than that of the much more celebrated Paul Robeson. He entertained our students several times, and they loved him, and for that I am profoundly grateful. But as time went on he became more difficult, and played "hard to get", refusing to commit himself one way or the other. Whilst awaiting his final "Yea" or "Nay" I chanced to meet at a party the Chinese artist Tsai-Chin, who had achieved great fame for her role in the musical "The World of Susie Wong." I gave her a lift home and on the way popped the question: Would she appear in my next show? Yes, she replied, provided that she could be the star, the final artist. Fair enough, she could be. I had no-one else firmly booked; and for days on end this conscientious actress came in with her accompanist to rehearse her final "spot".

The day before the Concert my telephone at home rang: "I find that after all I am able to take part in your show tomorrow. There is one problem, however. My accompanist has left me following a dispute between us. You will have to find me a competent pianist. Can you do this?"

"Well, yes, Edric," I replied, "it so happens that we have a most brilliant Brazilian who can play every type of music and I feel sure he will oblige. There is, however, just one matter that I ought to mention. You will not be the last item. I have promised that place to Tsai Chin, as I did not know whether you were coming."

"So I am not to be the star of the show."

"The star of the show, Edric, is the one who pleases the audience most and you undoubtedly have the capacity to fill that role. I shall put you on last but one, which is really a better position because, as you know, the show goes on late and people start leaving during the last item to catch the last bus or tube. I am sure you will be a great success, as usual."

"I see," remarked Edric heavily, using the two words that people often use when they have no intention of seeing the other person's point of view. But the rehearsal was arranged with the brave Brazilian, and from 2 o'clock to 7 on the day of the performance the building reverberated to the strains of "Ole Man River" and other Negro spirituals emanating from the Games Room and accompanied by the South American on a rather tiny piano.

Shortly before 11 the moment came for me to introduce Edric to the large international audience, and, realizing that he had been disappointed by the billing, I gave him a tremendous build-up, finishing with the words: "And now, Ladies and Gentlemen, I present to you the great Edric Connor." The Brazilian played the introductory bars of "Ole Man River" and Edric's giant and impressive bearded frame strode on to the stage. With a wave of his hand he silenced his gallant new accompanist, paused for a moment, and then addressed the assembled company as follows:–

"Ladies and Gentlemen, I have just made a great decision. I have decided that never again shall I perform in public, except perhaps in charity-performances for small children. The Lord is my shepherd; therefore I shall lack nothing. He maketh me to walk in green pastures ...." and he proceeded to recite the whole of the Twenty-third Psalm. That completed, he walked slowly through the audience towards the door, where he paused and looked back at me, hoping, I think, that I should implore him to return.

The audience had received this display of histrionics in stunned silence, and I, too, made a great decision – not to recall the tempestuous star.

"Ladies and Gentlemen," I said, "that WAS the great Edric Connor. Now we pass on to the last item on the programme, Tsai Chin ...."

Edric kept his rather macabre promise and did not perform again. He died a few months later.

The selection of items for the show was often difficult: there were always too many would-be artists offering themselves and a refusal to accept them could give offence. In the early 1960s an Egyptian student came to me with the news that the greatest of all Egyptian belly-dancers was in town, and might be prevailed upon to appear in my next show. He added, for good measure; "She was President Nasser's favourite artist" – which did not of itself seem a very strong recommendation. Had V still been there I would have been in no doubt as to what to do: I would have refused the offer. But the regime of George Mellors was far more liberal – indeed the title of my shows had by now even been changed from "Student Concerts" to "Student Cabarets" – so I accepted this offer and repaired one evening to a restaurant in Kensington where I watched this gyrating gymnast for hours on end, and I must say that I was impressed. When I tried to speak to her afterwards about my show she said that she was tired (understandably) and invited me to tea any afternoon the following week at her Kensington hotel. As Roy was still my clerk at that time I was available every afternoon, so there was no problem.

Over a prolonged pot of tea we discussed the lady's visa problems and I was also asked to recommend English language courses that she might attend. She readily agreed to take part in my next cabaret and we seemed to be getting on so well together that it would have seemed inappropriate – even churlish – to raise the sordid subject of expenses, although I would have been quite prepared to pay her return taxi fare between Kensington and Oxford Circus. Such a charming and talented creature could surely not be concerned about money!

On the night of my Cabaret, Fatima literally stopped the show. She was the last item and whirled on and on to the accompaniment of resounding cheers, especially from our Arab element. Eventually it was all over, and I will let my friend George Mellors take up the story from then on, as I have heard him relate it so often.

"Eric was helping himself to his second large whisky and congratulating himself on having presented a remarkable show when his belly dancer, now respectably dressed, appeared in the office.

"And when do I get my £100?" she demanded (I interrupt George to remark that £100 then would be the equivalent of nearly £1000 now). Eric gulped hard, (his mouth was half full of whisky), and he sobered up remarkably quickly. "I didn't promise you £100" he protested.

"Everybody knows that I never appear for less than £100," she persisted. "And I want it now – in cash."

"I am sorry, but you are not going to have £100, as I have never agreed to pay it to you."

"If you do not give me £100 I shall sue you – and the British Council," she threatened.

"Eric's eyes narrowed and an evil glint came into them. "Tell me," he asked quietly. "Do you get £100 every night at the restaurant in Kensington?"

"I do," she replied.

"And how long altogether are you performing there?"

"Three months so far – probably six. Why?"

"I was wondering if our income tax authorities know that you are receiving £600 a week .... I am sure they would be very interested."

"There was a long pause, during which the lady's hard mouth became even harder. "You are a bastard, aren't you?" were her final words as her ample hips flounced towards the door."

It was rather Machiavellian, I must admit, but I was not in a position to pay the £100 and I could not imagine the reaction of Accounts Department of the British Council to a petty cash voucher reading: "To the services of one belly-dancer, £100. Eric Crowther." I wonder what the Daily Express would have made of a semi-British Council "culture vulture" spending the tax-payers money on that!

This was not my only British Council encounter with an exotic dancer. Again I will let another friend of mine, Antony Wicken, tell the story. By now I had changed Chambers, and my clerk was Robert.

"It was the first day of my pupillage, and in the morning we did a case at London Sessions which finished just before one o'clock. "Do we have lunch now?" I asked .... "No," my learned pupil-master replied. "We're going to Ealing for a view." "Oh, are we going to see the site of a personal injury accident?" I asked. "No," he answered. "We are going to audition a hula-hula dancer for my next cabaret at the British Council."

"Is a hula-hula dancer respectable enough for a British Council performance?" I ventured. "Certainly," he said firmly. "She advertised her services in the Personal Column of "The Daily Telegraph.""

"So we set off by tube for South Ealing, and then had a half-hour walk in pouring rain to a mysterious detached house, where Eric rang the bell. I was expecting the door to be answered by a voluptuous willowy dusky young maiden from some South Seas island, but in fact what appeared was a rather short plump peroxide blonde from Australia. "Why, come on in, cobbers" she said, and took us into a downstairs room, drew the curtains, and disappeared. We sat in semi-darkness for a few moments after which she re-appeared garbed as if to greet American tourists arriving in Hawaii. She put on some soothing music and then proceeded to move seductively around the room. After about ten minutes she slumped down exhausted and said: "That's my number one show. It costs £15." My pupil master agreed to engage her for this fee, and gave her the place, date and time. By now she had recovered her breath and she made a further offer: "And I strip for twenty."

"Come on, Eric," I said encouragingly "let's see if the full show would be

suitable for the British Council."

"Definitely not," said my pupil-master severely. "We have an important conference in Chambers at half past four and are leaving for the Temple –immediately."

This dancer, too, was a sensation on the night, and, in her enthusiasm for the great reception that she got, she carried out uninvited and free of charge, before the international audience at the British Council Student Centre, the threat or promise she had made in Ealing. I was glad that night that V was no longer in command!

Chapter 6

"Neither Fish, nor Flesh, nor Fowl ....."

In the summer of 1952 Mew was ousted in one of those internal internecine feuds that beset the British Council in those days and for many years thereafter. The "victor" in this battle was the even more formidable Dame Nancy Parkinson, generally known as "The Dragon", who, in 1964, was to set up the brand new British Council Student Centre in Portland Place to be a rival to Dame Mary Trevelyan's already planned International Students House, just up the road at Park Crescent. If those two ladies had been more concerned with student welfare and less with their personal conflicts and aggrandisement one of those two organisations would have operated in South London –Brixton perhaps – instead of their both being established within a year and half a mile of each other.

Mew accepted her defeat graciously and left the Council and went to live in Paris with her friend, the very talented British Council representative there, Enid McLeod. Two years later, I visited Mew in the French capital. "Where would you like to go, my dear?" she asked invitingly. "I have an old jalopy if you'll risk my driving." At school I had been much attracted by the life and work of the romantic poet Alfred de Vigny, and I had written a thesis about him (so far unpublished!) Perhaps one thing that appealed to me was that he wrote so little: three plays (including one based on the life of HIS hero, the English poet Chatterton), three books (not exactly novels) and about ninety poems, some of which, like "La Mort du Loup" and "Eloa", are among the finest in the French language. "I would like to see de Vigny's home," I said, and Mew very generously drove me about forty miles to the Chateau de Vigny, only to find that it was closed on Mondays. I told Mew that she was sorely missed at the Student Centre in Hanover Street, and this was indeed so. I frequently did "door duty", which consisted mainly of preventing non-members from getting in, and Mew had often been there on Saturday and Sunday nights to greet those hundreds of young people from overseas who were entitled to enter, being bona fide full-time students who had paid their five shillings a year for membership. "And how are you my dear?" she would ask regally, greeting by name some shy student from a small West African state. "And how is your course in tropical hygiene going?" Somehow she always got right both the name and the subject of study, and the student was delighted to be made to feel so important by this supremely dignified lady. She was certainly the best ambassador for her country that I have ever met, and she also managed to hold Lawrence and V together and at bay in their separate corners in an atmosphere of comparative tranquility.

It was upon this reasonably happy scene that Will Byford descended as Mew's successor in the summer of 1952. His first act as Deputy Director was to call a staff meeting. "When I come upon a department that is working well, as this department is, I never interfere," he undertook. I have learned since that such general pronouncements, whether made by politicians, diplomats or lawyers, are never to be trusted. The interference started very soon. Will decided that he was not interested in anything that Lawrence did, and he left his activities alone. Lawrence wisely became a great friend of Will and they always went off to lunch together, so Lawrence's little world remained safe. It was poor V who was to suffer most. "Yours are the only activities here that interest me," he announced, "and they're running efficiently at the moment, but, by God, if I ever discover any slackness or inefficiency on your part, I'll have you out and take over." He spent much of his time trying to catch her out, a vain hope with someone as conscientious as V, but he succeeded in making her life a misery and her a nervous wreck. The tragedy was that V was eventually constrained by his persecution to apply for a transfer and was seconded to be warden of a girls' hostel in Birmingham, a job for which she was singularly unsuited but did remarkably well, her secondment taking place just after Byford had left and been replaced by the delightful and highly intelligent Richard Auty, whose relations with his staff were always happy.

Will Byford was a large man looking like a cross between Robert Maxwell and the late Aneuran Bevan. He oozed grease, from the palms of his sticky hands to the Brylcreem of his black plastered carefully parted hair, and he had a raucous laugh, normally to be heard just after one of his own jokes. He was quite the most pompous and conceited man I have ever met. The set-piece of the week was the Sunday evening lecture at 6 o'clock arranged by V but chaired up to Byford's arrival by Michael Catliff and me in turn. Byford decided to take over the introduction of these distinguished speakers. "It's too important to be left to be a part-timer," he explained to me. He was a great extrovert and an even greater bore. He liked to appear to be an expert on everything, but in fact he would look up the topic of the Sunday talk in the Encyclopaedia Britannica or some similar publication and deliver a sort of mini-lecture before the main speaker. Through my friend Michael Scott, who had been at school with that great actor, I got Paul Schofield to come and talk and perform on Shakespeare's birthday. His appearance was preceded by a long introduction by Byford explaining the technique of presenting and acting Shakespeare, as achieved by Byford himself in Jamaica. When eventually he was able to take the stage the aggrieved Paul Schofield started: "I feel inadequate to perform for you after that introduction," and afterwards he asked me, "Who was that buffoon who introduced me? I don't want to come here again while he is here." Worse was to happen when Lord (then Sir Robert) Boothby came to speak at V's invitation. Byford's introduction went on so long that when Sir Robert eventually rose he said to the audience: "Well, I came here to present a lecture on the British political system, but as it has already been given I'm going home. Good night;" and he left. After that I was back in the chair for two or three weeks.

Byford's covetous eyes alighted on another successful item on the programme: my international student cabarets. These functions, also, were too important to be presented by a part-timer, although he was quite content to leave to me the task of collating and rehearsing the items. At first he handed over the job of compering my show to a reluctant Gerry Lloyd Evans. Gerry was made of India rubber and was a real comic in the Harold Lloyd mould. On the night, while on stage, he kept forgetting (or pretending to forget) things that he should be saying, and then he would slap his own cheek, then fall to the ground, immediately bouncing back into a vertical position. How he failed to break several bones in the process I shall never know. The students loved his performance, but Byford did not. Gerry was summoned next day to his office to be given a piece of advice. "Lloyd," he admonished, "the ringmaster should not be the clown. It's obvious to me that both you and Eric are quite incompetent to present the students' concerts, so I shall have to take them on myself."

International students are not the easiest audiences before whom to perform. They make very clear their likes and dislikes, and they did not like Byford. His numerous jokes between items were accompanied by loud laughter – but only his own; and, as the introductions got longer than the items, there were cries of "Get on with it!" Next term I was back in charge of presenting my own cabarets.

But Byford could not leave well alone. V had appointed me to my various teaching jobs in the Council, so I had to be stripped of them, in the name of "reorganisation", as well as having my Saturday hours cut down (but not cut out). When I protested to Byford that the people who were being appointed in my place were less well qualified for their subjects than I (especially British Life and Institutions, for which I had laboriously produced copious notes) and that I desperately needed the money, he exclaimed angrily, "Why, you're nothing in the Council. You're neither fish, nor flesh, nor fowl, nor ...." "Nor good red herring," I volunteered helpfully, but Byford was not a man who liked to have his sentences finished for him, especially as he considered himself to be a Shakespearean scholar. "Get out," he shouted. "You're very lucky to be in the Council at all. I could have you out in no time if I wanted, and I shall if you come whining to me again." I knew there was something in what he said, and I left him alone for the rest of his six years, seeking teaching employment elsewhere in order to survive at the Bar. In the result I finished up lecturing almost every night of the week for the Greater London Council in dreary evening institutes on subjects in which I was not interested (I even lectured on Company Law! Some of my students came for the law; the majority for the company) to students who did not appear to be interested. The "lectures" often consisted of being a couple of pages ahead of the students in their recommended books – not a very difficult task as most of them did not read the books, anyway. But a marked change for the better was to come in 1958.

In that year Byford was transferred to some South American state ripe for revolution and his place was taken by the brilliant and immensely likeable Richard Auty, who was to become in due course one of the Council's top men. A man of catholic and cosmopolitan tastes, married to a French lady, he did nothing by halves. His was the only family I know to have had two au pair girls at the same time. Both were Yugoslav, both were very beautiful, and both are still good friends of ours.

In early 1959, after I had officially announced my engagement to Elke Winkelmann so that I might dance with her twice rather than once on Sunday afternoons, Richard Auty summoned me into the office from which I had once before been so abruptly expelled by his predecessor. "Eric. You are going to get married soon and there is a danger that we may lose your services. Elke won't want you to be away from home every weekend for six shillings an hour. I don't think you realise how valuable you are to the Council." (I certainly did not, after his predecessor's treatment of me.) "I'm going to try to make it worth your while for you to stay with us. I'm proposing that you shall be a half grade F Council officer, working half the time of a full Council officer, in other words seventeen and a half hours a week, and receiving half of a grade F salary and an appropriate Council pension. We shall also pay your National Insurance contributions. You will really be one of us. What do you say?"

"Well, Richard, it's very kind of you, but you know I'm just beginning to get busy at the Bar and I don't think I can spare seventeen and a half hours a week," I replied.

"I've thought of that," Richard retorted. "You can continue to do Saturday evenings and Sunday afternoons and evenings and Vera wants you back teaching British Life and Institutions and a couple of other classes. I'll fit all those lectures into one evening if you like. That will amount to about fourteen hours a week. Then we'd like you to run a law group for Commonwealth law students once a month and a weekly Debating Group. Do you like the Edinburgh Festival?" he interjected, surprisingly, "Immensely," I replied.

"Good," he said, "We organise three courses there every year; one for each of the three weeks of the Festival. We'll send you up there to run all three of them. It's really a twenty-four hour day. With three weeks paid holiday – half what a Grade F gets – you should be up to the required number of hours. What do you say?"

I talked it over with my wife-to-be and she agreed. Elke has always been very tolerant of my extra-mural activities – (and she still is) – because she and I met in the Student Centre. After eight years of working there, I was "in" the Council at last.

In a slightly Machiavelian way I tried to turn my Council work to my advantage. To my monthly Law Group I invited such distinguished speakers and wonderful men as Lord Denning, Lord (then Lord Justice) Scarman and Lord Justice Lawton and I decided to invite along Sir Frank Milton. I admired Sir Frank immensely, but I must confess that the thought passed through my mind that if the Chief Metropolitan Magistrate saw me, as chairman, handling well a young cosmopolitan audience just at the time when Great Britain was in the process of becoming a multi-racial society he might think that here was a man well suited to be one of his regular colleagues (I was already sitting as a deputy). At the end of Sir Frank's erudite and entertaining address to this large Commonwealth audience I, as chairman, invited questions, and a little Indian law student raised his hand, "Yes," I said encouragingly, "what is your question?" and my blood froze as he asked it, my imagining all my chances of being a stipendary vanishing as the Great Man thought: "Did he bring me here to be insulted?"

"Sir Frank," asked the questioner, "do you not lie awake at night worrying about all the people you have wrongly convicted?"

There was a long pause, it seemed like half an hour, but it was probably only half a minute, before Sir Frank gave a reply which I shall always remember, not only because of the tactlessness of the question, but also because the answer contained so much of value for all who presume to sit in judgment upon their fellowmen. Sir Frank replied, "No, the answer to your question is emphatically "No". I'm sorry if that sounds harsh and callous and isn't what you hoped to hear, but English law provides me with the answer. English law says that if at the end of the case I'm not happy, not sure, not certain – call it what you will – if I have any sort of lingering doubt whatsoever I simply say: "case dismissed" and if the policeman's back isn't broad enough to bear it he's not fit to be in uniform, anyway. Now, if you had wanted to ask me an intelligent question, and I imagine from the manner rather than the content of your interrogation that was your intention, you should have asked me: "Don't you worry about sentencing?" That is the real problem."

I have always tried to follow Sir Frank's precept that night about the burden of proof in my nearly two decades on the Bench.

Sir Frank of course was too great a man to be affected by the Indian student's question, and in due course in 1968 I was appointed as a London stipendiary. The question then troubled me: Was I entitled to continue working for the British Council? I put it to Frank. "I don't know", he replied ponderously. "We'll have to put it to the Lord Chancellor". A little later I received an invitation to tea at the House of Lords, Lord Gardiner looked magnificent in his robes, but it was clear that even he did not know the answer to my question, for he kept turning for advice to an eminence grige behind him whose name, I discovered, was Sir George Dobson. "I don't think we can possibly have a judicial officer, however lowly, as a grade F British Council official," said that individual rather pompously.

"Well, I can't be a grade A," I responded, "there's only one of those, and he's the Director-General."

The Lord Chancellor looked at me rather severely and approached the subject from a different angle. "Look here," he said, "the British Council is a fine organisation and you have done some very useful work for it" (He clearly had not been talking to Byford). "I want you to continue to work for the Council – but to receive no remuneration for doing so."

This came as rather a shock financially. I pointed out that I subscribed to a number of charities. Would it be all right if I got the Council to pay my subscriptions to those? Lord Gardiner looked at Sir George who replied, "I can see no objection to that." But the Council could. "Suppose you were to subscribe to a controversial charity – even a political one," they asked, "would we not then be involved in controversy?" I could not see Cancer Research, or the World Wildlife Fund, or the P.D.S.A. as being terribly controversial, or political, but the Council would not play ball. But I had spent ten very happy years at the Council with first Richard Auty and then with George Mellors (and with both for a time) and I decided to carry on with this enjoyable work, especially as the Lord Chancellor found it so "useful".

I decided to take advantage of the situation. "As the British Council is such a useful organisation that you want me to work there indefinitely and without remuneration, would you be prepared to come along one evening to give a talk to our students about your office?" I asked. The Lord Chancellor could hardly refuse, and one Sunday evening soon thereafter Lord Gardiner came to the Student Centre and gave an excellent talk on "A Day in the Life of the Lord Chancellor" – witty, warm, urbane, wholly delightful. Gerald

Gardiner had the reputation of being cold, retiring, unfriendly; he displayed none of these qualities with our overseas students, although I think that he is basically a modest and shy man. He is also immensely kind. In 1971 I was on a committee chaired by him – he was then no longer Lord Chancellor – a committee set up by "Justice", whose recommendations resulted in the passing of the Rehabilitation of Offenders Act. The meetings were held in Lord Gardiner's flat in the Temple. I omitted to attend on one occasion. Elke had been terribly ill and had an operation that day. Two surgeons had been in attendance and for five hours she hovered between life and death on the operating table. I just forgot to go to Lord Gardiner's flat that evening. When I realised what I had done (or, rather, not done) I wrote to apologise, of course, and I received from him the most gentle and consoling reply, full of good wishes for Elke's well-being, that can be imagined. On the night of Elke's operation I decided to stay in my flat in Lincoln's Inn so as to be near to the hospital in case her condition worsened – of course, that was the night that the telephone in the flat went out of order, but a sympathetic neighbour agreed to take any call from the hospital – and on my way there in the Inn I met Lord Denning. "You're looking very down in the mouth, Eric," he commented, accurately. "What's the matter?" When I told him Lord Denning said, "Well you can't be alone at a time like this. Come up to our flat and have a bit of supper with us. Joan's only making a little boiled chicken and rice but come and share it with us." Some of the great men of the law are really very kind.

Even so, I wish, that I had not been to see the Lord Chancellor, I feel certain that if, I had not raised the matter no-one would have been the wiser and I would have gone on earning thousands a year from the British Council for the next thirteen years. This would have been very useful because of a financial blow that was to fall in April 1969.

In 1967 Sir Frank Milton had asked me to tea in his office at Bow Street. Edgar Bradley, clerk to the Poole Justices, had just been appointed as a new stipe. In fact his appointment was announced on my birthday. I read of it in "The Times" on my way back from Ipswich where a good client of mine who twice before had been acquitted when I had defended him had gone down for five years because I had asked an ill-advised question in re-examination which the Recorder, Sebag Shaw Q.C., had latched on to in order to conduct a very disarming interrogation of his own. (The same Judge had presided in the two earlier cases that had resulted in acquittals.) The client had not blamed me for this bad result. He was a professional criminal and, like most of his kind, was philosophical about the risks involved in his work. "We can't win 'em all, can we?" he had remarked, but I knew that he knew that I had made a mistake. It was a sad birthday and Elke realized that I was sad when she met me at the station and invited me to dine in a specially nice Greek restaurant.

Over tea Frank remarked: "I'm awfully sorry, Eric. I got back from holiday and there was a list of all those who have been sitting recently as deputy stipes and I was asked to choose one of them. Somehow I missed your name on the list and, as I didn't know any of them, I told the Lord Chancellor's Office I'd leave it to them and they chose Bradley. I do regret it because when you used to appear before me at North London I used to think: "He's a natural for a stipe," and now I'm afraid, barring accidents, it will be a year before there's another appointment. I'll put your name forward but by then the new man, Tom Skyrme, will have found his feet and he may have his own nominees."

It was difficult not to feel resentful of Bradley, although during the year I was to appear before him several times and always found him exceedingly sound and fair. But he always seemed to be just one step ahead of me. Appointed exactly a year before me he spent that year at fascinating Bow Street (the "testing" Court) and managed to avoid going to the dreaded (because oh! so boring) Wells Street, whereas I was to have only three interesting weeks at Bow Street and fifteen monotonous months at Wells Street, during which I cried inwardly every day: "Why ever did I leave the Bar for this?" Bradley got his own Court, at Camberwell Green, as soon as that "Palais de Justice" opened, and it was convenient for travelling from his home address. After Wells Street I got sent to Thames which was a journey of nearly two hours from my home – but I loved Thames. I had been a magistrate five and a half years before I got transferred to the Court that I really wanted, West London, to which I could cycle from home. I was moved from there in 1984 after nearly eleven years.

But worst of all was the financial consequence: up to April 1968 if a barrister received a judicial appointment any Bar fees received thereafter were tax-free. This was the only "perk" that the Bar got of which I am aware. (As a stipendiary magistrate I get a free copy of "The Times" every day.) Solicitors pay slowly and a tremendous amount was owing to me from them when I was appointed. (Some fees are still owing nineteen years later!) This tax concession went, at, I believe, Lord Gardiner's suggestion, in the 1968 budget. As these old fees came in I was taxed on them in addition to my salary, and this put me well up in the Supertax class for several years. It really had the effect of impoverishing me (as in effect I was being taxed twice over) although not quite to the extent of the poverty that I had experienced in my days as a student and early on at the Bar, although now I got into debt – then never. It was only after my sister died late in 1974 and I inherited all her careful savings that my own finances got on to anything like an even keel again. Perhaps I should not complain too much: Sebag Shaw, Q.C. suffered far more on his appointment to the High Court Bench at about the same time from the withdrawal of this tax concession, he having been a much more successful advocate than I. But if only I had been appointed in August 1967 and Bradley the following year Bradley would have lost little, as he would have continued to work as a court clerk until his appointment to the Bench, and I would have been, for the only time in my life – rich! If Edgar ever reads this he may be surprised, so may I add that until he retired (also well ahead of me) I found him a charming colleague and I delighted in his dry, sardonic sense of humour.

It was not only on financial grounds that my tea-party with the Lord Chancellor was inopportune. By resigning from the Council as I did in the autumn of 1968, but complying with his injunction to remain, thereby becoming thereafter an "honorary student counsellor," I lost not only my salary but my cherished status as a "half grade F British Council officer." Once again I was "neither fish, nor flesh, nor fowl ...." Had I remained in paid employment the attacks which were to be made on me in the late sixties and early seventies would never have taken place, because those who perpetrated them subscribed to the doctrine that no worker must ever be dismissed, however bad he was (and they could not have imagined anyone worse than I).

The "happy years" at the Council ended with the departure of Richard Auty and, soon thereafter, of George Mellors. This coincided with my appointment to the metropolitan stipendiary bench in 1968. George and I felt that we had been such a successful team that we viewed with apprehension the appointment of George's successor, believing that all our work in creating an easy, homely atmosphere in the Student Centre might be wrecked by the arrival of some bureaucrat from the dreaded new headquarters in Spring Gardens, which always regarded the Student Centre as the Cinderella of the Council. So we sought our own nominee to succeed George and found him on (or rather within) our own doorstep. He was Ronald Dunmow.

We had known Ronald for about six years. He had arrived in London from the North of Scotland with impeccable references stating how helpful he had been on a voluntary basis in organising activities for overseas students in the small British Council office up there. He was made an honorary member of the Student Centre, and took over from George the teaching of Scottish Dancing, which he did extremely well. He was charming, with a quiet, sly sense of humour. He came to all our parties and never forgot to bring a present for our children. He got on well with the students. He seemed the ideal person to take over from George as the person in charge of the Centre. Another advantage was that he was almost permanently unemployed.

This, he explained, was because there was only one job that really appealed to him, that of a Programme Director in the BBC. Every year he applied for such a post; every year George and I wrote glowing references for him; every year the "Beeb" turned him down. How wise they were!

So, thanks to my efforts and those of George, Ronald took over the key position in the Student Centre in the late summer of 1968. In fairness to him, he seemed reluctant to accept it – he still coveted the job with the BBC – but we persuaded him to apply, saying that this would increase his chances for his preferred post.

George had a friendly, untidy desk. Ronald cleared it. Hardly ever did you see a piece of paper on it. In retrospect I have decided that I don't like people with tidy desks. My own, my wife describes as "that heap"; V's could better have been called "the mound". George had a spell of leave before his new posting to Zambia and spent quite a lot of time in his spiritual home, the Student Centre. Once when I was also there I heard him give his successor, very gently, a piece of good advice, based on his long experience of running the Centre. The reply from Ronald sent a chill down my spine:–

"Your term of office here ended on the last day of last month, and that was the last day on which your face was welcome in this building."

"Very well," replied George, "you won't see it here again"; and we didn't for many years.

If Ronald could treat George, a friend who had done so much for him, in that way, what was in store for me? Worse, far worse! I, as a magistrate, whatever my political views (or lack of them) was part of the "Establishment", and the Establishment was something reprehensible that had to be destroyed. I had to be removed.

To aid him in this and other important manoeuvres Ronald gathered around him a little cell of like-thinking people to organise the programme with him – to do the work that George and I had been doing. These comprised a young man called Sid Vague who combined the cunning of a fox and the venom of a viper. So great, in fact, was his cunning that he nearly failed his interview on account of it. Looking very pious, he said that he hoped that when doing Sunday duty he might be excused for an hour or so to slip away to Evensong. Mistakenly he assessed his interviewers as being profound practising Protestants. In fact George, chairing the Board, was a committed atheist as well as a strong Socialist and nearly rejected Sid on this account. He need not have worried. I doubt if Sid had been in a Church since the day of his baptism.

Next there was the coach driver, whom Ronald promoted. (I saw nothing wrong in this, and, left alone, Cliff would have been a very nice fellow, for he was basically decent and honest, and I feel sure that we could have been good friends; it was a matter of great regret to me that we were not); and then there was a fellow Scot, a girl, even more politically extreme than Ronald himself, who hated me more I believe than almost any other person has ever done – certainly more than any other woman – and for no good reason that I could see except that I was seen as part of the detestable "Establishment".

I have never held any strong political views, and neither did Sid: he just followed the course of self-interest. But Ronald and his compatriot and Cliff were deeply committed to the extreme left, and, with Sid joining them in every enterprise, a formidable gang of four was created. The doyens at Headquarters came to fear Ronald. Money poured into the Centre at an unprecedented rate for his projects. We, who had always prided ourselves on being a non-political organisation, had an evening devoted to songs and speeches against the. Greek Colonels. I did not like the Greek Colonels myself, but I found it shameful that we could be directing propaganda against an ostensibly friendly foreign power in the British Council Student Centre. Advertisements of our political activities in the "Agit-Prop" column of "Time Out" ensured a good, rabid, revolutionary turn-out. When a lady who had worked as a secretary in the Student Centre for many years attended one of these functions and complained to Ronald that a lot of the guests were smoking cannabis in the Centre and one of them had offered her a joint, the new Head of the Centre responded with: "And why didn't you accept it? It would have done you good, you old witch!"

The British Council's Charter stated that it should be a-political. V, had been, like almost every other Council officer I have met, a committed Socialist. Yet in her time we had only one "political" evening in the year and that was an "Any Questions" session on which the Labour, Conservative and Liberal viewpoints were all represented. However passionate her political views V, believed equally passionately in the dictum incorrectly attributed to Voltaire (but I cannot at the moment remember which noble Frenchman made it): "I disagree with every word that you say, but I would fight to the death for your right to say it." If there is one change that I regret above all others that has occurred in our British society in the last two decades, it is the almost complete departure from this principle.

Both George and Byford were committed Socialists, too. But neither of them had ever allowed their political persuasions to influence the content of the programme at the Student Centre. Under Ronald, however, it became what he had wanted the BBC to become, a nucleus for the dissemination of extreme left-wing or even anarchist propaganda. What was I to do?

My work as a metropolitan magistrate involves an implied commitment to be non-political: "to do right to all manner of people."

I have never found this very difficult; I am by nature an a-political animal. For seventeen years, although dominated by Socialists, the British Council Student Centre had either avoided politics or presented the viewpoints of all parties fairly and objectively. Within a few months of Ronald's becoming Head of the Centre (a title which he had created for himself) all this had changed and the

Centre had become a political machine. I desperately wanted it to return to its former political neutrality, and I decided that I could achieve my aim far better from within than without. I must stay, whatever the cost, despite what had happened to George.

And the cost was great. Ronald and his confederates used every device to get me out. Some of the staff remained loyal to me, and one of these photocopied a document produced by Ronald stating that I was too well-established to be dismissed from the organisation, but that I should be harrassed to such an extent that I would leave of my own accord if my life could be made sufficiently unbearable. The main things that I did at the Council then were the successor to Lawrence's Everyday English Class, my student counselling, and my end-of-term international cabarets; in addition I joined in Scottish Dancing (which I have always enjoyed and now teach) on Wednesday evenings after the Everyday English Class. These activities were assailed in the following ways: The Everyday English Class would be moved to different unsuitable rooms nearly every week; these rooms were normally at the top of the building and the lift would be put temporarily out of action so that both the students and I would have difficulty in reaching the classroom, often not equipped with blackboard and chalk when we arrived. Ronald wanted to insist on an appointments system for my student counselling, which he would control. This I successfully resisted with the Director, arguing that if a student has a problem he wants it resolved now, not on Wednesday week; but I was compelled for the first time to keep a record of all the students who came to me, along with the advice that I gave, to ensure that it was not subversive of the subversion that was going on. The date of the Students' Cabarets would be changed a few weeks before the event, in the hope that I would lose some of my artists in that way and the show would be less successful; and I was forbidden to leave my Scottish Dance clothing in the office on the ground that it was "unhygienic." All of this I endured without complaint, saying that I was sure that Ronald would not issue such edicts without good reason in the best interest of the Centre. This seemed to infuriate him even more – in this instance "the soft answer did not turn away wrath" – and for about two years I was "sent to Coventry" by the gang of four, although Cliff did usually reply monosyllabically when I spoke to him, and the students remained as friendly to me as ever.

But Ronald was eventually to overstep the mark. One term he ran a course called "The Alternative Society" on which each week some radical came to address the students. A left-wing lawyer came to speak on how to stand up for your rights against the police. A "hippy" doctor spoke on the benefits to be derived from smoking cannabis. Another lecturer, speaking on sex in society, advocated a permissive attitude towards sexual promiscuity; there were talks on the politics of protest and "Bomb Culture" and one of the editors of "Oz" came along and, in an impassioned account of the "Underground Press", freely punctuated with the better and the lesser known four letter words, strongly advised our overseas students to leave their parents as soon as possible, to do everything they could to destroy existing society, and never to trust anyone over the age of thirty. To an Indian student who asked the chairman whether he agreed with this last piece of advice Ronald, then in his mid-thirties, replied that he thought that the speaker had put the age of untrustworthiness a little too low.

Caroline Coon was due to lecture on her organisation "Release" (but did not turn up). I cannot remember the rest of the programme, comprising about ten talks. It was widely advertised and one of the leaflets came into the possession of Lord Boothby, whose own last visit to the Centre had not been an unqualified success. He sent it to the Director-General, with a note asking "What is this nonsense?", and soon thereafter Ronald was moved (after four years as Head of the Centre) to a post in a Communist country, where it was hoped that he would feel greater empathy.

His replacement was Norman Leigh. Norman met me one day shortly before taking office, and after we had spent an hour or two together he commented: "I've been told awful things about you, but you seem quite reasonable. I think we shall get on well together."

But he did not get on well with the remnants of the gang of four. He was what in modern parlance is called a "straight guy" and they despised him for it and determined to get rid of him. He survived for only a few months and was replaced as head of the centre by – Cliff. The war was on again!

Although Cliff was undoubtedly receiving advice if not orders from Ronald's headquarters abroad he fought a much cleaner campaign than his leader, because he was a much less devious person. His method was to gather as much support as possible from the rest of the staff and then to go to the Director and complain that it was impossible to work with me and to hint at the possibility of a strike.

The first of his Directors came up with a Machiavellian Council compromise that I would be asked to stay away on Saturday: this was the night when most students came for the discos and rock bands that were then current, and I refused to accept this.

Soon thereafter there was a change of Director. The new one was a kind, generous, honest man, but very weak. After one of these interminable meetings he invited me out to dinner, in a pub in Regents Park. It took him a long time to get round to what he had to say, but eventually it came out.

"Eric, there was another meeting about you yesterday. It went on nearly all day. Four of them are against you, four in your favour. I want to keep you, I assure you. I think you do invaluable work for us. But it can't go on like this. The atmosphere of strife is preventing any work from getting done. I'm not prepared to bar you from the Centre, as some of them want me to do, because I can't see that you've done anything wrong, but may I ask you, as an act of personal friendship to me, to take a year's Sabbatical? Then maybe there'll have been staff changes and you can come back and resume your good work in an atmosphere of harmony. It's the only way I can get peace back in my Department."

It was all put so appealingly, diplomatically, so plaintively almost, but I knew that if I left I would never go back. "Will you give me a week to think it over?" I asked, as we parted after that sad meal.

Occasionally God or Providence or Fortune smiles on all of us. (I happen to think of it in terms of God smiling; others like George would view the matter differently.) But the secret of success in life is good timing – or sometimes just the right thing happening at the right time.

In 1966 I had acquired the tenancy of a tiny ancient flat in Lincoln's Inn in circumstances that I will describe later. A few months before my fateful dinner in Regents Park a stipendiary colleague of mine, Bertie Clark, who had been a Clerk to the Justices in Devonshire and is now a Crown Court Judge, came to me with a request. His son was about to take his medical finals. Did I know of anywhere quiet in or near the City where he could reside and study during those last few intensive weeks? I was using the flat very little then, so I offered to let him have it. The young man moved in, worked hard in the peaceful atmosphere of the "village" of an Inn of Court, passed his examination with flying colours and left behind a box of excellent claret. Soon after he had gone Bertie got in touch with me again. "Eric," he said, "you'll think I'm very importunate, but would your flat by any chance be free for the next month? A friend of ours is coming up from Devon because he'a taking on a job with the British Council. He'll be buying a house in London but he wants a pied à terre for a few weeks while he looks around."

"What job is he going to do in the British Council?" I enquired.

"He's going to be director-general."

"I think I can manage to make the flat available," I said, "but it's a pied au ciel rather than a pied à terre, being up four flights of stairs"; and a few days later Sir Jack Llewellyn moved in.

Two days after my Regents Park dinner I finished my magisterial work feeling very depressed. I had something on in town in the evening and did not want to go home, and I made my way to the flat to relax, hoping that Sir Jack would not be there. He was, and noticed that I seemed upset and asked "What's up?" and I told him. I then sought his advice. "Do you think I should leave?" I asked. "I don't know," he replied. "Let's meet in two days' time. I'll tell you then."

When I returned to the flat Sir Jack had this to say to me:— "Look, I've been through all your files. You've been with the Council for over twenty years, longer than almost anyone else. All your annual reports were glowing except those from a man called Byford, and they weren't too bad really – until recently, and now it seems you can't do anything right. I don't think you can have changed all that much since you became a magistrate. I've spoken to a lot of people you've worked for in the past, and they are all of one opinion. You've got to stay on."

"Is that an order?" I asked.

"Yes, if you want it that way," Sir Jack replied, as he puffed away at his pipe with his avuncular smile.

So I returned to my director with my decision. "I'm not going," I said. He looked alarmed. "I've talked to the new D-G and he's given me an order to stay on. And we've all got to obey the D-G, haven't we?"

"Oh yes," replied the Director, with obvious relief, and he added enthusiastically: "And now I've got the necessary ammunition to support you. Yes, we've all got to support the new D-G.

In the remaining seven years there were no further serious efforts to get rid of me, but I do not think that mine were the only files to be examined by the new D-G. Shortly thereafter Sid was transferred to a routine job at headquarters which involved hard and rather tedious work and no contact with students and he left the Council soon thereafter, and Cliff was not there for much longer, although he is still in the Council and by all accounts does a very useful job. When he left, the final member of the gang of four, the most overtly hostile to me of them all – the female of the species – lost interest and ceased to attend the Centre, and comparative normality was soon to be restored.

After the cultural revolution the Student Centre became once more what Mew and Dame Nancy and other dedicated Council officers had always intended it to be: a haven of rest and recreation for students from all parts of the world where they could meet in an atmosphere of friendship and seek advice about their many problems. My role lay largely in providing the counselling service. The students problems were many and varied, and, thanks to Ronald's insistence, I have summaries of all those of the later years. I will give just one example, though this occurred in 1965, three years before Ronald assumed power. In June of that year I was approached by a Hungarian girl called Tunde.

Tunde was working as an au pair in Chelsea. Her father had been conductor of a Hungarian orchestra which had played several times with distinction at the Edinburgh Festival before the Second World War. Tunde herself loved music, and her father for sentimental reasons (which we English too often ignore) had urged her that whatever else she did in Britain she should attend that wonderful Festival. But there was a difficulty. Tunde's visa expired on 31st July 1965: and the Festival was due to begin in mid-August. So Tunde wrote to the Home Office asking for an extension of her visa. She received a curt refusal. She wrote again explaining her ambition in rather more detail. There arrived an even briefer, more discouraging reply. A determined girl, she wrote asking the reason for this apparently unfeeling attitude. The answer read: "The Secretary of State is not required to give reasons for his decisions and does not choose to do so in your case. You are reminded that you are required to leave the United Kingdom no later than 31st July 1965." It was in these circumstances that Tunde came to me, near to tears.

For many years I had been in Chambers with Anthony (now Sir

73

Anthony) Buck, Conservative Member of Parliament for Colchester and, more important, an excellent and ever-thoughtful godfather to our daughter, Evelyn. A Labour Government was in power at the time and Tony was delighted to be given a stick with which to goad the Home Secretary – I think James Callaghan or Mervyn Rees. "Would this girl mind publicity?" Tony asked. "She won't mind anything if she can go to the Festival," I replied. "It's become an obsession with her." "Good," he said, "send her along to the House to see me", and, conscious that I had left the matter in capable and sympathetic hands, I proceeded to forget about it.

But not for long. A few days later I was walking along the Strand when my eye fell on a copy of the mid-day edition of the "Evening Standard". The two left-hand columns of the newspaper were fully occupied with a picture of this tall and beautiful girl and the banner headline read: "WHY CAN'T HUNGARIAN TUNDE GO TO THE FESTIVAL?" Tony had asked a lengthy question in the House, the peroration of which comprised: "Does the Right Honourable Gentleman really imagine that this little (that epithet was not wholly accurate) Hungarian au pair is a latter-day Mata Hari?" The Home Secretary bashfully asked for further time to consider the matter and about a fortnight later Tunde received a rather ungracious letter extending her visa until the last day of the Festival, in mid-September, but warning her that under no circumstances would any further application for an extension be considered. Tunde did not care. She was happy. She could go the Festival; and in fact I got her on my British Council Edinburgh Festival course and she presented to me a large photograph of herself taken by the "Evening Standard" photographer. Under current Government regulations Tony would not have been allowed to take up her case as he was not her local Member, and if that Member declined to do so (as might well be the case if he supported the Government in power) Tunde would have returned to Hungary, sad and resentful, on 31st July 1965.

In fairness to the Home Office I should perhaps relate the sequel to the Tunde story. Some years later I was dining in Lincoln's Inn. There we eat in messes of four and the rules provide that one should not talk to anyone outside one's own mess. (There are sensible reasons for this.) This was a Guest Night and the barrister opposite me had as his guest a senior official of the Home Office. The combined effect of convivial company and generous libations of alcohol served to loosen that gentleman's normally discreet and diplomatic tongue. "Crowther," he suddenly remarked, pointing an accusing finger in my direction: "You're the fellow who caused us so much trouble over that wretched Hungarian girl."

"Tell me more," I replied curiously, and he did. Tunde was one of the two first Hungarian au pair girls permitted to come to England after the Revolution of 1956. One went to the North of England.

Tunde came to London. The British Government of the mid-1960s was very keen to open up the Iron Curtain by getting students from Eastern European countries over here, but as their own Governments usually allowed them only the equivalent of £2 to take out of the country (about enough to keep them in cups of coffee on the journey) the only ones who could come were girls prepared to be au pairs and to study English in local authority schools. So Tunde and the other Hungarian were the guinea-pigs, to be followed by hundreds of Polish girls, gasping for a breath of freedom. But Hungary, following its workers' revolution of 1956, was completely dominated by the Soviet Union and it was with Russia that the British Government had negotiated this pilot scheme. The Soviets had agreed to it, but subject to two conditions:–

1. That under no circumstances should the girls' visas be extended by the British Government beyond one year; and

2. That the terms of the agreement, including that just recited, should be kept completely secret.

So the Home Office had some excuse for its taciturnity.

When Tony Buck raised the matter in the House of Commons the Foreign Secretary communicated with the British Ambassador in Moscow, who was instructed to talk to Kruschev, and "get him in a good mood." This involved plying the Soviet leader with a good deal of vodka, and asking him to save the British Government from further embarrassment. Eventually Kruschev had had enough to feel generous, and murmured (no doubt in Russian): "Of course she can stay." There followed sighs of relief in Whitehall, in the House of Commons, in the British Council, but, most of all, in the heart of Tunde. So ended my first (and only) excursion into "haute politique".

Amazing coincidences do occur. My wife runs a School of English for three weeks every summer and I do a lot of the teaching, including speaking about British Life and Institutions. I talk about our Parliamentary system before taking the students on a visit to the House of Commons and the House of Lords, usually arranged by Sir Anthony Buck. In July 1985 I was speaking to our students about Question Time as a uniquely valuable British Institution and illustrating my theme by the story that I have just recited when my wife tried to call me away to the telephone. When I asked why the person could not ring back later Elke replied: "She says it's important. Her name is Tunde." Married now to an Englishman, but living and working in Hong Kong, Tunde was back in London and wanted to see the British Council official who, by doing so little, had done so much to make her happy.

But the Tunde story cannot now be repeated, due to the outlook of both the British Government and the British Council. Kruschev may have been prevailed upon to be generous in 1965 but the British Government certainly was not generous in 1981 when it introduced a regulation forbidding girls from Communist countries from coming here as au pairs. They did this despite an attack by that warm-hearted lawyer Lord Scarman on "this nasty, mean little measure", and they have maintained their stance although a former Chairman of the Conservative Party, Cecil Parkinson, has tried, since becoming Chairman of the Anglo-Polish Society, to persuade them to relent. Let it be clear. It is not the Russians who are preventing Poles and Hungarians from coming here: it is the British. I would have thought that in the propaganda war that is waged constantly between East and West the most valuable weapon would be the young student who returns to the East having had a breath of freedom. Instead, our Government prefers them to be cooped up behind the Iron Curtain, subjected to unremitting indoctrination. And why? I suspect, but do not know for certain, that the reason is that some of these students have annoyed the officials of the Home Office Immigration Department by making nuisances of themselves, applying for extensions, "doing a Tunde", not wanting to go back ....

The coal miner from Sheffield who stays on an extra day in the clear air of the Lake District has to be punished.

The Cultural Revolution over, my remaining years with the British Council were for the most part tranquil and happy. But after Cliff a Scottish lady became Head of the Centre. Although I am a great believer in equality of opportunity, I do not think that we are all the same. I entered the British Council in 1951 with a starry-eyed idealism that a person's nationality and background made absolutely no difference to his character, but I soon came to take the opposite view. There ARE Indian characteristics, and African outlooks, and Chinese customs, and English ways and so on, throughout the world – and this is what makes the world so richly rewarding and interesting. And the Scottish characteristic that I have most observed is not parsimony but rigidity. "Rules are rules," V used to say, but at least she interpreted them sensibly and fairly. Cliff's successor carried strictness to absurd, almost inhuman limits. One winter afternoon we were all there in the warmth of the centrally-heated Student Centre and a line of students was shivering outside in the biting East wind, so I let them in. This martinet turned them all out again. It was not yet the opening time of half past three! Security had been far too lax under Ronald and Cliff, when the acolytes of "Oz" and "Time Out" were raiding the Centre, and she had her instructions to tighten up. But under her regime a student had not only to prove that he was a member by producing his membership card, but also to prove that it was his membership card (we did not insist on photographs in those days: we did later on) and to prove that he was still a student. If this involved a journey back to Brent or Brentwood, so be it! and NO GUESTS were allowed in, not even old respected British Council scholars revisiting London and wanting to have a drink in their old club.

So, after a few months of this tyranny and the ordeal of her cross-examination at the door (what a contrast to Mew!) those attending the Saturday discotheque dropped from over four hundred to a number countable on the fingers of both hands, and, fortunately a broad-minded Director realised the harm that was being done and transferred this honourable but unsmiling lady to another Department where she would have little to do with what she least understood – people.

Thereafter I have nothing but praise for those with whom I worked –mostly young people motivated by the highest ideals and working harder than I have seen people working almost anywhere (certainly harder than anywhere else in the Council). In the late nineteen sixties and early seventies the threat to the British Council Student Centre came from the extreme left. Now a new threat was to come from the right –and from within the Council itself. The joint attack was to prove fatal.

In 1979 Mrs Thatcher's Conservative Party came to power with a thumping majority. Shortly afterwards Tony Buck, who had been Minister of the Navy in the Government of Edward Heath, told me:

"The nation is in for a shock. We've been looking at the books. Our country is on the verge of bankruptcy. If we are to survive as a great nation there will have to be massive cuts. They will be spread everywhere .... Even your beloved British Council will be affected and may have to go."

It was by no means the first time that covetous Treasury eyes had been cast on the British Council. The Callaghan Government had realized that we were on the verge of a national financial crisis but had been less forthcoming about it; and who knows even now why Harold Wilson resigned? So James Callaghan called for a report by the Central Policy Review Staff (sometimes called the "Think Tank") under the Chairmanship of Sir Kenneth Berrill, and the Berrill Report recommended in 1977 that the British Council should be abolished altogether or retained in a greatly reduced form (preferably the former).

But this Report was so biassed, so unbalanced, that the Government of the day did not act upon it, but merely reduced the Council's annual allowance. The new Conservative Government was to reduce it a great deal more, and a new Report was commissioned under the Chairmanship of Lord Seebohm. By 1980 drastic cuts in the Council's budget were threatened. This coincided with the retirement of Sir Jack Llewellyn as Director-General and his replacement by Sir John Burgh.

This combination of events was most unfortunate from the point of view of the future of the British Council Student Centre. It was going through its most glorious and useful phase, having over 4000 members, a tenth of whom one could expect to be visiting the Centre on any Saturday or Sunday. In the thirty years that I served the Council, over an eighth of a million students from more than 150 different countries passed through its portals and received advice, hospitality, kindness and entertainment there in an atmosphere of international amity. Dame Nancy Parkinson saw her building in Portland Place as the British Council's "showcase on the world". Others in the Council did not share her view, and it is amazing that in the Council's recently published official book "The British Council, The First Fifty Years" by Lady Donaldson (wife of the Master of the Rolls) there is only one mention of the Student Centre on any of its 422 pages, this being a brief reference to its closure, and no reference at all to almost any of the people of whom I have written except the Directors-General. Lady Donaldson depended, of course, for her otherwise very informative and interesting book, on what she was told by Council staff. Why was she told nothing (or little) of the work of the Student Centre? The answer is, I think, to be found on page 113 where she writes of Dame Nancy Parkinson as "one of the great names in the history of the British Council .... A compulsive worker, usually to be found at her desk in Hanover Street late into the night, she was often less popular with her own staff, who found her autocratic and rather bossy." This is the great understatement of the book. Within the Council Dame Nancy was almost universally loathed. This was because of the way in which she treated many of her underlings, although I must say that she was always fair and courteous to me.

Now the Council is a relatively small organisation, and in the nature of things people who start with humble positions like chauffeurs and porters can rise to positions of considerable influence and power, and some of those who felt that Dame Nancy had trodden them underfoot were to do so. Dame Nancy was credited, wrongly, with the creation of the British Council Student Centre: V and Lawrence and especially Mew had far more to do with its conception and inception. But certainly her energy and enthusiasm were mainly responsible for the move in 1964 from the small and homely premises in Hanover Street to the magnificent building opposite the BBC in Portland Place – which was so large that at first it was difficult to fill (a good example, perhaps, of Parkinson's Law). When Nancy died her enemies banded together and determined that whatever good she had done for overseas students and so for international relations and the reputation of this country abroad – and she had done a lot – her empire should topple, her memorial be destroyed. Sir Jack Llewelyn told me of many occasions when meetings that he attended would begin by his being asked some such question as: "When are we going to get rid of that wretched white elephant, the Student Centre?" "Never, so long as I am in charge," had always been his reply, for he was a man with a student background who recognised the correctness of the phrase that I was to utter frequently, and so unavailingly, thereafter: "The overseas student of to-day is the world leader of tomorrow. Treat him well, and he will be your friend and the friend of your country for life."

Sir John Burgh did not come from a student background: his working life had been spent in the Civil Service, and for this reason doubtless those to whom he came thought that he would be malleable, and would see things "the Council way". In this they were for the most part mistaken, for Sir John, a most brilliant man and a powerful speaker, was to prove very much his own master. There is only one matter on which I find myself in disagreement with Sir John, who has done a great deal for the Council: the decision to close the Student Centre.

In 1980 the Centre cost about £¼ million a year to run; less than half of one per cent of the Council's total budget. Most of this £¼ million related to the rent of the premises in Portland Place. Its value in terms of international goodwill was incalculable. I became the spokesman for the Student Centre in the fight to keep it going. I wrote to Sir Geoffrey Howe, then Chancellor of the Exchequer, asking for an interview, but he had no time to see me. I wrote to all the leaders of industry pointing out the benefits to this country of the Student Centre for future world trade and asking them to subsidise it. Those who found time to reply could not see their way to helping. I proposed that a substantial part of our splendid building in Portland Place should be turned over to a school for the teaching of English as a foreign language, – at that time my everyday English class was the only English class – the students paying fees for their tuition. Education Department would not hear of it: it might offend some of the private schools! (But shortly afterwards the Council was to assume the task of inspection and registration of English Language Schools, so it must claim some expertise in this sphere.) If we had done this, I am convinced that the Centre would not only have paid its way, but would have made a handsome profit.

There was a lot of correspondence between me and the new Director-General and finally a meeting was arranged at the magnificent Headquarters in Spring Gardens for 3.00 p.m. on 25th July 1980. "Beware," said my Director, Kelvin Nicholson, eyeing me meaningfully: "Sir John doesn't suffer fools gladly. You'll know when he's getting restive. He doesn't usually give audiences of more than half an hour."

Well, Sir John entertained me patiently for an hour and a quarter. The one argument that I could not overcome was the proximity of International Students' House to the Centre in Portland Place – five minutes walk away. "It's absurd," said Sir John; but of course they were so close because of the bitter rivalry of those two formidable Dames, Nancy Parkinson and Mary Trevelyan. "We can help the International Students' House. We can give them £10,000 a year for taking over our responsibilities, and we'll save £240,000. The rent of those premises is enormous."

"Cambridge is a much happier city than Oxford," I ventured. "Do you agree?" (I knew that Sir John had had his higher education in the London School of Economics.)

"Yes, but why?"

"Because Cambridge is devoted entirely to students, and Oxford is half students, half motor industry. Town and gown don't mix."

"I don't understand what you're talking about."

"International Students' House is largely residential. Those who live there are quite rightly, afforded great privileges. Our students are non-residential. They will resent being different. It won't work." (And it didn't.)

As Big Ben struck 4.15 across St James's Park a note of impatience crept into Sir John's voice. "You've made that point already. You're repeating yourself." I knew it was time to go, and I felt that I had lost. I had obtained one concession, though. Sir John had promised that the Centre would remain open for at least another year. And it did. The Student Centre closed its doors on the students on 31st July 1981 – and reopened as offices for Council staff on 3rd August (and is still used for this purpose, despite the high rent.)

During this time of discussion and decision an event happened that I thought – I hoped and prayed – could change everything. The Chairman of the British Council, Sir Charles Troughton, had been to see Mrs Thatcher and persuaded her to allow the Council to have an extra £4 million a year. I read this in my "Times" on my way to Court one morning and was immediately on the telephone to Sir John. "This is wonderful news," I exclaimed. "It means that the Student Centre can remain open, doesn't it? We need only a sixteenth of what Sir Charles has managed to get." "All that money has already been allocated," he replied abruptly. Those who were determined to bring about the end of the Student Centre had got in first.

I think that I worked for the British Council for longer than anyone else. For all its faults – the internal power struggles, the occasional "bitchiness", the temporary political intrusion – I think

81

of it as a wonderful organisation. How necessary it is to bring together the peoples of the world through the medium of culture, of hospitality and of mutual study. Through the Council I have met young people from almost every country in the world (not, alas, Albania) and I cannot think of any country with which I would like my nation to go to war. The events in and around the Falklands in April 1982 were a source of especial sorrow to me, having many dear Argentine friends. Most revolting of all did I find Rupert Murdoch's headline in "The Sun" (the most popular of all British newspapers – what does that say for us? alas!): "Up the Argies, Maggie." This was to be excelled by a further headline three years later in the same newspaper when a Middle Eastern Ambassador was expelled (quite justifiably, in my view): "Out. You Syrian Swine." How many lives did that save? Or (more important perhaps to Mr Murdoch) how many copies of "the Sun" did that sell?

Through the Council I have friends in almost every country of the world and many remain in communication with me, some after thirty-six years. I regularly send out over five hundred Christmas cards and receive a similar number. (I think that our postman deserves a bonus, especially at Christmas time, for he never complains). There are very few countries in the world where I would not be offered a bed in a private house and indeed, when I travel on legal conferences, as I frequently do, I rarely stay in hotels. The British Council itself has sponsored me on lecture tours in India, Poland, Finland and Paris. Even in the Soviet Union, in 1967, my wife and I received hospitality in the home of a teacher whom we had met in London and who had been a member of my Everyday English class. Here she came to one of our parties: it was the only occasion on which a couple of Russian guards have stood outside our house. But I fear that our visit to her and her family in Moscow may have had disastrous consequences, for thereafter all her greetings, and the presents she sent to our children for Christmas and their birthdays, ceased. A couple of years later a Ghanaian friend was going to study at Moscow University for a year on a scholarship, so I asked him to look Ludmilla up. On his return he came to see me. On calling at her address he had been told by the new occupants and all the neighbours: "She never lived here. She doesn't exist. You're imagining things." He told me that he had written to me to convey this information, but I have never received the letter ....

But in recalling so many good friends from all over the world, I must thank the Council most of all for introducing me to my wife, Elke, who has put up with my absence – and my presence – for nearly thirty years now and stood by me in so many crises and with loyalty and common-sense has helped me in so many ventures. The final programme at the Student Centre on 31st July 1981 included a mini-Cabaret which I put on, full of nostalgia. As I walked out of that building, so redolent with memories for the last time suddenly, unexpectedly the lyric and music of a song from the musical "Salad Days" came back to me. I had found "Salad Days" so enjoyable in the fifties that I saw it eleven times – with eleven different girls – probably from eleven different countries – the last of whom was Elke. The cast changed frequently during the many years of its run, but two of the principal couples came and performed in my International Student Cabarets (sorry, Concerts in those days!) and now I found myself at the head of the procession of students leaving the British Council Student Centre for the last time and started almost compulsively to sing this refrain:–

"We'll never be able to break the spell,
The magic will hold us still
Sometimes we may pretend to forget
But, of course, we never will.
"We mustn't say these were our happiest days
Whatever our memories are
We mustn't say these were our happiest days
But our happiest days so far.
"If I start looking behind me
And begin retracing my track
I'll remind you to remind me:
We said we wouldn't look back ...."

I think my final judgment on the British Council after those three decades would coincide with that of the American writer who said of her sojourn in England during the Second World War;

"I have seen much to hate here, much to forgive.
But in a world where
England is finished and dead,
I would not wish to live."

I think that, substituting "the Council" for "England", that epitomises my sentiments regarding the organisation for which I worked for thirty years.

Chapter 7

Summers at Dotheboys Hall

On my first evening at the British Council Student Centre in September 1951 I met and fell in love with the daughter of the Chief Justice of Austria, a beautiful and charming painter and graphologist. (She was responsible for the illuminated lettering and other illustrations of the official "Book of Austria"). Epi, was, up to that time, the most beautiful, charming and exciting girl I had ever met, and a lump still comes to my throat when I read that marvellous if sad book "Silas Marner" in which the heroine is the only other Epi of whom I have ever heard. The months of January 1952 (when Epi was my guest at a post-call party in Lincoln's Inn in which I was the speaker and she said that my address was "wonderful" – unfortunately she understood little English at that time!) to May of the same year were certainly among the most hectic of my life. The trouble was that many other men also found Epi beautiful, charming and exciting, and my strongest rivals were Filip, a wild Polish artist of great talent whom Epi always called "Fips," who used to give her piggy-backs and whom I liked immensely, and Peter, a dour Lithuanian student at the London School of Economics with whom Epi went "pot-holing," and whom I disliked intensely. I will not recite in detail the events of those first five months in 1952. The main purpose of writing is to get one's feelings off one's chest and for the only time in my adult life I kept a diary when Epi was in London, and "The Book of Epi" (in sombre black covers) runs to four volumes and is not for publication. My dear reader(s) now is/are expecting an autobiography, not a romantic novel. Unhappily, Epi was not as faithful to me as I was to her, and when she left London (for the last time) on 20th May 1952 all three of her musketeers – Peter, Fips and I – were there to see her off (although Fips, characteristically, was nearly too late). For once I arrived in

Chambers before 9.30 – and very tired, having slept little the previous night – but my pupil master was already in situ. I felt that some explanation of my unusually early arrival was called for and so I remarked: "I've been seeing a friend off to Vienna." "I'm sure that was much appreciated," replied Hugh Corner sardonically, yet perceptively. "Now let's hope that you can concentrate and get down to some work."

"You must come to visit me in Vienna," Epi told me repeatedly, and she frequently spoke of "when you come to Austria," but she often confused the "wenn" of "when" with the "wenn" of "if". Unfortunately she extended this invitation to other admirers, so many of them that I once opined: "Epi, when I go to buy my train ticket the travel agent will say: "I am sorry, sir, but all the trains for the rest of the year are fully booked with Epi's satellites." In fact I did get a place, having saved up the return train fare of £37 and other money for the holiday from my British Council salary. I am not sure that I would have bothered if I had realized that on the evening on which Epi was to meet me at Westbahnhof she had already visited that station earlier that day to celebrate the departure of Peter. (Fips never visited her because, as a Pole, he was afraid that he might not be readmitted to England). My sister supplied sandwiches and a thermos flask of tea sufficient for the 36 hour journey, my only memory of which is of a lengthy argument with an elderly Austrian lady as to whether London or Vienna were the larger city. Although I was more correct than she (I believe) we were equally childish in our chauvinism. Anyway, I was too preoccupied to notice Peter on the train travelling in the opposite direction.

Whilst Epi's greeting on arrival was warm and welcoming, it was soon clear that her interest in me had waned considerably in the preceding four months. For every proverb there is a counter-maxim. Of "Absence makes the heart grow fonder" and "While the cat's away, the mice will play" I prefer the former but believe in the latter, and although on my first night Epi whisked me through the Austrian rain to see the first European performance of "Porgy and Bess" at the Staatsoper, thereafter she had little of the next three weeks to spend with me. Enchanting though Vienna was, I found Epi's frequent absences frustrating, and after a week I decided to make another train journey, to Trieste, to visit my delightful Italian family who had been so good to me during the eighteen months immediately after the war, and who always referred to me as "Carol

Lloyd, nostro caro fratello." Epi could not believe it when I announced that I was leaving her the next day. "Erich. You are so English. No Austrian would ever leave a woman he has come a thousand miles to visit." But my mind was made up, and with sadness in my heart I went to the station (I cannot remember if it was the same one) next morning. Just as the train was about to leave I heard the unmistakeable musical voice of my love running along the platform shouting: "Erich, Erich, wo bist du?" I revealed myself, for Epi to tell me: "I am coming with you to Trieste, but get off the train at once. We are going by car to Munchen." My second suitcase left the compartment just in time and I made my way happily with Epi towards the station exit. My joy was short-lived, however, for at the barrier stood a handsome, hearty Austrian with an old sports car, greeting me with a vigorous "Grüss Gott" and a painful handshake. There followed the most hair-raising car-ride that I have ever embarked on, except for one that I had last summer in Andalucia. The roads were wet and greasy, Epi's latest "beau" drove at breakneck speed and very badly, having several near misses as he demonstrated this aspect of his prowess. The climax came when we skidded off the road, hit a telegraph pole, and finished up in a ditch. Almost immediately we were surrounded by soldiers: Russian soldiers, for we had crashed in the Russian zone. "Passports" demanded their leader solemnly, and those of Epi and her friend were produced and returned without comment and without a smile. My British one evinced a different reaction. The Russian soldier looked at the passport for a long time, stared at the photograph in it in disbelief, and said "Komm mit." I decided not to understand German; it is much better in such circumstances to be monolingual. "But I'm British," I protested. "Komm mit," he repeated more loudly, and the other soldiers surrounded and seized me and started marching me away, while Epi and her friend looked on in helpless alarm.

I was saved by what seemed like a miracle. Just at this moment a jeep pulled up and out jumped about half a dozen American soldiers. Their sergeant sauntered over and asked: "Hi! What's all this? You English? You in trouble?" I replied: "I've been in a car driven by a lunatic, we've just crashed into that telegraph pole, and we landed in that ditch and now the Russian Army is taking me I know not where. I think you might say I'm in trouble." "Okay" said the sergeant, and turning to the Russians, he said with a dismissive gesture: "Get outa it, beat it", and to my relief and astonishment, they did! "What's the explanation!" I asked my saviour, as soon as I could think clearly again, "because this is the Russian zone, isn't it?"

"Yeah, the Ruskies control the zone, but we control the highway, and they're not allowed to stop any vehicle going along this main road, and they know it. There'll be trouble over this."

My new-found friends righted our vehicle and got it started again; the damage to it seemed minimal, but I declared firmly: "I'm not putting up with any more of this driving. I think I'd rather go with the Russians." I didn't say: "I'd rather be red than dead," but that was the effect of what I was thinking at that moment. "If I continue in that car, I shall be driving to Munich." (I had once in England borrowed a car from a friend and let Epi drive, and this was another experience that I did not wish to repeat). So we made our leisurely way to the Bavarian capital, where we arrived at three in the morning, in the middle of the Oktoberfest. We did find somewhere to sleep – eventually – and I was surprised next morning to awaken and see opposite the signs of Woolworths and C and A Modes. I thought I was in Oxford Street.

The damage to the car was greater than we had believed, and, it being Oktoberfest, the garage to which we took it said that it would take at least three days to repair. This was a blessing in disguise in that its owner refused to leave it and travel by other means, and I refused to remain so long away from my beloved Trieste. Epi had to make the choice between him and me, and chose to come to Trieste by train with me. But she did not love Trieste as much as I did, nor did she love my sweet but rather unsophisticated Italian family – and they did not approve of her at all. So, two days later, Epi was on the train back to Vienna: via Munich .... I stayed on in Trieste for a nostalgic week, reviving old memories, revisiting old friends, before returning to Vienna for the last few days of my holiday. Epi greeted me at the station with the warmth that she reserved for someone she had not seen for a while, and this time the warmth remained for the rest of my brief stay.

In Trieste I had been to the cinema, Poleatami Rossetti, but I had had to pay for my ticket. This was unusual, because throughout my time in Trieste in the Navy I had always seen my films free. The Triestini were so grateful for being liberated from the Yugoslavs in the sort of mini-phoney-war that followed immediately after the real war that the Government of the Territorio Libero di Trieste said that all British and Americans could attend all places of entertainment free. (It was in Trieste that I acquired my love for opera, sitting with the padre in what had been once the Royal box). Initially they said that all drinks in the bars would be free also, but this policy was abandoned after a week during which the Triestini came to realize the extent of British and American thirsts. But as a result of this generosity I saw many fine films, some British – for this was the epoch of great British films – including two by Noel Coward: "Blithe Spirit" and "Brief Encounter".

"Brief Encounter" I regard as one of the most beautiful films ever made – Celia Johnson was an actress who could always be guaranteed to bring tears to my eyes – and I have seen it many times since. On the afternoon on which I repaired to the Poleatami Rossetti in Trieste to see it for the first time, it was preceded by a short film. I am unaware of the title of this film, as it had already started when I got there, but it had a most profound effect on my life. I had fallen in love with Trieste from the first day that, shortly before the end of the war, from a small landing-craft with nine men on board, I first saw the gleaming white city rising from the azure bay to the green hills of Opicina and the russet mountains beyond. I had the good fortune to meet my Italian "family" who had rented a flat just above the shop in Via Mazzini which the Navy had commandeered as a clothing store, and I had never before encountered such kind, warm, generous people.

Trieste is a small city, and I felt that I had come to know every stone of it. When the time came for my demobilisation I volunteered to stay on for an extra six months, so much did I enjoy the life there, and during those six months I was offered a job as interpreter for the Venezia Giulia police. This I had decided to accept, abandoning all prospects of practising at the English Bar (and of doing pupillage with Hugh Corner.)

When I went into the cinema I soon realised that the subject of the short film was familiar to me. It was a ride on a number 13 bus, dropping off at various famous tourist attractions like Regents Park, the Sherlock Holmes Room in Abbey House, Baker Street, at Selfridges', the statue of Eros, the National Gallery, Trafalgar Square, St. Paul's Cathedral and – the Law Courts and the Old Bailey. I had always used the 13 bus route to get between home and school, and buses were my hobby – more than a hobby, an obsession; and I still know a lot about them. I knew the driver in the film, I knew the conductor, I seemed to know every inch of the route. It was indeed a sentimental journey for me. Then followed "Brief Encounter" – so English in all its ways, and so moving. When I left the cinema, my mind was made up. I would return to my homeland after all, and would become an English barrister. Three weeks later I was on my way back to London. From a practical point of view this was just as well, as the Venezia Giulia Police Force was disbanded shortly afterwards, when Trieste became a part of Italy again.

But the parting from Trieste was heart-breaking. I remember Giovanni, our dear old honest shoemaker, rushing out to say goodbye as the naval transport took me away. "My wife say", observed Giovanni, who was much influenced by his wife: "Carol Lloyd go, good luck go". On my next visit to Trieste I learned that he was dead.

The parting from Epi was heart-breaking, too, in a different way. I remembered as we went to the station a line from "Brief Encounter": "This was the very last time that we should ever be together." I had realised by now from Epi's life-style that this must apply to our situation, too. In "Brief Encounter" the final parting in the dreary war-time railway waiting room is interrupted by the unexpected arrival of a talkative, gossipy acquaintance of Nora (Nora being the part played by Celia Johnson) and: "I felt the touch of his hand on my shoulder, and he was gone forever."

At the Westbahnhof in Vienna Epi's and my final embrace was interrupted by a raucous female American voice addressing me: "Oh, thank God I've found someone who talks English. These foreigners are so stupid. Listen, I gotta get to Switzerland but I don't want to go through Linz. I can't bear to have those Russians goin' through my bags again. Now, look, I gotta map here ...."

"How could you have been so patient?" Epi wrote in her letter that day, "while that woman was spoiling our last moments together?" I don't know, I really don't, but I got nearer to murder that morning than at any other time in my life. But the last words that Epi uttered orally to me on the platform of Westbahnhof were: "Eric, shall we ever again meet in this life?" I did not reply, but in my heart I knew that the answer was "No."

My Viennese visit was to be my last trip abroad for several years, apart from my forays to Paris with or on account of Michael Scott in 1954 and 1955. My next few summers were to be occupied otherwise. In the spring of 1953, V, who always had my welfare at heart, noticed in the personal column of "The Times" the following advertisement:

"TUTORS REQUIRED to teach English to Foreigners at Summer School on the Suffolk Coast. Salary dictated neither by Cresus nor by Harpagon. Return rail fare paid. Write for interview to the Headmaster, Sizewell Hall, Suffolk."

This was my introduction to holiday courses, to the incredible Harry Tuyn (pronounced as in the near-synonym for "city") and to the establishment which some of the less enchanted tutors rechristened "Dotheboys Hall" where I was to spend my summers for six of the next seven years, with the full approval of Roy, my clerk, as I was out of the way and not worrying about work. On my first approach for the interview, in a taxi from Leiston station with a garrulous taxidriver who called me "sir" every fifth word, I was reminded more of Daphne du Maurier than of Dickens as we wended our way down the winding tree-lined path to get a glimpse of what at first sight looked like Manderlay, but was in fact Sizewell Hall. Built in 1922, its mock Tudor windows made it appear much older, and its commanding position looked down over its private beach to the North Sea. I forget how many bedrooms it had, but Sizewell Hall accommodated a hundred students in dormitories for six weeks every summer, and from the profits of this enterprise Harry Tuyn, who resembled a cross between Peter Ustinov and Orson Welles in the role of "Citizen Kane", lived like a king for the rest of the year. And a king he seemed to be – another resemblance was to Henry VIII as portrayed by Robert Shaw in that wonderful film "A Man for All Seasons," with Sizewell Hall as his castle where, in the private sector, he and his wife Elaine lived in great splendour and luxury. The Tuyn kingdom extended for about two miles in every direction, including I felt sure, a fishing limit (or, rather, for reasons that I shall reveal, a non-fishing limit) of that distance out into the North Sea. There was a pub (out of bounds not only to students but also to tutors, because Harry Tuyn had quarrelled with the landlord) at Sizewell, but otherwise the nearest shops and habitations were at Leiston, nearly three miles away, and, up to there, Tuyn reigned supreme; and all of this he got for a little more than £3 a week (the salary that he paid to each of his tutors.)

During the second World War Tuyn had been a pacifist – although a less pacific person I never encountered. Being excused from military service he had looked around Cambridgeshire and Suffolk for somewhere to live and had lighted on Sizewell Hall. Colonel Ogilvie, the owner, preferred to have this great house occupied rather than left to go to rack and ruin, and let it under an informal arrangement to the Tuyns for the weekly sum of £3. Then came the Rent Act 1946 and the Tuyns were protected tenants, presiding over a gold mine, for Harry set up there the first summer school for foreign students learning English after the war, and by the time I arrived it was flourishing.

Tuyn had one great advantage: he was a foreigner himself, a Dutchman, so he was well acquainted with the difficulties that foreigners had in learning English, a language in which (as in French and German) he was perfect. On my first day there Tuyn said: "I want you to take some of the grammar classes." "Good, " I remarked, "I've always liked grammar." "Don't be so bloody stupid, " he retorted, "I'm not talking about the English grammar you studied at your puny public school. I'm talking about grammar for foreign students – a very different operation." I must have looked downcast, for he cheered me up by asking: "You consider yourself intelligent, don't you?" "Fairly," I replied, accurately rather than modestly. "Good, then you'll come to my study a quarter of an hour before each class begins and I will give you enough material, with the drilling you'll give the students, to last for the hour of the lesson." And he did, and excellent material it was, for he was a brilliant teacher. Perhaps I was more intelligent than Tuyn gave me credit for, because after each lesson I transposed what he had taught me and I had tried to teach the class into notes, and these notes were to form the basis for the grammar lessons of the Cromwell School of English, which Elke and I set up twenty years later, running similar (but much smaller) summer courses in our own home. Tuyn was a great authority on Shakespeare, his in-depth studies of his plays being the best that I ever heard after Lawrence's talk on "Romeo and Juliet."

Tuyn had his phobias, his predilections and his own peculiar, rather cruel sense of humour. His main aversions were fish and atomic power. His long-suffering, good-natured but garrulous wife had, when they were in a strange city, to walk ahead of him to ensure that he did not come within sniffing distance of a fishmonger or a fish and chip shop, for the smell of fish drove him beserk. I remember once strolling through Ipswich with him when we came upon a newly opened fishmonger and he charged through the street raging like a bull, cruelly tortured in the corrida. A student went out to sea in a small boat and caught a fish which he proudly (and innocently) brought into the school. He was immediately expelled. Tuyn was not a very fair man. He instituted a system of fines for breaches of the school's rules, starting at a shilling for speaking a language other than English and rising even to £5 (in 1953!) for such heinous offences as "snogging" (which Tuyn described as "eating hair") or answering back. This caused so much resentment that I persuaded him to set up a Fines Court, sitting once a week, to deal with appeals from allegedly unjust or unduly heavy fines. I presided over this tribunal, having with me on the bench a student and also an ostensibly "neutral" member of the staff like the secretary or the housekeeper. The students were allowed to select whomsoever they wished to represent them, and usually they would have the services of Tuyn, undoubtedly a barrister manqué, who could be guaranteed to put on a flamboyant performance somewhere between Rumpole and Perry Mason. The Fines Court took some of the sting out of the fining system (which was certainly a good idea in so far as it encouraged the speaking of only English in the school.)

Tuyn's other phobia was atomic power, of which he was terrified. It was a tragic irony that the country's biggest atomic power station was to open at Sizewell, less than a mile away from Sizewell Hall, and in 1960 he closed his school and divided the rest of his life between Canada (which he hated) Switzerland (which he liked, and where, for a time he had a girls' finishing school) and Oxford (which he loved, and found appropriate to his intellectual near-genius.) He suffered a heart attack in Canada, and died while receiving treatment for it in the United States.

"Eric, we do not have favourites," V was to tell me when I started to dance more than once with my future wife, but Tuyn had them, both among the staff and the students. If you were one of his favourites you sat for meals at the Headmaster's table to be regaled with his scintillating conversation, the "guests" at which table were carefully selected from photographs before the students arrived; and on Wednesdays you could stay "at home." All the students were equal, but some of them were more equal (and much more equal) than others. Perhaps the most equal of all was a beautiful, elegant, aristocratic, aloof German girl student with whom Tuyn disappeared for a week-end. The atmosphere was very tense while they were away but his tolerant and loving wife did not say anything when they returned (not publicly, anyway). Wednesday was excursion day, and most of the students and tutors went out from early in the morning until late at night. For the few who remained Tuyn cooked a Rijstafel unrivalled by the Bali or any other restaurant in Amsterdam: he was brilliant at everything he undertook, except speaking Italian. I was not invited to the Rijstafel during the first two years, but often partook of it after that.

As King of Sizewell he was a despot, and knew (and felt he had to know) everything that was going on. Because he wanted the reputation of his school to be unsullied in the locality he insisted that as soon as the excursion bus reached Leiston on its return journey the interior lights should be switched on. (Up to then the students could be "snogging" to their hearts' content). One Wednesday night I succumbed to their blandishments and left the lights extinguished until we reached the outer gate of Sizewell Hall. Next morning Tuyn sent for me: "I tailed your bus from Leiston last night. You kept the light off until you entered the grounds. I expect my orders to be obeyed. If it happens again you will leave here – without pay."

Apart from that incident life proceeded fairly quietly for me during my first year. I was not part of the "inner circle" comprising the deputy headmaster, the chief administrator, the senior tutor, the housekeeper, the secretary and the cook (every one of whom, except the secretary, was subsequently and separately sued by him) who joined Mr and Mrs Tuyn night after night for Remy Martin and raucous laughter about the day's events; I did my job and went my way.

My main tormentor was Baggott. Most of the boys slept in a large cottage about half a mile away from the school and I was in charge of them. After the evening activity – a lesson, a session of games, a visit to the cinema at Aldburgh, or a dance – I had to take the boys up to "The Homestead" and Tuyn warned me that I must keep them quiet on the way. On the first or second night at about 1.00 a.m., the telephone beside my bed rang just as I was dropping off to sleep and a strong Suffolk accent addressed me thus:

"That you, sir? Mr Crow, sir? I'm Baggott, sir. Mr Baggott. I'm not one to complain, sir, and I know boys will be boys but them boys of yours made a terrible noise on their way up to the Homestead tonight, and my poor Minnie she's expecting – in fact she's overdue, and you wouldn't like her to lose her baby would you, Mr Crow, sir? You wouldn't like that on yer conscience when we've been trying these ten years? Do you think you're capable of controlling these young animals, sir? They're hooligans aren't they? – and foreign hooligans at that! Have you got the necessary experience, sir?"

"Yes, Mr Baggott, I'm quite capable of controlling them and I'll see that they're quieter in the future."

I then heard screams in the background. "Oh excuse me, Mr Crow, sir. I think this is the moment. I think she's coming. Get off the line, sir. I must call the doctor."

The baby did not arrive that morning and Baggott's nocturnal complaints continued.

"They are quieter, Mr Crow, sir, and I know you're doing your best, but they've been in my garden scrumping the apples."

"I think they were drunk, sir. Did you take them to the pub? I thought it was out of bounds, sir."

"They broke my window with the football sir. And my poor Minnie a fortnight overdue."

I decided that I did not wish my sleep to be interrupted every night. I had to see Baggott face to face and settle matters once and for all, so I asked all the regular staff where he lived. I got varying replies: at the Sizewell pub, in Leiston, on a nearby farm, in the lighthouse. I decided that Baggott did not exist. But if there were no Baggott, who was Baggott? The solution to that problem came the next night when the inevitable telephone call came even later than usual.

"Excuse me, sir, Mr Crow, sir. You and I are men of the world sir. Don't you think Mr Tewin's a bit hard on the students, a bit cruel to them, a bit of a sadist? You sir, Mr Crow, sir, what do you think of the Headmaster?"

"Baggott," I replied, "I am not prepared to discuss the Headmaster with you at three o'clock in the morning or at any other hour. Goodnight!"

During that day I became sure. Baggott's calls were getting later each night, so I stayed awake until two o'clock and then I rang the Headmaster's study. After a few moments my call was answered, and I addressed the unmistakeable voice on the other end in an exaggerated Suffolk accent:

"You sir, Mr Tewin, sir, what do you think of Mr Crow, sir?"

The reply was cold and firm. "I think he's a bloody sight too clever. Come and see me first thing in the morning, Crowther."

When I did, he was very affable, and invited me to return to the study in the afternoon. Then all the "Inner Circle" were there, and we listened to the "Homestead Tapes". I had never heard a recording of my voice before, and I thought that it sounded like a poor imitation of me. Tuyn had clearly been impressed by my refusal to discuss the Headmaster with Baggott "at three o'clock in the morning or at any other hour" – "a strong, loyal tutor" he observed to his admirers. We then heard the tapes of the other tutors who, unwittingly, had been subjected to this torture. One was a mild and lanky young man called Gerald Walter, who spent his not very considerable free time stalking and crawling through the rushes of the marshes with binoculars to gain a sight of rare birds. Baggott began his first nocturnal call on Gerald in this way:

"That you sir? Mr Wall sir. I'm Baggott, sir. Mr Baggott." (The caller did not leave Gerald time to ask the obvious question: "And who is Baggott?" but continued immediately): "I've noticed you sir, creeping about in the long grasses with your spy-glasses. You're after the birds, aren't you Mr Wally, sir? Well, sir, I was wondering if we could go out together some time. I'm a bit of an orthinologist myself. I wanted to ask you something, sir. Do you know what I saw this afternoon, sir? There was a group of white birds out to sea all with their heads down in the water and their little bottoms bobblin' about up top. Do you think they'd be puffins, sir?"

"Oh no, Mr Baggott," Gerald replied earnestly, "I don't think there are any puffins to be found on this part of the coast."

"Well, sir, what do you think they're doin', bobblin' about with their bottoms like that. Do you think they get some sort of sexual satisfaction out of it?"

"No, Mr Baggott, I don't. It may be ...."

"My Minnie says they're masturating themselves, but she's like that, my Minnie. Do you think they'd be masturating, Mr Wally, sir?"

"No, I don't think so, Mr Baggott, "Gerald replied rather prudishly. "I have no knowledge of any such activities on the part of birds."

And so it went on, for hours in Gerald's case, for he was more patient than I. All the temporary tutors fell into the trap of responding in detail to Baggott's invitation to criticise Harry Tuyn, and all did so rather unfavourably. In Gerald's case it went like this:

"You sir, Mr Wally, sir, what do you think of the Headmaster?"

Gerald replied along these lines: "Well, he's obviously a very brilliant man and he runs a highly successful school, but I wish he'd be kinder to the students and not shout at them so. I really don't like all this bullying and I'm not sure that I agree with the system of fines. Another thing is that I think with all the money he takes from the students he ought to feed them better. I've noticed that the food on his table is always rather better than that on the rest of the tables and this really isn't fair. I have to say that I find him rather mean ...."

Gerald and the other "temps" were not to be invited to return to Sizewell Hall.

Tuyn was an excellent mimic and had a formidably cruel sense of humour based on exploiting the weaknesses of others. I once heard Edward Clarke, then an Old Bailey Judge, begin an address to Bar students of Lincoln's Inn at Cumberland Lodge with the words: "Now I happen to have been gifted with a very beautiful voice." It was not, I think, for this reason that I was asked always to read out the fines at lunch time and at dinner to announce the evening activities, but simply because I was a barrister and it was thought that I could do so in sufficiently stentorian tones. But my style did not give Tuyn total satisfaction, for on one occasion I caught him giving an imitation of me to the Inner Circle in the study. "And then that pompous bastard from the Bar got up and announced: "After dinner you have a choice of activity: Mr Tuyn will be talking about Shakespeare in his study whereas I shall be delivering a LECTURE on British Life and Institutions in the Library."

All went well with Tuyn as long as one flattered and admired him and did what he wanted. His wife, a kind, generous (but at times quite tiresome) woman – when I wanted something out of Harry I always got it through her – genuinely worshipped him and usually referred to him as "God." There was in the establishment a young Persian girl called Haleh. She had been dumped at Sizewell at the age of about twelve by her father on the occasion of his second marriage to a woman much younger than he, on terms that Tuyn would educate her and the father would pay whatever was asked of him (and I am sure that it was a lot.) Haleh really seemed like a sort of slave, working a lot in the kitchen, and eventually taking over all the cooking for the hundred or so students.

Nevertheless under Tuyn's tutelage she turned into a most delightful and sophisticated woman, exceptionally well-read, especially in Shakespeare. Tuyn wanted her to marry Geoffrey – by far the least desirable member of his entourage – a local electrician, because Geoffrey would always come out in the middle of the night to mend a fuse or cure an electrical fault. To have a permanent electrician on site, married to the cook, would be extremely useful; but Haleh developed a mind of her own and married the son of the local doctor, and they live not far from Sizewell and have two children and appear supremely happy when we go to visit them. A previous cook did marry the senior tutor at Tuyn's behest, but that did not work out well, for Tuyn was to dismiss them both and sue them for alleged dishonesty.

Tuyn had plans for me, too. I was to marry Ankie, a Dutch nurse who was a very conscientious "ladymaid." She would then become his nurse-cum-housekeeper and I would be permanently around as senior tutor. The fact that we were not mutually attracted was neither here nor there in his eyes, but it was in ours, and to his dismay bordering on horror we both refused to comply with this mandatory injunction. When I took a girlfriend called Helena to Sizewell to stay the weekend there Tuyn expressed himself strongly on her unsuitability for me as a wife. He may have been right. Later on I went shopping with Helena when she sought to buy a pair of shoes. All along Oxford Street and Regent Street we left piles of boxes and distracted shoe salesmen in her three hour unsuccessful quest. I think it might be quite a good test of a spouse's suitability to say: "Come on, I'm going to buy you a pair of shoes." I did not take Elke to meet Tuyn before we were married, and he neither attended our wedding nor acknowledged the invitation. I feared that he would not "recognise" our marriage, as it interfered with his plans, but ultimately he did.

Tuyn loved to be engaged in battles, and so litigation was almost a hobby with him, and I became his "standing counsel." Despite Vice-Chancellor Megarry's rather inelegant analogy between the practising barrister and the "cabbie on the rank", I refused to appear for Tuyn against any of the people I had worked with at Sizewell Hall. He found this hard to accept: "You know all their little foibles, Mr Crow, sir. You can exploit them and get them angry." The "cabbie on the rank" in those days was compelled to go only six miles, and being briefed to appear against one's friends or acquaintances was being asked to go too far. But we had many actions in the Ipswich and Saxmundham County Courts, usually against the parents of children at Sizewell. The local Judge was a courteous, charming, and an erudite man, but he could usually be relied upon to come to the wrong decision. This was good for the lawyers on both sides, of course, because nearly all his cases seemed to finish up in the Court of Appeal. And it was one of his decisions that took me for the first time into that august appellate Court which on that occasion found that the Judge had reached the right decision but for the wrong reasons. The case achieved the Law Report in "The Times" under the title "Parents Beware." In the second chapter of "Advocacy for the Advocate" I recited the extraordinary events preceding the hearing of the argument in *Tuyn v Creasey*, so I will not repeat them here. I think that I lost as many cases as I won for Tuyn, but although he was an extremely bad loser at all forms of sport (especially volleyball) he was always a good loser in litigation; but *Tuyn v Creasey* we won, both in the County Court and the Court of Appeal. This afforded satisfaction to Tuyn not only at the time, but also doubtless during the long winter evenings that were to follow, with Tuyn exercising his talent for mimicry, as he acted out the drama of the hearing for the Inner Circle night after night. His imitation of Lord Denning's Hampshire "burr" was better than my own – and mine is good enough for Lord Denning to have asked to hear it – and then there would intrude the polite insinuation of Lord Justice Norman Birkett and the down to earth, commonsense pronouncements of Lord Justice Hodson. "I liked Hodson" said Tuyn firmly, "He was on my side from the start."

That evening we had a celebration dinner in Tuyn's favourite London restaurant, the Pastoria, and Tuyn began to rehearse his one-man show. *Tuyn v Creasey* arose because an irate parent complained that the school did not live up to the claims of the brochure; our contention was that the brochure was just a form of advertisement, the statements in it mere "puff", and that the terms of the contract were to be found elsewhere. The other diners at the Pastoria were a little surprised when Tuyn suddenly rose during his narrative and, holding up the menu, declaimed: "And then that pompous Crowther got up and declared: "My Lords, it says here in the brochure that Suffolk is the driest part of England. Is the Headmaster to be blamed if it RAINS?" "I'm not sure about that analogy", said the cautious Birkett; "U-r-r-r-r" said Denning; and Hodson, the best judge, went "Ha! ha! ha!" "

Laughter in Court was to cause me trouble in another Tuyn case.

Harry was once again suing for damages for breach of contract and I called him as the first witness. Difficulties arose immediately when he declared his unwillingness to take the oath. When the Judge enquired the reason, Tuyn replied that he was a Quaker and therefore wished to affirm. This sudden conversion to any form of Christianity on Tuyn's part came as a great surprise to me, but he explained afterwards that he thought the Judge looked religious and religious people always believed and trusted the Quakers. That hurdle overcome, I asked the Plaintiff:

"Are you Harry Tuyn, the headmaster of Sizewell Hall, Suffolk?"

"I am he," came the dignified reply.

"And are you a Master of Arts of the University of Oxford, and a Master of Arts of the University of Utrecht?"

"Yussir," answered the unmistakeable voice of Baggott.

At this point I roared with laughter at the sudden incongruity of it all, to be severely rebuked by the Judge, who had not noticed the Baggottism in the answer. Tuyn meanwhile regarded the Judge with a hurt expression, which seemed appealingly to ask: "How can I expect justice when I have a mad counsel who screams with laughter at my qualifications?" Somehow we got through the case, and won it.

My first Sizewell summer ended in mid-September 1953 and after lunch on my last day Tuyn came over and said coldly: "I've ordered you a taxi for two o'clock in front of the Hall. Goodbye." Rather disconsolately I collected my luggage from the Homestead and walked with it up the path to the front of the main building, where Mr Garrod, the loquacious local taxi-driver, arrived promptly on time. As I climbed into the vehicle there was a shout from above and Tuyn emerged on the balcony.

"Are you coming back next year?" he demanded.

"Do you want me to?" I enquired.

"Of course I want you to, you bloody fool. I wouldn't be asking you if I didn't would I? See you next July."

Although I no longer had Baggott to contend with, Sizewell 1954 was much less peaceful than 1953. This was mainly due to an eighteen year old French boy called Gérard Dosmond, who was constantly with me. He slept in the Homestead, where I was in charge at night, he ate at my table ("the Table in the Hall," the title of a sketch that I performed in a cabaret at the end of the course, because in 1954 there were more students than the previous year and an extra and larger dining table had to be set up outside the refectory) and he was in my class. Gérard was very tall, very thin and had unkempt hair and a lugubrious face which never smiled. He wore ill-fitting clothes, including a jacket that was far too long and drainpipe trousers that were far too short and a black cord for a tie. He looked and behaved, like a younger version of Jacques Tati. He arrived at Sizewell with only two words of English and left having succeeded in his determination to learn no more. His two words, one of which was unusual – but he used them all the time – were "Inadmissable, sir" with the second "i" being pronounced very long. Whenever he was fined, which was very frequently, the protest: "Inadmissable, sir" rang out, followed usually by a series of oaths, uttered in French of course. Whenever there was trouble, Gérard was in it. He was strongly suspected of a not very successful arson attack on the Sizewell public house, but the evidence against him was indeed largely "inadmissable," and Tuyn did not like the pub owner anyway. A ladder was erected one day in the hall for some redecoration. Gérard arrived late for lunch (as usual) making the most tremendous noise as he did a long slide towards his place at my table, in the course of which his foot just caught the bottom of the ladder. The noise had attracted the attention of the (very severe) senior tutor who came rushing out just at the wrong moment, for the ladder fell on him, impaling his head. "That will cost you £5" shouted the senior tutor from between the rungs. "Non, sir. Inadmissable, sir," responded Gérard indignantly. I think that I reduced the fine to £3 on the appeal against sentence in the Fines Court.

But another incident resulted in my imposing a fine of £5 on Gérard, who by now had become a Sizewell recidivist. I do not know what sixth sense of something amiss caused me to awaken as dawn broke that bright morning, but, looking out of my window, I was amazed to see the unmistakeable stooping figure of Gérard creeping around the house carrying a bucket. A second later he threw the cold water in it through an open window over the sleeping body of a German boy whose screams of drenched horror lasted several minutes. I descended rapidly to Gérard's bed where the perpetrator of this assault was convincingly feigning sleep. When I succeeded in "rousing" him he complained loudly "Non, sir. Inadmissable, sir. Il est seulement cinq heures et demie. Sir, vous êtes fou. Inadmissable, sir." But he could not explain, in English or in French, why his slippers were warm.

So, Sizewell 1954 was hectic and chaotic, thanks mainly to this clown with the sad face. He was so remarkable that I felt that I had to get to know him better, and one afternoon had a long conversation with him – in French, of course, quite contrary to the regulations. He explained to me that his parents had just separated, neither wanted him around during the summer, so he had been sent to Sizewell to learn English. This he determined not to do ("pas un seul mot") but he had heard before coming about the fines for breaking the rules and had to have one expression available to protest each time he would be fined: "Inadmissable, sir!" His great love was for mathematics and science (not my subjects at all) and my afternoon with him convinced me that he was really a very brilliant if somewhat sad and lonely young man. After we had both left Sizewell he wrote to me from Paris for a while – in French, naturellement. It was pleasing eventually to have got to know him as a friend – but he was exhausting!

The next time I went to Sizewell I had been promoted to the exalted rank of senior tutor, at the greatly increased salary of £10 per week, the previous incumbent of this office having been dismissed, and sued (unsuccessfully). This year one of my students was another French citizen, Sabine, an ardent Protestant and as interesting as Gérard, but much more diffident and less difficult. Sabine was fifteen years of age then, but maintained contact with me, and seven or eight years later, returned to London to perfect her English, and then I saw a lot of her at the British Council Student Centre, which, until its closure, did so much good for private overseas students like her with no strong links with this country. But by then inflation was beginning to take its toll and Sabine, who lived in comparative luxury in a flat in Knightsbridge, found it difficult to make ends meet, and sought my advice. I suggested that she should advertise in the Personal Column of "The Times" her availability to give French lessons. In those halcyon days (as they now seem) "The Times" was still a respectable newspaper and "French lessons" had no sinister connotation; moreover "gay" still meant happy. Even then "The Times" was claiming that each advertiser received hundreds of replies: Sabine got just one, from a private banker called Robert, who wished to improve his French because his bank believed, underestimating the hostility to his wartime hosts of General de Gaulle, that Britain was about to enter the Common

Market. The lessons took place about three or four times a week, and Robert engineered quite a lot of extra-mural studies: dinners with his mother, theatres, sporting activites, visits to the country, etc. In the result the teacher fell in love with her pupil.

Some months later she rang me and asked me to see her. "Erique," she said (Sabine has until today retained her charming French accent): "I do not understand him. He takes me everywhere, and I do not think that he has another girlfriend, but he never DOES anything. I love him, I want to marry him, but he never says anything about our future, and he never shows any – passion! What is the matter with him?" "He is English," I explained.

"Yes, but what can I do? I can't go on like this. I am so happy and so unhappy at the same time. I am so frustrated."

By now I had had quite a lot of experience of giving advice on all sorts of problems at Legal Advice Centres.

"Are you prepared to take a risk?" I asked. "This is a situation in which you could win all or lose all."

"I am prepared to risk losing all if there is a chance to win all," Sabine replied.

"Good," I said. "Then say this to Robert: "I'm afraid you will have to find yourself another French teacher." He will ask "Why?" "Because I am going back to France on 1st August" (or whatever date quite soon you may decide). "Why?" he will ask, "Well, there is nothing to keep me here" you will answer. Then he MAY say: "What about me?", and you ask: "What do you mean?", and he may declare his intentions to you. But you are taking a risk. He may not protest at your going, and then you will have to go; otherwise you will lose all credibility in his eyes. Are you prepared to take this risk?" "Yes," Sabine replied.

A little later she rang me again in great distress. She had followed my instructions to the letter, and everything has gone exactly as predicted – up to a point. That point arose when she had observed: "Well, there is nothing to keep me here," and instead of responding with: "What about me?" Robert had said: "Oh, what a pity! By the way, are you free on Saturday to come to the point-to-point?"

"What can I do?" sighed Sabine.

"Nothing," I said. "We've failed."

But we hadn't! A couple of weeks later Sabine phoned me again in a state of ecstacy: "Erique. Do you know what happened after our French lesson yesterday? Robert said: "I've been thinking about what you said a fortnight ago, when you said there was nothing to keep you here. What about me? Would you like to marry me and become an Englishwoman?" Erique. We are going to be married. Will you and Elke come to the wedding?"

So we went to the little protestant church in Mazamet, in Toulouse-Lautrec country, and have remained close friends of Robert and Sabine ever since. And whenever we go over there for dinner I look at their three teenage daughters and I think: "But for me, you would not be in this world – not in your present form, anyway."

Unhappily this was my only effort at match-making that achieved permanent success. Three other couples who met at our parties were to be set asunder by Judges of the Probate, Divorce and Admiralty Division, while the only other couple who have remained together have become such appalling snobs that they do not acknowledge anybody who has neither a title nor a country-house (or preferably both) – which rules us out, although the man was one of my former pupils and the woman one of Elke's best friends.

I did not go to work for Tuyn in 1958. On 30th June, Elke's birthday, she and I had become engaged and I did not want her to be rejected and return dejected from the Kingdom of Sizewell, so I declared my unavailability. We went instead for a week-end in Guernsey.

In March of the next year we married – not in a Quaker Meeting House, nor in the Chapel of Lincoln's Inn (which, on reflection, would have been a good place to have celebrated our wedding), but at St Mary's Parish Church, Hendon, a very beautiful old church at which I had worshipped since my Confirmation nearly twenty years earlier. We did this without blessing of Tuyn and, as he did not acknowledge the invitation to the wedding, I felt that he did not approve and I should never hear from him again. I was wrong. He rang me up early one morning shortly afterwards and said: "Elaine bought a pair of gloves from Harrods and they split the first time she put them on. I've started proceedings in the Westminster County Court but I can't get down, so please go along there this morning. "Bull" (his tame solicitor) "will be there with a backsheet".

"Harry, I can't. I'm in the middle of a murder at the Old Bailey." (The "Rainbow murder", for readers of "Advocacy for the Advocate.")

"Well, get someone else to take that over. This should only take an hour or so, and Elaine will get hysterical if you're not there."

"Harry, I can't, and I won't. Goodbye."

That surely did have to be "Adios", but – no! At the beginning of July there was another telephone call: "My summer course has just begun and I've decided I can't stand the students this year. I'm leaving tomorrow with Elaine for Switzerland for two months. Kathleen" (the ever-faithful secretary) "will take over for a few days but she can't cope with the school all the time. I'm appointing you Headmaster, and I'm going to be generous with you, and you will have discretion to do things exactly as you wish. Your salary will be £25 per week. When are you coming?"

"I don't know. I'm married now."

"Yes, I heard about that, but it doesn't matter. Your wife can come up if you like. I'll give you a nice little cottage to live in, in the grounds."

Near Baggott, I wondered; but I said: "I shall have to talk to the two most important people in my life, my wife and my clerk. I'll let you know."

Roy, my lazy clerk, agreed most readily. The idea of having me out of the way for the two traditionally slack summer months at the Bar, and not worrying him about work, delighted him. "Don't you worry, sir. I'll send all the papers that come in on to you – by registered post." I don't remember receiving any. Elke was working as a secretary, less than a hundred yards from my present Court, and following our three week honeymoon could get away only at weekends, but she came up on Friday evenings and left every Sunday night. Fortunately one of the Italian students had a brother (an ex-Sizewellian) who was staying in London, and this former student transported Elke both ways at high speed in his Alfa-Romeo – happily and surprisingly without any accident.

Given as I believed a free hand I set up something which I had always thought was needed at Sizewell: a Student Committee which met every day just after lunch in the Headmaster's study to discuss problems, actual and potential. One member of this committee was a Danish girl who became my confidante – uncharitable people might regard her as a sneak – and through her I got to know everything that was going on and was able to avert trouble before it arose. Elke used to complain that this girl was always in my study, but she was useful.

Kathleen found herself in an invidious position. She adored Tuyn

– to her he really was God – and for his sake she wanted Sizewell '59 to be a success, and she also wanted very much to collaborate with me. But each evening there was a telephone call to Switzerland to report on the day's events and Tuyn was not pleased by what he heard. My regime was far too "liberal"; I had told Haleh to spend more on food for the students; and, from afar, Tuyn ordered that the Student Committee should be disbanded. The idea of any form of democracy in the Sizewell autocracy appalled him. I, however, realised that I depended on the Student Committee to get me through the summer without disaster, and I refused to disband it. On the first Friday when I asked Kathleen for my weekly salary she replied: "Mr Tuyn says that I am not to give it to you. He says that you are changing the whole character of the school, and undermining his authority. He says that the matter will have to be settled in the Courts, after the course is over."

"The matter will have to be settled this evening," I replied. "Either I receive my £25 and an undertaking that I can run this course in my own way without interference, as I was promised, or I leave tonight."

When Elke arrived with Ildefonso I asked her not to unpack her bags. "We may be leaving," I said. "I believe the Norfolk Broads are very restful and I've booked provisionally for the weekend there. If we go, we shall not be returning to Sizewell."

The matter was not resolved until after ten that night, but then Kathleen came to me, after what seemed to have been interminable international telephone call, with £25 in her hand, and said: "Mr Tuyn wants you to stay on." It was the only time in my life that I have ever threatened strike action, and, I must say, it was effective. Kathleen and I worked well as a team, she being by nature loyal and extremely conscientious, and I heard no more from Tuyn, either during or after the course – or ever again. I was however to receive a sad letter from Elaine reporting his death. I could not imagine how she would survive without him. He really was her whole life. The next year was to see the last course at Sizewell Hall – in that year the atomic power station began to be built – and once again Tuyn decided to be an absentee Headmaster. I was not to be asked to deputise again, but I did get a telephone call from Bull, the solicitor, that autumn, telling me that Tuyn was suing my successor, and asking if I would accept the brief. I declined.

After the first week Sizewell '59 proceeded smoothly and

happily. I think that I was lucky; the weather was beautiful most of that summer (it rained on only one day, my birthday) and so when the students got raucous and rowdy the staff could always chase them into the sea. There was only one really drastic incident. On the course there was an eighteen year old Dutch girl who bore a remarkable physical resemblance to the then very popular Brigitte Bardot. Her provocative pout apparently appealed to one of the six tutors, and "Brigitte" complained to me of an indecent assault upon her. Her "evidence" of this was supported by two other students who said that they had witnessed the occurrence. The tutor concerned denied the incident – or, more accurately, indulged in "confession and avoidance", alleging an element of consent, but I came to the conclusion that it had happened as she said and I sent him away on the first train from Leiston. This had two consequences: I, who had seen myself in the role merely of an administrator for the summer, had to take over the naughty tutor's teaching duties additionally; and, a few days later, I received a letter from the National Union of Teachers stating that unless I wrote an unqualified apology for my high-handed and unjustified treatment of their member I should face proceedings for wrongful dismissal and defamation of character. I replied that I had not the slightest intention of apologising for *my* conduct, but that I had spoken again to the girl and if the tutor concerned wanted a legal airing of the matter the student was quite prepared to take out a summons in the local Magistrates' Court. I did not hear from the National Union of Teachers again.

Otherwise, Sizewell '59 was a happy year, and Elke, during one of her week-end visits, remarked: "You missed your vocation. You ought to have been a teacher"; words of which I often remind her now. The farewell party, always lavishly laced with food and punch, was a tremendous success, but I was a bit alarmed when at 3.00 a.m. that final Sunday I could not find any of the hundred or more Sizewell students! My relief was considerable when, as dawn broke on the morning of that blissful last day, I heard an international choir singing (not very melodiously) what had become "the song of the year": "This old man came rolling home"; and I saw on the horizon this small polyglot army marching cheerfully back, intact, to Sizewell Hall. That afternoon, when the last student had gone, I fell on my knees on the lawn by the discobulus in front of the still standing school and uttered a prayer of gratitude: "Thank you, God, that it's all over and nothing went seriously wrong."

It was nearly fourteen years later that I took Elke up on her rash comment made in the cottage at Sizewell Hall that summer, and in 1973 we set up our own summer course of English for foreign students, and it has been running every summer since under the name of "The Cromwell School of English" – not because I am a Republican (quite the reverse), but simply because Elke had lived in Cromwell Road, Earls Court, before we married. The first two students to register for the Cromwell School were Epi's children.

Chapter 8

Pupillage:

The Colonel and his Batmen

"La prim'amore non si dimentica" say the romantic Italians, and I shall never forget my first year in the British Council, which coincided with my first year at the Bar, the year of pupillage. Both were exciting experiences, but in quite different ways.

In the early 1950s the newly-called barrister had just one problem: how to get work. He found himself in a vicious circle, what nowadays would be called a "Catch 22" situation. He was allowed to accept work only from solicitors. Solicitors would not brief an unknown, inexperienced barrister. But how could the barrister get experience and become known if solicitors would not brief him? This was the young barrister's dilemma. It took me at least six years to resolve it, by which I mean that for the first six years of my life at the Bar I did not cover my expenses (rent of Chambers and clerk's fees) from my earnings at the Bar. I had to depend on my extra-mural activities with the British Council, lecturing in evening institutes, and various other jobs like gardening and working in a factory. In those days, however, although one was expected to do a period of pupillage of between six months to two years, one could practise in the Courts immediately after Call. In theory it was possible to be called to the Bar on a Thursday night and, after a highly alcoholic celebration of one's success with one's contemporaries and the Benchers in one's Inn, to be defending in a serious case at the Old Bailey on the Friday morning and, occasionally, – very occasionally, – it happened. Now the unknowing public is protected to the extent that no barrister is allowed to practise until he has done at least six months pupillage with a practising barrister – perusing and working on his papers, attending all his conferences, and accompanying him on all his Court appearances.

But the newly-called barrister of today faces two crises:– finding a Master (I am unaware of any lady barristers who take male pupils, which is just as well, since this might lead to insuperable difficulties of nomenclature) and – even more difficult – then finding a seat in Chambers. "Many are called but few survive" has always been the maxim of the Bar, but the young Common Law barrister who now succeeeds in overcoming both these hurdles – I do not profess to be an expert on the fortunes of the more rarified Chancery Bar – can, if he finishes up with a place in average or above average Chambers look forward to a reasonably secure life financially only a year or two after Call. This is due to the increase in crime, and the availability of legal aid in nearly all criminal cases. Since the 1960s crime has been our great growth industry in Britain. In the mid-1950s there were fourteen Courtrooms in and around London dealing with serious crime, and the fourteen regular Judges sitting there felt hard done by if they sat more than twenty weeks a year. Now there are over one hundred and forty Courtrooms in the same area close to London (many in newly constructed buildings) and of the four hundred or so Crown Court Judges more than half adjudicate on the South-Eastern circuit, where the Courts sit continuously and there are often waits of a year or more to get a case on for hearing. No wonder there are more people in prison! I will leave it to the politicians and the sociologists to work out the underlying reasons for this massive increase in crime, whilst proffering my own perhaps too simple solution that it may have something to do with the fact that schoolchildren are usually not now taught the difference between right and wrong in their schools – they are taught their rights but not their duties to their fellow citizens – and how they suffer for it in terms of human happiness!

What qualities go to make the right sort of person to be a successful Common Law barrister? asked Professor Glanville Williams in "Learning the Law" – still regarded as essential reading for all would-be lawyers. He answered his own question by quoting from Samuel Warren: "On the physical side a melodious voice, a commanding appearance, and an iron constitution; on the mental, perseverance, logical thought, quick perceptions, a retentive memory, sound judgment, presence of mind, self-reliance, self-control, and that ductility, elasticity, activity; that expansive and contractile power of mind which can adapt itself to everything, and pass in a moment from one engagement to another, of the most different character, from labyrinth to labyrinth – with unwearied energy, with a mind unconfused."

I think one can get by without one or two of those qualities – I did! –but he might have added that you ought to know people established in both branches of the legal profession. This I did not. The only lawyer I knew was Lord Justice Jenkins, whom I had to visit twice a year under the terms of my Tancred studentship, but he had spent all his life at the Chancery Bar and could not help me with advice about a Common Law pupillage. So I sought an interview with the Director of the Council of Legal Education, the ancient and immaculate William Cleveland– Stevens, KC., and he provided me with a list of four names of barristers who had said that they were "willing to consider taking pupils". I approached the first of these and, during a pleasant and even jovial interview, was accepted. I have often wondered how different my life would have been if I had chosen to go to the second on the list, Geoffrey Howard. He was to become a County Court Judge, and a very meticulous one – I often had to appear before him later on – and he had the reputation of being a really tough pupil master who drove his pupils hard but also cared a lot about their futures. This would have been good for me on both counts.

Hugh Corner did not drive his pupils very hard and did not care much about their futures. An ex-Indian Army Colonel, with a military bearing and manner, he had come to the Bar late in life – just before World War II and had acquired a vast practice while younger men were away fighting. This practice was mainly in the field of divorce, and Hugh needed young "devils" to draft his numerous petitions for him, and he normally had four pupils for this purpose. He was exceptionally mean, and it was hard to resist the conclusion that he took on so many pupils at a hundred guineas each so as to get through this mound of very tedious work on the cheap, for we were never paid for devilling for him. Whilst he did give us the opportunity of seeing his "corrections" to our pleadings, it did not take me very long to realise that his own petitions were not very good – I had to wait to share a room with Bill Kee later on to see how a divorce petition should really be drafted – nor was Hugh a particularly brilliant advocate. But he was busy, so the four of us got around a lot. His room was quite crowded, as he shared it also with two other members of the Chambers, of which he was the Head, so there were often seven of us beavering away there. One of my first tasks there was to dust all the books in his library.

So, in the summer of 1951, I was accepted as his pupil by Hugh, who seemed easy and affable, and my good friend Michael Scott was looking for pupillage at that time, so I recommended that he applied to Hugh, and he was also accepted, joining Hugh's troupe shortly after I did. This was not good advice that I gave to Michael, and he was to suffer for it, for he and Hugh never saw eye to eye.

Michael was an Irishman, with all the best qualities of that nation, being witty, talkative, friendly, and resourceful. He could make the funniest comments with the straightest of faces. I remember that on the day that King George VI died he told us solemnly: "The signwriter is already changing the name "King's Bench Walk" to "Queen's Bench Walk": and when we swallowed that one, he added, for good measure: And British Rail has announced that in future King's Cross Station will be called "Queen's Angry". This whimsy did not appeal to Hugh, who had no sense of humour, and deplored Michael's habit of writing his divorce petitions in green ink. Hugh also insisted that his pupils addressed him as "sir", in which we all acquiesced except Michael, who produced some Bar Regulation which, emphasising the equality of all members of the Bar, stated that the correct form of address between the pupil and his master (and vice versa) was by use of surnames. (Somehow I could never bring myself to address Hugh as "Corner".)

Chambers were a riot of fun when Hugh was not there. He was a director of many business institutions and belonged to a number of City Livery Companies and was often away after lunch for a substantial part of the afternoon. The other two barristers were one of the most attractive women I have ever met – whose husband, an estate agent, was gaoled for three years for fraud during the period of our pupillage – and a very able and handsome young barrister called David Green, who looked remarkably like Stewart Granger (if one regards Stewart Granger as handsome). Alas, David was to be involved in a terrible car crash that New Year's Eve as a result of which he became virtually a cabbage and spent the rest of his days in Stoke Manderville Hospital – a great loss to the Bar.

The lady barrister had a good sense of humour and joined in the fun but David Green used to complain sometimes: "When you four young animals are here roaring about it's more like a circus than a set of Chambers''.

Perhaps Michael did not take his position as a pupil as seriously as he might have done. Hugh was Standing Counsel to the Court of Protection and, as such, had to look after the interests of all those who had the misfortune to be divorced on the ground of incurable insanity. All these undefended cases were heard on the first and third Monday morning of each month and, where the Petitioner was the husband, Hugh used to have to rise up and ask him: "Are you prepared to pay the sum of four shillings and tuppence per week for extra comforts for your wife?" He asked this question in such a stern and demanding tone that I never heard a Petitioner give a negative answer, but it was not a very inspiring morning for us four pupils, and one Friday afternoon Michael asked Hugh: "Do we have to turn up on Monday? After all, it's lunatic day". Hugh was furious. "I will not have my practice denigrated in that way," he declared. "Certainly you have to be there."

Nor did Hugh think very highly of Michael's pleadings, drafted as they continued to be in the inevitable green ink. On one occasion he hurled a divorce petition back at Michael with the comment: "When you give up practice at the Bar, as I imagine you will do quite soon, may I recommend that you take up writing short stories for children, as your pleadings suggest that you have a particular aptitude for that type of literature?"

"Thank you, Corner," replied Michael with studied irony, "that's a very helpful suggestion and one which I shall seriously consider."

In one sense I had my first case in Court – or at least my first forensic mention – with Michael. A devout Catholic, Michael went weekly to give advice at a Legal Advice Centre run by the Roman Catholic Church, and he was briefed by a solicitor there to appear, free of charge, in a matrimonial case called Kelly v Kelly at Tower Bridge Magistrates' Court, on the afternoon of Christmas Eve 1951. It found its place "Last on the List" before that formidable lady stipendiary magistrate, Sybil Campbell. The ground on which Mrs Kelly was seeking a separation order from her errant husband was an unusual one, brought under the Licensing Act 1872, that of habitual drunkenness. Michael invited me to go along to watch his first efforts in advocacy and to give him moral support. What we had not realised was that matrimonial cases in Magistrates' Courts are held in private, and the gaoler made efforts to keep me out. Michael protested eloquently and effectively, and the gaoler said: "Well, you'll have to justify him to her Ladyship. She's a stickler for etiquette, you know."

Michael got over this particular difficulty by opening the case when it was called upon with these words: "May it please you, Madam, in this case I appear for the complainant Mrs Kelly, with my learned friend Mr Eric Crowther acting as my junior." It all looked a bit oppressive, as the bewildered Mr Kelly was appearing in person. Michael went on to open the case at considerable length, explaining that the grounds were unusual.

"Yes" observed the magistrate, "I have not had such a case in all my years on the bench. You must give me a few minutes to look up the relevant law."

I decided that the time had come for me to justify my presence, so I rose to say: "I think that I might be able to help you, Madam, if you would lend me your copy of Rayden on Divorce. Miss Campbell beamed at me in whatever is the female equivalent of an avuncular way, but unfortunately as it descended from the Bench I in my nervousness dropped the heavy and precious volume, out of which Sybil's Christmas cards fell all over the floor, the usher scurrying across to pick them up. The case bristled with difficulties and at the close of the complainant's evidence there seemed to be a danger of the magistrate's holding that there was no case to answer, but, prompted by me, Michael succeeded in dissuading her from such a drastic course (although by now it was past five o'clock) and the Respondent made his way unsteadily across to the witness-box to give his account of this sad little marriage. He had not got far with his evidence when Michael and I watched with amazement as, leaning against one of the wooden pillars at the corner of the witness box, Mr Kelly slowly sank lower and lower until eventually he collapsed in a drunken and somnolent heap on the floor and proceeded audibly but invisibly to snore. "I don't think I need to hear any more of this case," announced the magistrate with dignity. "I find the allegation of habitual drunkenness proved, and I shall make a separation order, and I order the Respondent to pay to the Complainant by way of maintenance the sum of one shilling per week."

"There is no application for costs," murmured Michael.

"I should hope not" said the magistrate severely as she swept out of Court without responding to Michael's and my duet of good wishes for the festive season.

By the time we left the Court, thankful to the inebriated Mr Kelly, whom we last saw lying in the arms of the Court Matron, for having won our first joint case for us (it was in fact to be Michael's only case at the English Bar), it was half past five and we had to hurry back to the Temple.

I was on duty that night helping to run for the first time the British Council's Christmas Party for the overseas students. Michael Catliff should have been assisting also, but he wanted the evening off, and I had asked Lawrence if Michael Scott could come and work in his stead. Lawrence had not only agreed, but said that Michael (Scott) would be paid at the top rate of six shillings an hour, although it was not a Saturday or Sunday, so this was to be a really big day for Irish Michael. But Lawrence had added a proviso. "He has got a dinner jacket, hasn't he? I do think we ought to put on a black tie for these occasions, don't you? The students expect a bit of formality from the English." So Michael and I each had a dinner jacket, back in Chambers, but when we got there around six o'clock, the offices were locked and in darkness. It being Christmas Eve everyone, even Douglas, the hard-working clerk, had gone home. Michael had the solution. He climbed down into the basement and prised open the window there with his penknife, and we both clambered in and ascended to the ground floor to retrieve our coveted evening dress. I did feel that it might have been a rather disastrous Christmas for us if a passing policeman had observed our movements that dark night and had taken us to Bow Street, leaving us to languish in a cell until Boxing Day on an attempted burglary charge, but happily no one saw us. It was about six weeks later that I did my own first case, fully robed in a County Court, but as the facts of that epic trial are set out in the first chapter of my earlier book "Advocacy for the Advocate", (published by Barry Rose) I will not weary the reader with them here. Suffice it to say that the brief was a return of the beautiful lady barrister; it was marked a guinea; I was promised half the fee for devilling; and I haven't been paid yet! She is not the only beautiful lady in my life to have let me down ....

A few weeks after my first triumphant appearance on my own in an English Court of Law the other two pupils, Chris and Josef, who very wisely had booked to stay with Hugh for only six months, left Hugh's Chambers for fresh fields and pastures new (abroad, as it happened). The morning after their departure Hugh addressed the two of us in solemn tones: "Now listen, you boys. There's an object lesson to be learned from those two who left yesterday. Josefides is a diligent and conscientious worker. He profited a lot from his pupillage with me and he will go far. As for that other fellow, that dilettante butterfly, he's no good at all and the Bar holds no future for him. He's just a lazy lay about."

I listened respectfully to his judgment on my fellow-pupils but Michael, who had been closer to Chris than I had been, did not. Looking straight at Hugh from above his poised green pen Michael said:

"I don't think you ought to say nasty things about people behind their backs when they're not present."

It was then that the explosion occurred. Hugh's normally red face became crimson and his toothbrush moustache bristled as he rose and pointed imperiously towards the door. "Get out," he roared. "Get out, and don't come back. I hope I never see you again."

"No," replied Michael mildly, "I'm not going. I've paid for a year's pupillage and I've still got six months to do. I'm staying."

"You're not," bellowed Hugh and came and seized hold of Michael and started to propel him vigorously towards the door. Michael resisted and the two struggled.

"Get Douglas," ordered Hugh, and, as there seemed no harm in this, I did as I was bidden and the clerk and I watched in horror as the two barristers exchanged blows. It was just at this moment, 9.45 a.m., that Tony arrived. Tony was one of the two new pupils, taken on to replace Chris and Josef. He was, and is, a man of great bearing and dignity, now a High Court Judge. He has described his first morning of pupillage as follows:– "I arrived, entered the room and hung up my bowler and my umbrella on the hatstand in the corner. I then saw that my pupilmaster and a fellow pupil were engaged in a bout of fisticuffs. I retook possession of my bowler and my umbrella, and repaired to the Kardomah for coffee. When I returned the battle was over, and the fellow-pupil had gone."

During a brief pause in the struggle Hugh had shouted to the amazed Douglas: "I have told Scott that his pupillage is terminated as from this morning." Michael saw that further resistance was hopeless, so he decided on different tactics. "This is a gross breach of contract," he declared, "and I want my hundred guineas back." "Certainly not, you impudent puppy." was Hugh's response.

"Then I'll go to the Bar Council," retorted Michael, "and I 'll go now – this minute."

I do not know what was in the letter which arrived on Hugh's desk a few days later, the envelope of which was embossed "General Council of the Bar of England and Wales", but judging by Hugh's expression as he read it, the contents were not wholly pleasing. I understood (from Michael – not from Hugh) that the "action" was compromised on terms that Hugh repaid fifty guineas to Michael, which seemed fair, as, after all, Michael had had the "benefit" of Hugh's pupillage for half the prescribed term. Douglas, the clerk, offered to return half of his ten guineas pupillage fee but Michael declined to accept this on the ground that Douglas was a "good fellow" – a judgment with which I wholeheartedly agreed.

The manner in which Michael severed his ties with the Colonel had a profound effect on the life of my friend, with whom I remained on close terms for some years thereafter. Initially he took a job as legal advisor to British Road Services, a nationalised industry which fell victim to the incoming Conservative Government's denationalisation policy. Disillusioned with the Bar, he applied to be disbarred, and then studied and qualified to be a solicitor – a much more elaborate procedure in those days than now but he did not enjoy his "articles" (although his reaction to that period was much less violent than his ultimate response to pupillage) and he did not engage in practice in that branch of the profession. Instead he lectured on law for some years at the Polytechnic of Central London (where he got me some evening work) and became part author of "O"–Level English Law" (and later "A"– Level English Law") by Scott and Sims, the standard text-books for those just taking up legal studies. In 1954 he and I drove together on what was my first visit to Paris, and in 1955 I was back in France for Michael's wedding in Versailles to Anne – the daughter of a French General! Eventually he rather than Anne tired of England and they moved to France where he qualified for the French Bar and took up a lecturing post at a French University. It was then, somewhere around the mid-sixties, that Michael and I lost contact for many years, during which he became a high official of the European Court in Luxembourg. From there he wrote to me again in the late seventies, saying that he was organising a week-end visit to England by a group of European Judges and would like them to spend the Saturday watching the proceedings with me presiding at West London Magistrates' Court. Alas, on the day on which they were due to come, and on which I would have seen Michael again after so long – and for the last time – I was flying off to give a lecture – at the British Council in Paris! The next that I heard of Michael was in 1983 when I read with great sadness a glowingly laudatory obituary to his varied and ultimately highly successful life in "The Times", he having suffered a heart attack on his way to visit his beloved Ireland.

Just before Christmas 1986 his widow Anne telephoned me to say that she was staying for the festive season with her daughter, Alicia, who lives no more than a quarter of a mile from us! The result was that we spent a lot of both Christmas and New Year's Eve together in reminiscences at once sad and laughing over the life of a man who had clearly been a wonderful husband and father, as well as a very great friend.

Hugh's predictions concerning Josefides and Chris also proved reasonably accurate. The former became a High Court Judge in Cyprus where Elke and I enjoyed a delightful dinner with him and his family in their home in 1969. Chris, too, left England, to go to North Africa to draft a Constitution for the Republic of Libya. It can't have been a very good one if it let Colonel Gadaffi take over!

Their replacements were Tony, already described, who was (and is) a perfect gentleman, and Michael Fish, who certainly was not. Stocky, unkempt and bearded like the pard, he was – I nearly wrote "a very different kettle of Fish." An aggressive little fellow, he made it quite clear from an early stage that he had no intention of addressing his pupilmaster as "sir". "I'm Fish and you're Corner," he informed an outraged Hugh, who took this piece of information with anguished calm after his experiences with the other Michael, but the atmosphere between them was not cordial. Matters came to a head in the Divorce Court at Lewes, where Hugh was conducting a defended divorce before a rather unpleasant and sarcastic Judge, also ex-Colonial, Sir Reginald Sharpe. Hugh opened the case with these words:–

"May it please your Lordship, this is a wife's petition on the ground of cruelty. I should advise your Lordship straight away that the Respondent in this case is a great big man, six foot four in height and broad in proportion, a Sergeant-Major in the Irish Guards."

At this point the Judge intervened: "All right, Mr Corner, don't frighten me."

Michael Fish burst into prolonged, uncontrolled, loud guffaws of laughter. Hugh turned on him angrily: "Be quiet, you silly fellow. If you can't control yourself, get out of the Court. Get out and don't come back." (an ominous phrase that I had heard only a few weeks before).

"Wait a minute," said Sir Reginald. "This is my Court and I am in control of it and I rather like it if people appreciate my little jokes. He can stay if he wishes."

"No he cannot" Hugh snapped. "He's my pupil – unfortunately –and I'm in charge of him, and he cannot stay. Get out this moment!"

The new Michael did then decide that discretion might be the better part of valour, but he was lurking in the robing room when the day's proceedings were ended.

"What are you doing here?" Hugh demanded.

"Waiting for a lift back to London," the pupil replied.

"Well, you're not getting one from me," Hugh said firmly. "Get out at once. I never want to see you again. Your pupillage is terminated forthwith."

"Then give me the fare back to London. You're supposed to look after your pupils."

"I shall do no such thing," Hugh asserted. "Get out of my way." It ended up with my lending Michael Fish the fare to London.

I arrived too late to observe the sequel that occurred next morning, but for Tony it was a repeat performance of what he had observed about a month before, except that this time the protagonists were armed:–

"I entered the room of my pupilmaster at about 9.45 a.m. and hung up my bowler and my umbrella on the hatstand in the corner. I then saw that my pupilmaster and a fellow pupil were engaged in a pitched battle, each armed with a broomstick. I retook possession of my bowler and my umbrella, and repaired to the Kardomah for coffee. When I returned the battle was over, and the fellow pupil was gone, but before leaving I did hear the words: "It's the Bar Council for you, Corner." "

I saw the second Michael only once more when he came back to Chambers a few weeks later to return the fare that I had lent him on the day of the ill-advised laughter in Lewes.

"How are things with you, Michael?" I enquired apprehensively.

"Marvellous. Couldn't be better. Got a job as legal advisor to the

Ministry. Thoroughly enjoying it.''

''Which Ministry?'' I enquired. I suppose the answer was inevitable.

''Why, the Ministry of Agriculture and Fish.''

I had witnessed the departure of Michael Fish with few regrets, but life in Chambers was much less interesting and less enjoyable without the Michael who was my good friend. I think that what went wrong between him and his pupilmaster was that Michael had such a rich sense of humour while Hugh had none. A sense of humour involves two things: warm generosity and a sense of proportion, and Hugh had neither. He was, in every sense of the term, a small man. Douglas, his clerk, a far warmer and more approachable personality, was even smaller in stature than Hugh, neither being more than about five feet six inches in height. I remember once walking with them both across to the High Court and Douglas was complaining to Hugh about the conduct of some other barrister. ''He's a little man, Douglas,'' commented Hugh, as I strode along towering over them, ''a little man. They're all like that.''

Nowadays pupil masters no longer charge fees of their pupils, regarding it as their duty gratuitously to perpetuate the species, but in the early fifties they still did, the amount being fifty guineas per six months, plus five more guineas for the clerk — a lot of money for someone in the position of Michael or myself. However, out of this it was expected that the pupil master would provide lunch for his pupil whenever they were together. This Hugh never did. But once we had been in an outlying Court (I think Uxbridge; it was usually Uxbridge when things went disastrously wrong) and Hugh had lost a case which I thought he should have won. He had put a great deal of effort into his presentation and I felt that the magistrates had come to a perverse decision by convicting. ''I think if I may say so that you did that case very well,'' I commented as we left the Court. ''I think you deserved to win it.'' Hugh was pleased and smiled broadly. (We all like to be flattered and what I said was true). ''You showed great perception by that remark, my boy. I think you'll do well at the Bar. Come along, I'll buy you some refreshment.''

It was one o'clock, and I was hungry, and wondering what sort of a restaurant Hugh would take me to. I was a little disappointed when we entered the A.B.C., even more so when Hugh swept past the food counters to where the beverages were being served. "I'll buy you a coffee, my boy," Hugh offered. "Large or small?" asked the girl behind the counter, but before I could answer Hugh said: "He'll have a small one."

But on the whole I got on well with my pupil master in those remaining six months, and apart from his lack of generosity, his lack of a sense of humour and the lack of variety in his work I had only one other matter to complain about. There was, however, one day on which he had cause to be angry with me. He was defending in an important one-day case at Kingston Quarter Sessions and was particularly anxious that I should be there to take a note and remind him of the salient points of the evidence for his closing speech. I had a case of my own that day (a "Cambridge House" case – more of this later) and he recognised that I would learn more by arguing a case myself than by listening to him, and he readily agreed to my going to Marylebone County Court in the morning, provided that I used every endeavour to join him at Kingston by 2 o'clock. I found that the best and cheapest way to get there from near the Court was by 715 Green Line bus. I had it all timed to a nicety, but as I ran towards the bus stop the bus was already there, five minutes early. The driver waited until I was about ten yards away from his vehicle before moving off his bus half empty with a broad grin on his face. (This was a game that London bus drivers enjoyed playing much more thirty-five years ago than now.) Whether his smile was so broad because he realised that the next bus had been "cut out" I do not know. All that I do know is that I arrived very late at the Kingston Quarter Sessions. Then I had to discover which Court Hugh was in. This was not difficult, as Hugh had a habit of whistling through his teeth while addressing the Court and I soon heard that high-pitched sound, denoting that he had embarked on his closing address. He was not pleased. "Thank you for all your help," he said dourly afterwards. "You've been of great assistance to me, I must say." He did not speak to me at all after the case and I wondered if I should receive the Michael Fish treatment in respect of the journey back to London as I carried his robes and books and we walked, defeated and dejected, back to his car. But I was allowed to board that elderly, battered vehicle. However, the hour-long journey back to London took place in complete silence. The tension was more than I could bear. As we crossed Westminster Bridge I decided to make a joke. I looked repeatedly and obviously at the clock in the

Tower of the House of Commons and then at my own wristwatch and then, pointing to Big Ben, I remarked cheerfully: "That clock's right today."

"You silly fellow," said Hugh. "It's always right."

The other matter concerning my pupillage of which I complain is that Hugh did nothing to help me after it was over. I could never get a straight answer from him as to whether I would be allowed to stay on in Chambers – which I would have liked to have done, for Douglas was a good, honest clerk – and he gave me no assistance regarding obtaining a tenancy elsewhere. This I consider to be a fundamental duty of any pupil master, and I flatter myself that no pupil of mine who wanted to continue in practice at the English Bar ever failed to find a place in good Chambers. If Hugh had done his duty in this respect I would not have finished up with Roy as my clerk. Strangely enough, I did not see Hugh again for many, many years although he continued to practise at the Bar until his ninetieth birthday. Then his loyal tenants gave him a dinner in his Inn of Court to celebrate his retirement, and most of his former pupils were also invited, although I did not notice anyone there with the Christian name of Michael. It was a splendid, and quite moving, occasion after which Hugh came up to me and was as pleasant and jovial as at our first meeting, a quarter of a century before. Addressing me for the first time by my Christian name, he said: "Eric, I always knew you'd make it, and you certainly did." I contented myself with replying: "Thank you, Hugh," although I almost found myself adding "sir".

His death occurred about three years later, after Hugh had been knocked down by a car. The question attributed to one of his tenants: "And was the vehicle a total wreck?" was, I believe, not prompted by malice, but was intended as a tribute to the extraordinary vigour, resilience and courage of a man who continued fighting cases in the Courts as a junior counsel until his ninetieth year. The Colonel was certainly a character, and one whom I will not forget.

Chapter 9

"Are you the poor Lawyer, sir?"

The door would open a little way, a troubled head would appear, and a nervous voice would enquire: "Are you the poor lawyer, sir?" This was a situation that I encountered two or three times a week for the first eight impecunious years of my life at the Bar. Michael Scott and Brian Calwell (the expert on lecturing activities for unemployed barristers) introduced me to the world of the Poor Man's Lawyer, later re-christened the Legal Advice Centres and later still the Law Centres, although these were unfortunately to become politically orientated when they came to depend for financial support on the local authorities. Some of these Law Centres, for example, refuse to advise landlords on landlord and tenant problems, although I have known of cases of poor and elderly landlords being terrorised by greedy and vicious young tenants. It is wrong when lawyers put labels on potential clients and decide in general terms whom they will and will not serve.

My three "P.M.Ls" were Cambridge House in Camberwell; Toynbee Hall in Commercial Street, E.1., and one attached to the Citizens' Advice Bureau in Croydon. After advising there on Friday mornings I used to do a "Meals on Wheels" service in the Surrey borough, to which Michael also introduced me. He knew that I loved driving, and I had no car. I think that I must have been a rather reckless driver, as one or two of the old dears of the Women's Royal Voluntary Service refused to accompany me, but another – the oldest of the lot – said that the ride in the van with me was the most exciting event of the week. And there were no seat-belts in those days....

The first Poor Man's Lawyer that I attended was Cambridge House. It was well organised by an elderly lady secretary, Miss Harman, who charged a fee of three shillings (15p) for advice. I have statistics for one year of its operation, produced when the Greater London Council was threatening to withdraw its grant. In the period 1953/4 no fewer than 3,363 new clients came to Cambridge House, 7,773 interviews took place, 11,643 letters were written and 405 cases were conducted in Court. Most important of all £12,500 (less 63p) was recovered for clients by negotiation, without litigation. And this success rate was achieved against a background of the oddest permanent legal staff imaginable, supported by part-time barristers like Brian Calwell and myself attending for half a day a week.

My half day was Monday afternoon, and I shared a room with a solicitor called Ronald Brown. It would be more accurate to say that I shared the room for part of the time, as Mr Brown, whose legal qualifications derived from Dublin, never returned until after 3.00 when the local hostelries closed, and for much of the rest of the afternoon he slept, while a strong odour of alcohol pervaded the consulting room. One afternoon Mr Brown did not get back. He had been knocked down and injured by a car on his return from drinking his lunch. When he wished to take proceedings against the car driver I had to advise him that the degree of contributory negligence likely to be found could amount to one hundred per cent.

Another of the regular staff left under a cloud having, it was said, embezzled a large part of the funds. He was replaced by John Wintersgill, an intelligent young solicitor who came from the Automobile Association whose legal department does not normally provide the brightest stars in the legal firmament. John was a good lawyer, organised excellent parties at his flat in Chelsea, sent me on my only legal trip abroad (to Holland, for a conference, in a case that ended up in the Chancery Division) and, as best man at my wedding, made the most tactless speech that can be imagined, enumerating every one of my love affairs of which he was aware (and that was the majority). I was glad that Elke's parents did not understand English, and happy and relieved that Elke herself did not run away. I think she was rooted to the spot in horror.

Strangest of all was Robert Hines, who was in charge. He was a rather seedy-looking man with a walrus moustache who, nevertheless, walked with gigantic strides. He was an excellent lawyer but very bad on public relations, and usually wrong in his predictions. Before being accepted as an advisor myself I had to sit in with Hines "to learn how to handle these people." His first case

123

that afternoon was that of a rather pathetic woman who expressed her problem thus:

"Me 'usband's left me and I want 'im back 'cos I love 'im. Can you 'elp me get 'im back?"

Hines had a swivel chair. When he gave advice he always swung round so that it was the back of his head that addressed the client, as he clasped his hands in front of him and closed his eyes. The advice – basically sound in law – came in these terms:

"Madam. The law of England knoweth of no means whereby to compel one spouse to cohabit with the other."

"I see," said the unfortunate woman, uttering that expression that people usually employ when they don't; "but I love 'im and I want 'im back."

Hines revolved to face his victim: "Madam I have given you my advice. If you are not content therewith may I suggest that you repair to a solicitor in private practice? Good-day to you."

"That's the way to treat them" he informed me, and I decided at that moment that I would never treat another human being like that, although I did not say so, as I wanted to stay on.

I met Hines only once socially, or quasi-socially. We were queueing up together one Friday evening at Lyons' Corner House in the Strand, my being on my way to my evening duty at the British Council. "There are two good things about this place" he said, closing his eyes. "It's cheap and they don't poison you." I did not find it cheap and that weekend I went down with food poisoning.

Cambridge House and Toynbee Hall used to brief the barristers who attended to give advice. (The Croydon Centre did not.) For Cambridge House we wrote opinions and did pleadings free. The last of Hines's briefs to me began with the words:

"The Plaintiff is one of the unemployable unemployed. He is a vexatious litigant who is an unmitigated scoundrel and whose case against the Southwark Borough Council has no merit"; and it finished "This is not an action that counsel should try hard to win."

I took a different view and did win the case, before that very fair and delightful tribunal, Judge Daynes Q.C. (who looked like everybody's idea of a bishop) to the astonishment of my opponent, that fine advocate Donald Keating, and to the intense dismay of Hines, who never briefed me again. But I did receive briefs, always marked two guineas, from Brown and John Wintersgill, and they proved to be among my most rewarding cases.

How, though, would Hines have dealt with this middle-aged lady, who came to me a few months later?

She sat down, eyed me very earnestly, and said, impressively and impassively: "I want an injunction against my doctor. I went to him for treatment a couple of years ago and ever since then he's been sending me these thought waves, and I can't stand it any longer." I listened to her story at length, for by now I had learned the important lesson that the best way to give advice is to listen and not to talk. Often the mere fact of having to explain the problem to another person will enable a confused client to see the real source of his trouble for the first time, and from his recognition of its nature will spring also his realisation of its solution; and it is also the case that the simpler the person, the more complex are the problems in which he is liable to get involved. Often the trouble is the one which is hardest to cure: loneliness and the desire to have some friend in whom to confide. More than once after reaching a satisfactory conclusion to a case – for we did have our occasional successes – we would hand over a cheque to a client whom we expected to be delighted to have reached the end of his legal journey. But his expression has been downcast: "Does this mean?" he has asked, "that I can't come and see you any more?" Christopher McCoustra, probably the best of our Toynbee barristers, did so much for one of his clients that he really made a new man out of a piece of human wreckage. When the legal action had been successfully concluded, this elderly character came into Toynbee Hall sporting a rather battered and unsuitable top hat. "Bought it for sixpence down the Lane, guv'nor," he told Christopher triumphantly. "Now I look a proper barrister, don't I?"

So, for many of our clients the weekly visit to the Poor Man's Lawyer was a social occasion, and many of the problems with which we had to deal were psychological rather than legal, like that of the lady with the thought waves. The advice that I gave her went something like this: "I think the treatment that your doctor gave you was good treatment. The only trouble is that he gave it to you too strong, so that some of these thought waves are still in your mind long after they should have left. They are still in your mind and they have got to be driven from your mind. The only way you can drive them out of your mind is by putting something else there instead. If you have something else occupying your mind there will be no place for these stale thought waves which ought to have gone long ago.

What I want you to do is to find a part-time job. When you get it, devote all your enthusiasm and energy to it. If you give it all your attention and concentration you will find that there is no longer any room in your mind for these oppressive thought waves, and they will quickly die away."

She came to see me a month or so later. By now she was working in a shop (work was easier to find in the early fifties than now – except for barristers ...) She seemed really happy on her return visit and reported that the thought waves had almost gone. "You've no idea," she added, "what a weight you've taken off my mind."

The clients often wanted to proceed for injunctions, but we did not encourage applications for this remedy, perhaps because none of us were Chancery lawyers. One mild little lady told me confidentially: "I want an injunction against the people living upstairs. They're making atom bombs. I'm not one to complain, but it's so dangerous." The senior solicitor at Toynbee was John Pym, who, alas, died very young, and he was a man of infinite patience, to such an extent that he took over this case from me and spent the whole of one night in her flat listening out for sounds of this terrifying activity. All was as quiet as the tomb. "I think you're mistaken," he pronounced soon after dawn. "No I'm not," she replied. "They saw you coming. I noticed their curtains move. They gave it up for tonight. That's how cunning and wicked they are."

Miss Harman conducted a rather rigorous "means test" before accepting clients at Cambridge House, but just occasionally the rich man (or woman) would get through the needle's eye. I was looking out of the window during one of my few slack moments when I saw a taxi – in those days a rare sight in Camberwell Road – pull up outside and a rather stately middle-aged lady in a magnificent fur coat – if fur coats can ever be magnificent – swept up the steps of Cambridge House. "Miss Harman will soon get rid of her," I thought; but, no, a few minutes later she made such an impressive entrance to my room that even Mr Brown woke up.

"I want to divorce my husband on the grounds of mental cruelty," she announced, and a shudder went down my spine, for "mental cruelty" was hardly recognised as a ground for dissolution of marriage in the early fifties; in contrast to today when mere incompatability will suffice; e.g. the loss of the man's income or the woman's pat-ability.

"Tell me what form his cruelty takes."

"Well, to begin with he allows me only £15 a week." (This, let it be remembered, was in 1952, and the figure mentioned far exceeded my own average gross earnings.) "Then he's moved the whole family to Orpington, which is a social desert, and, worst of all, he's now encouraging my daughter, who stays at home to look after me, to become a nurse."

I listened to her other trivial complaints at some length and then I said: "I was going to advise you to go to a solicitor in private practice, which I am satisfied you can well afford to do, but as I think you have no case at all, you should save your money."

"Save my money!" she exclaimed indignantly. "You're quite hopeless. I've come twelve miles by taxi to receive useless advice from you. Call me a taxi to take me home!"

People came a long way to get our advice, but very different from the anti-Orpington lady was another lady whom I saw in conference at Cambridge House prior to appearing for her at Watford Magistrates' Court. I expressed surprise that after many years of desertion by her husband she had not taken proceedings for dissolution of the marriage, and she replied primly and firmly that she did not believe in divorce.

"Well," I said cheerfully at the end of the conference, "I'll see you on Friday in Court."

"I'd much rather see you on Sunday in Church, young man," she pronounced severely. "That would be a far better place for you."

We did not get that sort of person at Toynbee Hall, which I attended every Wednesday evening, the sessions there often continuing well after midnight, but the clients were equally unpredictable. One man entered the room there and greeted me with the words: "I'm off me 'ead. I may go off me 'ead any moment as I stand here."

"Well, you'd better sit down," I advised.

Another man came in brandishing a letter. "Did you write this to me?" he demanded.

I took it and saw my initials on it and agreed that I had done so.

"Good," he said. "I'm going to beat you up. I'm going to thump you into next week."

Edging my way past him I asked: "Would you mind waiting there while I get some witnesses? It's always helpful in cases of assault."

When I returned he had gone. It is true that I took quite a long time to get back. He was a rather powerfully built man ....

127

Women often brought their children to Toynbee, and this sometimes proved a distraction. On one occasion I had great difficulty in concentrating on the matrimonial history of a woman with a young child in her arms, because he screamed continuously throughout the conference.

"Your child does cry a lot," I commented, at last.

"Yes," she said compassionately. "The poor little mite. He's got scarlet fever."

I terminated that interview rather quickly.

Doing the solicitor's work, writing letters for clients, could be quite fun, despite the experience just recited. A shy twenty-one year old Indian student came to see me at Toynbee in great distress. He had been inveigled into the Arthur Murray School of Dancing for a "free trial lesson" and, before he left, he had been induced to sign a "non-cancellable agreement" for dancing lessons at a total price of £370 (in the 1950s!) He did not have the money and had been put off dancing forever. He had just not gone back and was now receiving ever more threatening letters from their rogue solicitors. I wrote to them on his behalf using such expressions as "signed under duress" and "an agreement that comes near to fraud." This evinced a pained and angry reply from the solicitors who said that this was a disgraceful imputation on the character of their internationally respected clients and that unless I retracted these remarks immediately I would receive a writ for libel and be reported to the Law Society. I replied that I would do neither: even I knew that correspondence between lawyers was privileged, and I would have been delighted to be brought to the attention of the Law Society, very few members of which were at that time aware of my existence.

While this bitter and protracted correspondence was going on, a strange thing happened. I was at home one morning – I had by now realised the futility of going early into Chambers in the hope of finding work, so I stayed at home during most mornings preparing lectures – when the telephone rang and a seductive female voice addressed me: "You Mr Crowther? Mr Crowther, this is the Arthur Murray School of Dancing. It is my pleasant duty to inform you that you have been awarded a free trial lesson in ballroom dancing in our Kensington studio. Ballroom dancing is the key to success in life, and could change everything for you. Will you accept?"

My life could have done with a change at that time, so I said:

"Well, yes," and thus I was invited into the same lions' den (or rather lionesses' den) into which my young Indian client had been seduced. "Seduced" is probably the right word. I was greeted on arrival by an extremely buxom young lady with an American or Canadian accent and an exceedingly low cut gown.

"You an experienced dancer?" she enquired.

"No, " I replied, not completely truthfully: I was experienced, but I was not good.

"We'll try the cha-cha-cha." she pronounced, and we did, she dancing remarkably close to me for a comparative stranger.

"Say," she observed admiringly as she led me round the floor. "You're wonderful. Have you ever done this dance before?"

"No," I answered, completely truthfully this time.

"Well, you're amazing," she added. "Just a moment, I'm going to call the manager," and, when he arrived, she assessed the situation thus: "Say, this guy's marvellous. He's not experienced, he's never done the cha-cha before, yet he moves like gossamer" (I think I weighed even more then than I do now). "I was going to suggest that he entered for our Silver Medal Course, but I think he might qualify for the Gold."

"Let's see yer dance," demanded the rather sinister individual to whom I had been introduced. I did not like him, I did not like the set-up, and I was even beginning not to like my partner, so I decided that quite deliberately I would dance even worse than I usually do, and during the "demonstration" I tripped over my partner's feet on at least three occasions.

"This is incredible," the manager judged at the end of my performance. "I agree with Lisa" – I think this was the girl's name – "that you're Gold Medal material. What that means is that Lisa will be your teacher and companion at all times. Do you agree to that Lisa?" he asked considerately, and not altogether to my surprise she nodded vigorously. "In a year from now you'll be doing exhibition dancing in all the main capitals of Europe – Berlin, Rome, Vienna. Have you visited them?"

"I've been to Vienna," I replied nostalgically.

"Good, well it's all agreed." He snapped his fingers and another girl appeared with a lengthy document on which my name and address had already been typed. I was ushered over to a table and chair, and I noticed with apprehension the sudden appearance of two rather heavy, rough-looking gentlemen who stood behind me.

"Just sign there," said the manager, "and all your troubles will be over."

"I'd just like to read it through," I remarked, boringly. "I always like to read things through before I sign them."

Lisa put her arm around me. "I'm so looking forward to being with you in Berlin, and Rome – and Vienna, " she sighed.

Despite this intervention I was able to notice that the Arthur Murray School of Dancing obviously thought more highly of my prospects (financial or terpsichorean?) than of those of the Indian, for the figure that I was being asked to sign away was over £500, (I think £520).

I read the document through carefully, in an atmosphere of growing tension. Then I said: "I want time to think about this. I'll let you know."

The manager's attitude changed. "You'll sign now," he ordered, and the two "heavies" moved closer to me.

"No, I don't think so," I replied. "As a matter of fact I don't think I like dancing, after all. I'm going."

"No you're not" said the manager, "You've swindled us out of a lesson. If you don't sign now, I'll call the police."

"Do that," I challenged. "There's no one I'd like to see more than the police just now."

At a signal from the manager the two "heavies" grabbed hold of me and propelled me to the top of the stairs. They did not actually push me down, and I did not sue for assault. As I had told the gentleman who had come in response to my letter, you really need witnesses to prosecute such a case.

This invitation at this time had been a remarkable coincidence. John Pym had signed the letters that I had written on the Indian's behalf, and only my initials had appeared at the top, so clearly my "free trial lesson" arose from a random selection in the telephone book. But it enabled me to return to the Indian's case with renewed vigour and enthusiasm. It was unfortunate that he had just passed his twenty-first birthday. Had he still been a minor he could not have been proceeded against, as dancing lessons could hardly be regarded as necessaries. Now the age of majority has been reduced to eighteen, recognising the earlier advent of "maturity". I confess that I find it a little odd that at about the same time Parliament (or the Home Office?) should have raised the age of criminal responsibility from eight to ten. It would seem that children are more retarded now in the first decade of their lives, but then advance to maturity by leaps and bounds.

The correspondence with Arthur Murray's solicitors continued with increasing acrimony. Towards the end of it they wrote: "We note with interest that at the time of signing the contract your client was a student of law, so that he clearly understood the implications of what he was doing." I enjoyed dealing with that one: "At the time of signing the so-called contract our client was a student of Roman Law, a subject in which allegedly non-cancellable contracts for dancing lessons does not form a very significant part."

The other side began to cave in after that. "Our clients have instructed us," they wrote hypocritically, "that in the interest of good customer relations they are prepared to waive their claim, provided that your client pays them the sum of £5 within seven days to cover our costs." I strongly advised the Indian against this but he insisted on settling the matter and having no more worry about it. He was now studying for his next Part I Bar paper – Contract and Tort! It was a pity; I should have loved to have gone as a witness and described my experience at the Arthur Murray School of Dancing. But let me be fair: Lisa did teach me to do the cha-cha in a manner that I've never forgotten. It's probably the only dance, apart from Scottish Dances, (which I teach and love) that I do well.

Nevertheless, I was glad to observe the closure of Arthur Murray's Kensington premises, sorry to see that they had opened up in Oxford, and not surprised last year to observe their offices all over the United States. Thank Heaven (and the Home Office!) for the Consumer Protection Act.

With Toynbee clients one reached those parts that other lawyers never reached. How otherwise would I have found myself in the dilapidated flat where lived a prostitute and her young baby in conditions of abject squalor, with leaking pipes, peeling wallpaper and a cracked lavatory pan? It was hard to believe that her landlord was, as he claimed, a Rabbi; indeed Judge Engelbach in the Shoreditch County Court found it hard to believe anything that this man said, despite his clerical garb.

Another of my Toynbee clients was accused of controlling a prostitute and living on her immoral earnings. James Dow, a non-lawyer and a very gentle person, had replaced the patient John Pym as organiser by now, and Mr Pace must have satisfied James that he was not living on immoral earnings to have got my services at

131

Thames Court for two guineas. Mr Pace said that the police could not possibly have seen up to the girl's flat from the street and the girl confirmed this, so I went with both of them to observe for myself, and I agreed with them. At the hearing I therefore asked the magistrate, Leo Gradwell, to come on a view. Although known as "Papa Gradwell" among the East Enders, Mr Gradwell was neither very kindly nor very paternalistic. He was also highly unpredictable, much seeming to depend upon the extent to which an old war wound in his leg was playing up on the day of the hearing. Nevertheless he did manage to clamber up the narrow stairs to the little top flat from which the girl was allegedly operating. As he ascended the last flight he gasped: "I think I should have lost all my enthusiasm by the time I got up here."

The police case was that they had been standing in plain clothes in the street and, each time a man had ascended to the flat the girl had come to the window and signalled with her fingers to Pace who was standing on a corner opposite to indicate how many pounds she was taking from the client, and he was occasionally indicating that she should ask for more. It was manifest that not only could the police not have seen the girl in the flat from where they had been standing but also that Pace on the corner would not have been visible to her. Even so, back in Court, Papa convicted Pace, commenting in his tiresome way out of the side of his mouth to his clerk rather than to the public at large: "All these Maltese live off the girls. I don't see why he should be the exception." And he sentenced Pace, a man of good character, to three months. Pace took the verdict and sentence stoically, but the girl cried.

The other Thames magistrate of those days was Colonel Batt. Despite his fiery manner, which made him much more feared by advocates, the Colonel was loved and admired by the East Enders, as I was to discover twenty years later when I became their magistrate. He was not a cruel man but patience was not his strongest virtue, and he did not have much time for "mental cruelty". "Harsh words break no bones," he used to declare. But he thought husbands ought to pay maintenance to their wives. A Toynbee client of mine stopped paying his wife when he took up spiritualism, saying that his spiritual adviser had told him to give up work and to give his wife nothing. The Colonel had not much time for that sort of thing, and made an order of £5 a week – a high amount in those days. "How am I going to pay that when I've got no income?" asked the man plaintively. "You'd better ask the spirits," growled the Colonel, "because if you don't pay I'll put you in prison, and you can have them in there with you if you like."

The Colonel did not believe in hearing assault summonses. His policy was to compel the parties to be bound over, which sometimes was a shame because the parties had been looking forward so much to a slanging match in Court. One Saturday afternoon there were cross-summonses for assault by most of the residents of one side of an East End street against most of the occupants of the other side. Dick Body, now a Member of Parliament and a farmer, was instructed by University House (another Poor Man's Lawyer) for street side A, while I was instructed by Toynbee for street side B. Honours were equally balanced: there were twelve protagonists on one side and twelve on the other, all with summonses and cross-summonses. In each case the P.M.L. had been induced to charge only one two guinea fee, so that the litigants were getting our services for less than a florin a head. In the event they were not worth much more than that, although at the outset it looked like being a long hearing, as we each had lots of proofs of evidence from "independent" witnesses.

Ignoring the lawyers in the case, the Colonel drew up his own plan of campaign. "All men from the North side of the street, go and stand to the left of the dock, and all men from the South side to the right," he commanded. When they were thus arraigned he selected the weakest looking man from the North side and eyed him ferociously; "Now, you. You'll agree to be bound over for one year in the sum of ten pounds, won't you?" "Er, yes," replied the victim nervously. "Good, very wise," observed the Colonel. "Any of you men on that side disagree with that decision?" In the three seconds that he allowed for answer, no one dared to speak, so he now turned his batteries on to the South side. "Are there any of you men stupid enough to want to take a different course?" he demanded menacingly. "Good. Very sensible. You're all of you bound over in £10 for the next year. Good afternoon, gentlemen."

"Let's go," advised Dick wisely, and we made off quickly in his car with two dozen irate East Enders running after us demanding their fees back.

During the journey we reached the conclusion that the hearing had not been wholly satisfactory and if a similar situation arose we would not again be browbeaten in this way. Our opportunity was to come very soon. We were both back before the Colonel on cross-summonses for assault a Saturday or two later, but this time there was only one party on each side.

"Are you two ladies prepared to be bound over?" began the Colonel.

With some trepidation I intervened. "I'm afraid that won't be possible in this case, sir. From the complainant's point of view a matter of principle is involved."

"A matter of principle!" expostulated the Colonel. "What possible principle can there be in an assault case, except to try my patience beyond endurance?" Then, seeing that I was not going to give way, he turned his fire on Dick: – "Your client's prepared to be reasonable, isn't she? She'll agree to be bound over."

"I'm afraid not, sir," replied Dick. "You see, she's come here with her four witnesses ...."

"Four witnesses!" the Colonel exploded. "You don't think I'm going to listen to four witnesses on a Saturday afternoon."

"It may not be necessary to call them all," said Dick, retreating slightly.

"It had better not be," threatened the Colonel in a voice of thunder.

After these initial exchanges the trial got under way, and it is fair to say that apart from occasional grunts and groans the Colonel did not intervene any more. Instead, he affected to go to sleep. At last it was all over, including Dick's closing speech about the burden of proof, that "golden thread running through the English criminal law", – I think that he had even brought Woolmington v. the D.P.P. with him –and the moment came for the Colonel to give his judgment. It went as follows:

"The case against each of you two vexatious litigants is dismissed, but you'll each of you be bound over in the sum of £10 to keep the peace and be of good behaviour for a year, which is what should have happened an hour and a half ago if your counsel had a grain of sense between them." Then his voice rising from a growl to a snarl he added, eyeing each of them in turn: "And the next time you two nasty little Jewish women have some trivial little quarrel about some unimportant matter, take it to the Beth'din. Don't bring it to me!"

Of course, no magistrate would get away with such outrageous comments now. After the Colonel retired from the metropolitan

Bench he went and sat as Chairman of the Bench in a country town in Devon. I'm sure he livened things up there!

Another difficult magistrate of those days was Geoffrey Raphael at Marylebone. Indeed it was before him that I had my most unpleasant Court experience of all time, which I will describe later, but when I appeared before him for a Toynbee client it was the defendant, not the magistrate, who was aggressive. The allegation was the very serious one of failing to pay National Insurance contributions.

"Are you Thomas Brown?" began the clerk of the Court.

"No, I'm not. I'm Tom Brown, and don't you dare call me anything else."

The clerk appeared nervous. "And what is your occupation. er – Mr Brown?"

"Thievin' and idlin'?" came the surprisingly frank reply.

The Magistrate looked quizzically at the prosecutor. "Are those insurable occupations?" he asked.

After my first case, which I devilled for a member of the Chambers where I was a pupil, my next ten cases came from Cambridge House and I won them all. I began to think that I was invincible. Then Ronald Brown briefed me in the case of Hartmann v. Strickland, and the rot set in. This case provided me with my first encounter with Judge Wilfrid Clothier, Q.C., at the Lambeth County Court. I found him a most unpleasant tribunal before which to appear. He was very sarcastic, and had a habit of baring his yellow teeth as though about to swallow up witnesses whom he did not like, or young advocates. He had a number of marked prejudices: tenants, judgment debtors, foreigners and black people in particular. I never saw a tenant win in a landlord and tenant dispute before him except when the landlord was black. Then the Judge's prejudices seemed to operate quite evenly, and a fair trial would ensue. In dealing with judgment debtors he displayed a degree of cruelty bordering on sadism: and yet I always felt that his bark was worse than his bite: at the end of a bullying harangue he would usually give the reluctant debtor "one last chance" to avoid prison by paying up. On the credit side, although impatient, he appeared to try cases carefully and did not hurry the advocates unduly (although he did harass them.) He was an excellent lawyer, and therefore it was surprising that he invariably wrapped up his decisions in findings of fact to avoid appeal.

Maria Hartmann was an Austrian refugee who was dissatisfied with her lodgers, Mr and Mrs Strickland, and brought proceedings against them – not for possession (she would have won if she had done that) but for damages, under numerous headings of breach of contract. The proceedings began inauspiciously as I read out the pleadings.

"The Plaintiff runs a boarding house at number 5 Cambria Road," I recited.

"Runs a boarding house?" echoed the Judge. "Runs a boarding house?" (In those days I was learning pleading in the rather slapdash military style of Hugh Corner; later I was to acquire some of the precision of the art of Bill Kee in such matters.) "Whatever does that mean?"

Before I could explain he looked at the end of the document and remarked: "I see the name of Eric Crowther here. Tell me, was this drafted by counsel?"

"Yes, Your Honour," I replied assertively. "It was drafted by me."

"O-o-o-oh," exclaimed Judge Clothier, using the whole range of his voice to express his astonishment. "I am surprised."

And the trial went on like that for all of five days. The Judge divided his fury approximately equally between me and the Plaintiff, who was, I must concede, a most tiresome witness who invariably equivocated in giving her answers. The Judge intervened a lot during her evidence:

"Madam, will you just do me the courtesy of giving a straight answer to a straight question, if you are capable of such a feat of concentration," he thundered.

"Now, is the answer to my question "Yes" or is it "No"?"

Mrs Hartmann pondered that assault for a long time, and then she replied slowly:

"I am thinking maybe "Yes", and I am thinking maybe "No"."

Each of those terrible days when I got off the 159 bus opposite the Granada Cinema in Lambeth Mrs Hartmann was waiting for me with some new instructions, resulting in a revised set of pleadings which ultimately ran into several different colours. I am sure that if she had known my home address she would have been at Hendon Central to meet me.

My opponent was a barrister called Gabriel Cohen – older, more experienced, and wiser than I. He was both able and fair, and never objected to receiving these amended pleadings, realizing that they infuriated the Judge and could only reduce the Plaintiff's credibility. Instead he used to accept them from me each day, putting his arm round my shoulder, and saying, sympathetically: "You know, Crowther, my heart bleeds for you."

In recent times I have seen Gabriel Cohen appearing before me defending in minor matters like careless driving and ticket frauds and "paper commitals", and I cannot understand why such an able advocate should not have done better in his career. Perhaps his clerk was a cousin of Roy; or was he being punished by the equivalent of Robert for making a long visit to Israel? More of Roy and Robert in the next chapter.

The final day of Hartmann v Strickland was a Friday, an extremely hot day in April 1952. Judge Clothier observed fiercely that he intended "to finish this wretched case today, come what may." He was no slacker, and it was after six o'clock when I completed my closing address, punctuated by many sardonic interventions from the learned Judge. As, wearily I resumed my seat, feeling (correctly) that all had been lost, a cry came from my lay client, as she re-entered the witness box to impart to the Judge the piece of information that she had been so keen that I should give him and which I had excluded because, even if time (which I doubted) permitted, it seemed quite irrelevant.

"No, don't sit down," she screamed. "There is much more to be said. Mr Strickland is an Army deserter vot vent to Ireland during the var. God save the Queen and Your Honour. Maria Hartmann." At this point she produced from her bosom a Union Jack, which she waved enthusiastically at the Judge, who displayed fury.

"Stand down, Madam. Stand down immediately or I shall hold you in contempt. How dare you, a foreigner, wave our British flag at me? Your action is dismissed, on all counts, with costs. Stand down, I say."

He may have been especially exercised because, a few weeks earlier, another discontented litigant had thrown a dead cat at him. To this he had reacted remarkably mildly, merely warning her: "Madam, don't you ever do that in my Court again."

Mrs Hartmann did rather more than was required of her. She not only stood down but she lay down in the well of the Court. Fearing that she had had a heart attack I moved towards here. "Leave her alone," the Judge ordered fiercely. "She's shamming, as she has been throughout this trial.'' He then proceeded for about twenty minutes to give a reasoned judgment (all wrapped up in fact!) on the seventeen issues appearing on the oft re-amended Particulars of Claim, finding against her on every single matter.

When the Judge had withdrawn I moved over towards the recumbent figure of the Plaintiff. In all the time that I had known her, Maria Hartmann had not remained still and silent for so long, and despite the Judge's admonition, I feared that this might be a case for the Coroner. Gabriel Cohen also approached from the other side, but it was me that he was worried about. "Crowther," he said. "My heart's been bleeding for you so much that I'm suffering from pernicious anaemia. Come on, I'll buy you a pint of beer. We both need it. And then I'll drive you to the Temple."

At this moment Maria Hartmann opened her eyes and rose in her wrath. "Vy are you talking to that fat pig, our enemy?" she demanded, prodding my opponent in his ample stomach.

"Crowther, I'm going," he announced. "I'm not going to be insulted by this woman." And I got neither my beer nor my car ride. Instead I stayed talking to Mrs Hartmann explaining that the Judge had so skilfully cocooned his findings in fact that no appeal was possible. She left the Courtroom, apparently convinced, and I made my weary, vanquished way to the now empty robing room, from which I heard the sound of smashing glass. When I descended the stairs I observed that every pane in the telephone box on the ground floor had been broken. But I never saw Maria Hartmann again.

I was, however, to appear many more times before Judge Clothier –always for Cambridge House clients, always for tenants, and I always lost. The one exception to this catalogue of failure was the last case that I did before him, which also was his last trial. It was an extremely difficult and complex case, and it lasted three days. It was, for me, a very important matter, for it was one of the very few cases that Roy got for me, from a busy firm of solicitors in Peckham called Hepburns, who remained loyal to me for the rest of my days at the Bar. Harry Taylor, one of their managing clerks, a most modest but brilliant man, who died young (probably through smoking too much) leaving a lovely wife and six adolescent sons, remained a close friend of Elke and me until his death. ("I liked you Eric," he said. "when I took you out for some refreshment after we had just done our first case together. We went to a workmen's cafe and you didn't turn your nose up at it. When I offered you coffee

you asked: "Can I have a cup of tea?" I like people who drink tea."
On such things success at the Bar depends.)

The case would turn largely on scientific evidence, and our
scientific expert was a German. Knowing Judge Clothier's
prejudices against all foreigners I suggested to Eric Clay, the bluff
managing clerk who was instructing me in this case, that we should
look for another expert. "No," said Clay firmly. "He's the best
in the country – and we've paid him." I felt sure we should lose
on this ground, especially as Clothier was one of those Judges who
thought that he knew everything about everything. But I had
reckoned without one factor: he was a Judge who, when he was not
shouting, would listen, especially to those who were prepared to
stand up to him – a quality not to be found in all Judges and
magistrates, I fear.

My worst fears were confirmed by our expert's heavy foreign
accent, as strong as that of the late George Mikes on an off-day.
With heavy irony Clothier bared his yellow fangs and remarked:
"Some of us have a little scientific knowledge, Mr Gunter" – and
then went on to ask what he believed to be (and so did I!) a
devastatingly loaded question.

"All that your question proves iz that a little scientific knowledge
iz a dangerous thing," countered Herr Gunter. "I vill now proceed
to show you how wrong you are" – and he did, while Clothier sat as
silent and hypnotised as a rabbit before a boa constrictor. So Herr
Gunter broke my record of failure before one of my least favourite
Judges.

Although I won Judge Clothier's last case – my first win before
him – he wanted to make it a Pyrrhic victory by not awarding the
Plaintiffs (for whom I appeared) their full costs, and when I started
to argue about this he became restive and said that if I was going to
be "difficult" he would put the case over to another day and come
out of retirement to have the issue of costs fully debated. This was
what he did, and the discussion went on for an hour and a half until
about midday when he finally gave way and justice prevailed and we
got our full costs. It so happened that I had another case that day in
the Lambeth County Court, which I accepted because I thought it
would follow on Clothier's last case with a new Judge, as there was
only one Judges' Court at Lambeth. In fact Judge John Barrington
was sitting in the Registrar's Court and waited for me from 10.30.
Most Judges would have been furious, but Judge Barrington, before

whom I was appearing for the first time, was courteous and disarmingly charming: "These things do happen," he said, and I went on, without fuss, to win the case. I was to appear before him many times thereafter, and never lost in his Court.

Judge Barrington was, like his predecessor, a good lawyer, but there the resemblance between the two men ceased. John Barrington was polite, quiet, and utterly just. He seldom interrupted, but there was usually a humorous twinkle in his bright blue eyes as he listened attentively and made careful notes. It was a delight to appear before him, and only once in the many cases that I was still to do in the Lambeth County Court was there any contretemps between us. On that occasion a fairly important witness failed to turn up at Court, but his prospective testimony was contained in a letter that he had written, and my instructing solicitor was very keen that I should try to get this piece of evidence in by a side-wind. At my first attempt the Judge said: "I'm afraid that's hearsay," but then, most improperly, but to placate the solicitor, I put the letter to a witness on the other side and asked him to comment on it. "What you are doing is quite wrong," said the Judge, "and I would have expected counsel of your experience to know better"; and, although we won the case, he referred again to this effort on my part to put inadmissable evidence before him when he came to give judgment. I have never felt so ashamed in Court, because this was a Judge I greatly respected.

On another occasion the plaintiff in a civil action, in which I was for the defendant, was a serving prisoner, brought up to the Court by prison staff. He went to have lunch in the same cheap restaurant to which I always went with Harry Taylor, and came over to us. "What's going to happen in my case?" he asked me. "I'm not sure what the result is going to be," I replied, "but this is the one Judge in the country of whom I can say it with certainty that justice will be done."

The prisoner lost his action and afterwards Harry and I were having our usual cup of tea in the same "caff" and the unsuccessful litigant was again there, with his wife and the two prison officers. "Bad luck," I said "but your side put up a good fight." "Yes, and that Judge was very fair." he commented. "I wish I'd had him on my criminal trial. Then I might have been at home with my wife, and not having to meet her here. I only brought this claim to get a day out, I never expected to get legal aid. But he's nice, that Judge."

He was, and I was very pleased when he accepted my invitation to address my Law Group at the British Council on "A Day in the Life of a County Court Judge." He gave an agreeable address with great modesty, a quality not always to be found in lawyers. But I was even more delighted when he invited my wife and me to dinner in his sweet little house in Barnes. On that occasion, the memory of which I still cherish, John Barrington told us how that day there had appeared before him as a defendant in a landlord and tenant dispute an old newspaper vendor who had his pitch outside the Oval Station. The case was a complicated one, and the Judge had advised the defendant that he needed the services of a lawyer. "In that case," the old man had said, "I'll go and see Mr Crowther, the King of Cambridge House." (I realise as I recount that story that the modesty which I found so admirable in Judge Barrington is not always particularly conspicuous in me....) Sadly, soon after that evening at his home John's dear wife died, but he was to remarry, his second spouse being a charming lady, much devoted to works of charity. John himself did not enjoy the best of health – he frequently had to bear the pain of a duodenal ulcer – and he was to die in harness and far too young; a great loss to the cause of justice.

The high opinion held of me by the old newspaperman was not shared by another Cambridge House client, a Chinese landlord. He wanted to get rid of his tenants, two old ladies, who had become "possessed of the evil spirits." During the interview it became apparent that these devils had entered into the two elderly tenants just after their landlord had served upon them a notice demanding a massive – and illegal – increase in rent.

"What have you yourself done about this?" I enquired knowing by now something of the remedy of self-help that is frequently available in Eastern cultures.

"Nothing," he replied, "except cut off their gas and electricity and water, but the demons are so strong that the women are still there."

After that I refused to advise the Chinaman anymore, and he demanded his three shillings back, but I thought that Cambridge House should retain it. "You will regret this," he warned me, appearing to set his own evil eye upon me. "You will pay for this."

I gave no heed to his threat until the Cambridge House Trust in general and I in particular were served with a writ of Mandamus to compel us to continue to act for the Chinaman, and I went along, in amazed trepidation, for the first time to the Queen's Bench Division of the High Court. I was not, however, called upon to address that formidable tribunal. The presiding Judge was Lord Goddard, the rich man's Colonel Batt. After hearing the Chinaman for about three minutes the Lord Chief Justice roared: "We're not going to listen to any more of this rubbish. Get out, and take your spirits with you. And take my advice. You leave your tenants alone, or you'll finish up in gaol." The Chinaman passed me on his way out, uttering some comments about justice that are not to be found in the sayings of Confucius.

If the people of Lambeth had the surprise of the change from Judge Clothier to Judge Barrington as their Judge, the people around Stepney had a comparable shock when Judge Engelbach was replaced by Judge MacMillan. Engelbach was warm-hearted, robust, fair and generally genial, although I do remember on one occasion his bellowing at a judgment debtor who was taking the oath: "Take your filthy hands off our Holy Book. How dare you come here covered in grime?" I felt rather sorry for the witness, who may have rushed into Court straight from work. But the Toynbee barristers enjoyed appearing before Judge Engelbach, who was courteous, good-humoured and decisive. His successor on his retirement was none of these things: very tiny, Judge MacMillan peered over the Bench like some small but interfering bird, constantly sipping from the cup of tea which the lady Associate had to replenish at half-hourly intervals in between his pecking at advocates. This tardiness enabled him to make the smallest possible number of decisions: a great many of his cases were transferred to his very much speedier Registrar. It was said that Judge MacMillan was so averse to making decisions because he feared being reversed on appeal: if so, this was strange, because he was an excellent lawyer, and County Court Judges could not be appealed on their findings of fact. But in nearly every case at some stage, usually before the defendant went into the witness box, he would say, in his strong Scottish accent: "I shall rise now for half an hour, during which time I shall expect the parties to get together and come to a sensible compromise. I hope that commonsense will prevail in this case." There are few better ways of causing dissatisfaction among both litigants and lawyers!

Judge MacMillan did not like Toynbee cases. He was the only Judge before whom my friends and I appeared who queried the propriety of our being instructed by the solicitor at the legal advice centres. In one case which he did not want to try he told me: "I shall adjourn this case for a month to find out from the Law Society whether it is proper for you to appear in this case. I feel it is my duty to protect the interests of local solicitors from improper encroachment on their preserves. In the meantime I express the hope that commonsense will prevail and that this matter will be settled."

This development worried me enough for me to approach the Law Society myself. The reply that I got was that the Law Society was delighted for barristers to be accepting briefs from solicitors acting for the legal advice centres, as many of the clients were types whom the solicitors did not want in their offices anyway.

Armed with this information I returned to the Shoreditch Court determined that, come what may, the case should go on.

"Before resuming this matter, Your Honour," I enquired, "I wonder if the Law Society has given Your Honour a ruling on the question of the propriety of my continuing to appear."

"You will be pleased to hear," announced the learned Judge, "that I have been successful in obtaining a dispensation enabling you and your colleagues to continue to act in these case."

"I am very much obliged," I said with a heavy irony which I hope did not escape him. "Your Honour is really *too* kind."

I came to the conclusion that MacMillan's aversion to Toynbee cases derived from his unwillingness to make decisions. Without us, many litigants would have been in person, and it was easier to persuade litigants without lawyers to settle their cases. I use the word "persuade" advisedly. The Judge's technique in disposing of cases in this way was very skilful and courteous; never bullying like his military counterpart in the Magistrates' Court a mile down the Mile End Road.

Judge MacMillan, a stickler for tradition, was trying to overturn tradition when he took on the Toynbee Hall Legal Advice Centre. Last year I was unable to attend its centenary, but a quarter of a century earlier I attended the dinner to celebrate its seventy-fifth anniversary. John Clark from my Chambers was there. He reminded me of his introduction to Toynbee, when one Wednesday I said to him: "Come on John. Tonight I'm going to show you what the law is really all about." John stayed on to be Toynbee's longest serving legal adviser — sixteen years, I think. It was a privileged position. Norman Birkett and Frank Milton had both advised for Toynbee, as had an old boy of ninety-two who attended that seventy-fifth celebration dinner, and in those impecunious days many unemployed barristers wanted to be taken on in the hope of getting those occasional two guinea briefs. One such came to me in Chambers one Wednesday but I told him, as was the fact, that the Toynbee Poor Man's Lawyer was full. Although we were working until very late at night (and sometimes into the early hours of Thursday morning) there was physically just no room for more advisors. However, he hung about outside my Chambers and followed me on the 15 bus to Toynbee Hall, where, without further words to me, he presented himself to John Pym, the organiser. It so happened that Christopher McCoustra had just telephoned to say that he was ill and could not come that night, so this lawyer was allowed in — and stayed for several years! He is now a highly successful tax barrister. Determined demands yield dividends!

I was sad to miss the Toynbee centenary, but a group of the longest-serving advisors meets for a reunion dinner every year, this usually being organised by John Clark or James Dow. Towards the end of the evening, when everyone is pretty merry, there is invariably a shout by someone, taken up as a chant by the others, of: "Eric. The mackintosh. Tell the story of the man in the Mackintosh," the account of my grimmest encounter with Judge MacMillan at his most awkward; and all the other customers at the restaurant have to listen to a tale that has been heard at least thirty times by all the Toynbee members present. But my readers will not have heard it before, so I will reserve it for the forthcoming chapter on "Different Kinds of Judges, " for Judge MacMillan was a difficult Judge.

Even more troublesome than the Cambridge House case of Hartmann v. Strickland was the Toynbee saga of Laufer v. Ciantar, where the main problem was that neither party spoke any English. Mr Laufer, like Mrs Hartmann, was Austrian, and I took Epi along to interpret for him, but unfortunately she did not speak the obsolescent Yiddish dialect into which he lapsed that day, so, finding her presence otiose, Epi left. The Maltese defendant also spoke no English and had no interpreter. (A fuller account of that devastating day appears on pages 53 and 54 of my earlier book "Advocacy for the Advocate.") Fortunately the case came before Judge Engelbach and not Judge MacMillan, and somehow we struggled through it and won, but at the end of it all I was very weary. It was therefore with relief that I sank down late that afternoon into the only vacant seat on the 76 bus which would take me back to Chambers, but my peace was short-lived, for the little voice of the passenger next to me murmured: "You know, those people in the flat upstairs are still making atom bombs."

At moments like that, if anyone had asked me: "Are you the poor lawyer, sir?" I would have answered, "Yes."

Chapter 10

A Tale of Two Clerks:

Reminiscences of the Bore War

They are the best of men; they are the worst of men. It is the age of wisdom; it is the age of foolishness. It is the epoch of belief; it is the epoch of incredulity. It is the season of light; it is the season of darkness. It is the spring of hope; it is the winter of despair. These are the feelings that beset the young barrister at the beginning of his career, especially in his relations with his clerk.

In about 1971 I was on a plane heading for a legal conference in Yugoslavia. Sitting next to me was a large black man. In every respect other than his colour he was very English, so we did not speak at all. Suddenly an announcement came through the loudspeaker system, uttered with that degree of controlled calm which signifies imminent danger: "This is your Captain speaking. There is nothing to worry about. We are about to make an unscheduled landing. When we do so will all passengers please leave the plane as quickly and as quietly as possible? I repeat, there is nothing to worry about. Please keep your seatbelts securely fastened until landing." After a few minutes of considerable anxiety we landed bumpily in a German field to see fuel leaking from the fuselage all over the cabbages, and it was many hours before another plane took us on our way from Frankfurt to Belgrade. This incident had the advantage of breaking the ice between me and my (up to then) taciturn neighbour, and as a result I became great friends with Mr Justice Evan Rees of Trinidad, who soon thereafter was to try the notorious Malcolm X and his only slightly less villainous companions so impeccably that the Judge received an accolade for his handling of the case from the Privy Council (Malcolm X and the group were executed within a few hours of the Judges in the Privy

Council tendering their advice to Her Majesty). Now Evan Rees is the first Ombudsman of Trinidad and Tobago.

The "Judges" on the conference were to meet President Tito on his island. The "lawyers" were not. Into which category did I, as a metropolitan stipendiary magistrate, fall? I believed the latter. Evan took the contrary view, so determinedly and forcefully that I received a coveted invitation to meet the man whom, in my small way, a quarter of a century earlier, I had been trying to keep out of Trieste. Evan, with typical generosity, invited me to be his guest in Trinidad; I, with typical opportunism, turned up the following year and he and his English born wife gave me a wonderful time. The visit afforded me the chance to see many old friends from my student days, including of course Masa and his natural wife, and their lots of natural children, and Masa's and my good friend, Bholan, another barrister. Bholan took me to his Chambers, a rather bare, functional office with a sparse collection of law books. While I was there the telephone rang; a client wanting his services. Of course I heard only one side of the conversation, but it went something like this: "Yes, I'm very experienced in that type of work. My fee would be 75 dollars .... No, I couldn't possibly do it for 50 dollars .... Well, everyone will tell you I'm worth more than that .... The absolute minimum for which I'll go into Court in this sort of case is 65 ...." I think in the end they settled for 60 dollars.

That day I appreciated, if I had never done so before, the value of the English clerk system. I was never any good at selling either insurance or brushes, and I could never have sold myself. The clerk is a kind of confidential secretary, fee negotiator and publicity agent all combined. His only qualification — I say "his" because even now when there are so many women barristers there are very few female clerks — appears to be to have been born in the Temple or at least to have worked there since leaving school at the age of 16. The Temple is, of course, the smallest village in the country and he is required to know all the latest gossip. Junior clerks earn a pittance, paid to them by the senior clerk, who generally has great wealth —often more than the Head of Chambers —and wields enormous power. One of my barrister friends, returning from his honeymoon, broke down on the N1 in France in his small pre-war car. He was delighted when a large modern Daimler with English number plates stopped just in front of him, surprised when his clerk stopped out and asked: "Can I help you, sir?" My first clerk Roy, when we dared to complain to him, as occasionally happened, would remind us: "Don't forget, I can make you or break you, sir." The trouble was that it was true — at any rate so far as the second verb was concerned: one of the few statements that he made to us that was true. I was never quite sure whether the appellation "sir" was uttered respectfully or ironically. When once there was a Chambers meeting, held specifically to discuss the deficiencies in the clerking we were getting, the Head of Chambers (who was to become the Solicitor-General) went to leave the room for some temporary purpose and to his surprise found Roy with his ear beside the keyhole. When he dismissed Roy on the spot the latter warned him: "I shall go straight to the Barristers' Clerks' Association, and nobody in these Chambers will ever have a clerk again." Roy was reinstated next morning by the man who would soon be the third most powerful lawyer in Parliament.

In my seventeen years at the Bar I had only two clerks, if I exclude Douglas, the excellent clerk to my pupil master, Hugh Corner. As my year's pupillage drew to its close I wondered if I could stay on in those Chambers, but I could never get a straight answer from either Hugh or Douglas. Hugh would always say: "You'll have to discuss the matter with Douglas, my boy — it affects him more than it affects me"; whereas Douglas always replied: "I'd like to have you, sir, but it's a matter entirely for Mr Corner." Somehow I could never get the two of them together to discuss my future, and when, after eleven months of my pupillage had passed, one of my fellow-pupils decided to give up the Bar and told me that he had negotiated a place in Chambers opposite, which tenancy would now be available, I hastened across to the basement which was to become my prison for the next ten years.

Roy was alone in the Chambers when I dropped in at about half-past five to enquire if the Chambers would like me as a tenant. "Sit you down sir," he said soothingly, "and tell me what you did during the war." "I was in the Navy," I said proudly. He looked disappointed. "I was in the RAF myself, Bomber Command, Wing-Commander, raids all over Germany, got the D.S.O., mentioned in despatches, but one doesn't want to talk about these things, does one, sir?" "No," I agreed, having acquired no decorations and never having been mentioned in despatches – not favourably anyway. At half-past nine I was still there, listening to Roy's wartime exploits. It was getting dark and I indicated that I thought I should be going, but what about the matter on which I had called, my joining the Chambers? "Oh, that's all right, sir," said Roy, "when would you like to come?" "Shouldn't I meet the head of Chambers or something?" I enquired. "Oh no, sir, he leaves everything to me. What I say goes. I'll tell him you're joining us. When will you be coming?" I thought of my projected holiday with Epi in Vienna. "Would October 1st be all right?" "Certainly sir, you come in whenever you like." I had passed the first endurance test of listening to Roy's bombing raids on Germany: there were to be many more such occasions.

I met the Head of Chambers only once, and he died soon thereafter. He was a grand old boy of 92 – practice at the Bar often leads to longevity – who had had a very good divorce practice but now did only the occasional undefended case, for which he drove up to the Temple in his 1924 Bean car, a magnificent creature. His death led to a hiatus in Chambers. Roy was very Right-Wing in his views, yet he negotiated with John Platts Mills to take over the Chambers, the latter deciding against it at the last moment, and eventually, after a gap of nearly two years another extremely Left-Wing politician, a close friend of Harold Wilson, came to the rescue.

Roy had never been demobilised. Every night – and every day – he was over Berlin shouting: "Bombs Away". "And then there was that night we got hit by flac but old Tubby Johnson got stuck between the seats and couldn't get into his parachute so eventually we landed on one engine at Hendon. Chug-chug-chug." How often did I hear that story, and other similar adventures! I said to him one day: "You know, Roy, I think I know your war history better than my own." But he did not take the hint. Instead he replied: "Well, sir, I suppose it was more exciting." A minimum of two hours every afternoon was spent in listening to these stories, and being fair-minded people, the members of Chambers tried to take it in turn to provide the audience, offering relief to the one who had sat through it the previous day. Occasionally – not very often – the telephone would ring; a solicitor wanting one of us to do some work, a possible line of escape. More often than not Roy would tell the caller: " Could you ring back later, sir? We're discussing something rather important," – and then, turning back to us: "And then Old Nobby Clark stepped out of the cockpit and said "Did you hear about that rookie who ....?" " And so it went on.

Roy was an unusual clerk. He was not a greedy man. Indeed he seemed to have no interest in money. He had (presumably) an R.A.F. pension to live on and, at the height of the wartime bombing when nobody else would risk investment he had purchased six large detached houses in South-West London for £100 each. His gamble paid off. They suffered no damage during the air raids, apart from a few roof tiles being blown off, and now they were let in flatlets, at a substantial profit. Well-dressed, well-spoken, debonair in the Gary Cooper style and presentable, clerking was a hobby for him. He resented those who tried to convert it into a form of work. I was far too active, restless and energetic. Many were the times that he would address me thus as I entered his room to enquire about the prospects of work next day: – "Sit you down, sir, and have a chat. You're buzzing around like the proverbial blue-arsed fly." (My subsequent studies of the Book of Proverbs have failed to reveal any reference to this quaintly-coloured creature.) "Do you think, Roy, that I'll ever make it? I've been here three years now and I've only had one brief through Chambers."

" 'Course you will, sir. I've seen slow starters before. They turn out to be high flyers in the end. Remember the story of the tortoise and the hare." But I got tired of living on lettuce. In fact I lunched every day, for two shillings and twopence, in Mick's Cafe in Fleet Street. One day Roy saw me coming out of there. He was deeply shocked. "How can you expect to get on at the Bar, sir if you eat in places like that? And look at you, sir. Look at that suit. I bet it's the one the Navy gave you when you were demobbed." (He was right.) "I'm trying to get you work, but how can you expect respectable solicitors to brief you when you dress like that and eat in Mick's Caff?" "I wish the solicitors who are so interested in my welfare would provide me with the wherewithal to dress and to eat properly," I remarked somewhat bitterly, but it made no difference. In my first five years at the Bar I got only three briefs through Chambers, although I did manage to acquire some work of my own through legal advice centres and occasionally being briefed by solicitors who had been my opponents in County and Magistrates' Courts. My sister had a solicitor friend who briefed me once in an affiliation case, which I lost: he died soon thereafter; and a schoolfriend who had become a solicitor sent me all his litigious cases, but, as he was primarily a conveyancer, these amounted to about one case a year. In the result it was more than six years before

I covered my expenses (rent of Chambers and clerk's fees) from what I earned as a barrister. During one of my fits of depression my friend Michael Scott, who was now working as a legal advisor for the Road Haulage Association, had come to me with a possible solution to my problem. Another nationalised industry, British Rail, was advertising for legal assistants, and I could apply there. If successful, I would have a salary of £900 a year and free travel and pension rights and could even buy a car. The work consisted entirely of advocacy in Magistrates' Courts, and I have always found them the most interesting. So I applied, and in due course was sent a letter inviting me to an interview, at 3.00 p.m. one Tuesday afternoon in office A on Platform Number 1 at Paddington Station.

I arrived early and had a cup of tea in a restaurant, contemplating with very mixed feelings my possible new life. At about ten to three I sauntered across to the station and asked a porter: "Could you please direct me to office A on Platform Number 1?"

"There ain't no office A here, mate," he answered firmly. "At any rate there's not been one in the ten years I've worked here."

"Of course there is," I rejoined. "Just look at this letter."

"Yes," he replied with satisfaction. "That says Office A on Platform 1 at Paddington. This is St Pancras."

I rushed for a taxi which got involved in heavy traffic jams, and as the clock struck 3.30 I arrived at Paddington. I dashed up to the nearest porter, but there was another man in front of me. "Excuse me," he was asking politely, "but could you tell me where is Office A on Platform 1? I have an appointment there at 3.30 and I'm afraid I'm a little late." I listened carefully to the directions, ran on ahead, and knocked on the door of the elusive office. "Come in," said a stern voice, and I faced a table of five angry-looking men. "I'm sorry I'm late," I said. I gave no explanation. Somehow mixing up Paddington and St Pancras did not seem a very auspicious beginning to a career with British Rail.

"Well, sit down now that you are here," said the chairman of the committee in a not very encouraging manner. "We want to ask you some questions." It was a long interview, and as time went on I had the feeling that it was going well. At last the chairman, smiling now, said: "Now we've asked you a lot. Is there anything else you would like to say to us?" Suddenly I felt that I was going to get the job, and I realised all that I would be losing, especially the independence and the companionship of the Bar. "Yes," I replied boldly. "I don't

151

think the money is good enough. I should want £1350." The solemn frowns returned, and the chairman said: "You'd better retire for a few minutes." I sat down in the corridor next to the man I had overtaken half an hour earlier, a rather older candidate than I. "They're taking a long time over you," he complained nervously. "I've been waiting here since half past three." At that moment I was called back in and the chairman said: "We've decided to offer you the job – at £1350 a year. Can you start on Monday?"

"Yes," I murmured wistfully. This experience confirmed a view I had long held. Never appear eager to have something in England. The British are very suspicious about people who seem to want things very much. I had drifted in half an hour late, and indicated that I would take the position only if offered an immediately fifty per cent salary increase – so I got the job.

It was a sunny afternoon as I returned to Chambers and never had the Temple Gardens looked so beautiful, but my heart was heavy. I had bought security, but at what a price?

As I entered Bill's and my room I could not believe my eyes. There, in the centre of my table, was lying a fat brief, privately paid (at four guineas) for a case in the Maidstone Assizes the following Monday, the brief coming from a very reputable solicitor in Sevenoaks whom I had been hoping to cultivate for years. Unlike the two guinea briefs that I sometimes got from the "Poor Man's Lawyers" it had red tape around it, and looked very opulent. It was the first "private" brief that I had had for nearly a year and I recognised it as a sign from Heaven. I must not now join British Rail.

So that night I wrote a letter to BR's senior solicitor saying that I had thought about it and was not coming after all. I fully expected to be sued for breach of contract (in which I clearly was) but instead I got a charming letter back saying that if I felt I would not be happy in BR's office I had made the right decision.

The case which caused me to abandon my new-found career did not turn out to be an unqualified success. The defendant, Mr Bailey, was charged with incest with his two young daughters, over many years. The main plank of my mitigation was a letter that Mrs Bailey had written to her husband in prison saying that she had forgiven him and would be waiting for him when he would be free again. I had a proof of evidence from the wife whom I fully expected to be at Court to give evidence on her husband's behalf. But she was not there when the case was called on, and I went ahead without her.

(One just did not ask for adjournments in those days: they are sought – and granted – far too readily now.) I quoted from Mrs Bailey's proof and handed up the letter. The very solemn Judge, Mr Justice Austin Jones, was not impressed, and sentenced the defendant, a man of otherwise good character with an excellent war record, to six years – a bad result and the longest sentence that anybody I represented ever received. But the solicitor, Norman Farmar, remained loyal: all his junior work came to me; all cases requiring senior counsel went to Leslie Scarman. (It is an odd fact that for solicitors to remain loyal, barristers should get bad results: win the case that everyone is expecting you to lose and you are unlikely ever to see your instructing solicitor again.)

I felt rather despondent as Norman and I walked down the steps of the Maidstone Assizes, when a bustling little woman came rushing up:

"Excuse me, has the case of Bailey been heard yet? I'm his wife."

"Well," I said, "you ought to have been here half an hour ago. You might have helped us get a better result."

"What did he get?" she demanded.

"I'm sorry to say that he received a sentence of six years imprisonment."

"The dirty devil," she exclaimed. "He ought to have got life!"

It was many years later (perhaps twenty years later) that an advocate appeared before me at West London prosecuting in six rail fraud cases. The pattern was always the same: "The defendant left the Underground at Barons Court saying that he had travelled from Earls Court whereas in fact he had boarded the train at Piccadilly. The fare avoided is 30 pence and I ask for compensation in that sum and costs in Your Worship's discretion." Dreary cases to try, drearier to prosecute. But for me there was interest in the fact that I recognised in the prosecutor the man I had overtaken twenty years earlier at Paddington, and had sat beside momentarily outside Office A on Platform 1. As he completed his sixth case he received a note from the magistrate, containing an invitation to lunch, which he accepted with surprise and gratitude. "What's your job like?" I enquired solicitously, as I helped him to a second glass of wine. "Well, it gives me a living," he said unenthusiastically, "and there's security and a pension at the end of it, which is more than you can say of the Bar. I must say I was glad when I got it. It was strange, you know. They only gave me a short interview – about five minutes, while the chap in front of me was in there for over an hour. Then they said they'd let me know, and I was sure I hadn't got it, but then about a week later this letter came offering me the job." "Have another glass of wine," I said, but he declined, graciously: "I must go. I've got six more of these to do this afternoon at Ealing." ("The defendant left the Underground at Ealing Broadway saying that he had boarded the train at Hammersmith. The fare avoided ....") "But you have been kind," he added. "Do you know, you're the first magistrate who's ever invited me to lunch?" I did not tell him that I was salving my conscience for that day I had by-passed him at Paddington. I have not seen him lately, and I think that he may be regulating the great railway network in the skies. ("The defendant boarded the comet at Saturn, my Lord, saying that he had travelled along the Milky Way, whereas in fact he had just come from Venus ....")

The tragedy about my first small set of Chambers was that its members were, on the whole, the writer excepted, so able. The Head of Chambers, Sir Arthur Irvine, Q.C., became Solicitor-General, and was an expert in planning work. Sir Frank Layfield, who conducted the Sizewell Enquiry, was there as his pupil and stayed on, for a time. Sitting opposite to the very Left-wing Head of Chambers was Sir Antony Buck, Conservative MP for Colchester, who was to become Minister for the Navy in Edward Heath's Government – an excellent advocate. Then there was John Clark, a brilliant lawyer, though not a very good advocate, who became Secretary to the National Association for Parish Councils and who, like Tony Buck, is often to be heard on the "To-day" programme, which I like so much. Two advocates did specialist work. This was because, in their impecunious days, they had edited or written books to survive: Victor Wellings, Q.C. editing Woodfall on "Landlord and Tenant" and Bill Kee being co-author of a case-book on Divorce. Victor is now a senior member of the Lands Tribunal and Bill is a Crown Court Judge in Kent, where he has always lived. So narrow was Roy's perspective that he believed that because these two exceptionally able men edited or wrote books on their respective subjects they were incapable of dealing with any other matters, and so Victor became the Landlord and Tenant expert in Chambers while Bill was consigned and confined to the Divorce Courts. (I can still see him ploughing his way through piles of undefended divorce petitions far into the evening.) This was a pity,

because Bill was quite the best common lawyer I have ever known –
even better, I think, than John Clark – and a man of sound
judgment, good common-sense and complete integrity. Dear Bill! I
learned so much from you in the ten years that we shared a room,
and to me you will always be the complete gentleman. I have never
seen you in action as a Judge, but how fortunate must be those who
come before you, seeking justice.

I joined the Chambers in 1952 and my fortunes changed in every
respect about the time that I started going out with my wife. In
addition to the specialists that I have mentioned (all of whom – like
so many others – except the faithful Bill left the Chambers in
despair before Roy finally departed to become a clerk at London
Sessions – for a very short time) there was always one knockabout
counsel available to do the common assaults, the minor motoring
cases, and exciting things like that. Roy was a man who always put
all his (rather small) eggs into one basket, and for my first five years
Giles Best, now a Crown Court Judge in the West Country –
another able advocate – was the recipient of this meagre bounty.
One evening when I was working late preparing a lecture, Roy came
into my room. "I think your're in luck, sir," he said rather dolefully.
I wondered which particular night over Germany I was to be regaled
with, but this time it was different. "Mr Best is betraying me after all
I've done for him. He's left us tonight, and good riddance. But this
could be the turning-point for you, sir." In fact he was right. I
inherited a lot of poorly paid work – poor old John Clark, who was
next in line of succession! – but gained a lot of experience in the
lower Courts. Shortly after my marriage I had two five guinea briefs
in one day, one in North London, the other in Bromley. I managed
both of them, and my wife and I celebrated with dinner in a
restaurant. (The trouble with the Bar is that, if you enjoy life, you
are liable to celebrate both when you get a good brief and months
(or years) later when you get paid for it, with the result that you save
nothing!) But Giles' unexpected departure in 1957 or 1958 indeed
marked the turn of the tide, and happened, happily, to coincide with
my plans for matrimony.

On this latter matter the path of true love did not run completely
smooth. Elke came from a small mediaeval town in mid-Germany. If
the Russians had been allowed to advance another six kilometres we
should never have met. Everyone there expected her to marry
Wolfgang, rich son of the owner of the local rubber factory.

Wolfgang expected this too, and treated Elke rather casually. But when she became engaged to me his interest in her somewhat perversely revived, and Christmas 1958 in Hann-Münden was a traumatic experience. Wolfgang invited us both to a Christmas party in the big house there, during which he took me on one side and tried to persuade me to give up my fiancée, his ex-girlfriend. (I was reminded of an occasion in Trieste when I attended a ball with Evalina. That night two of our frigates were sunk by mines laid by our Yugoslav allies and I was required to leave the dance to issue loan clothing and bedding to the survivors. I noticed with alarm a very romantic Lieutenant-Commander with a dreadful reputation as a ladies' man eyeing my partner in a predatory manner as I departed. Returning some hours later, my duties completed, I learned to my concern that the two had left the building together. Feeling very angry, I entered his office next morning and said: "Look here, sir, I want a man-to-man talk with you." He looked up mildly and his reply, which disarmed me completely was: "Certainly. Bring the two men in.") With Wolfgang and me the situation was somewhat reversed, but I must have disarmed him as he promised to have nothing further to do with Elke.

He did not keep his promise, however. Three months later at half past seven on the Monday morning of the week in which we were to get married Elke rang me in great alarm: "Eric, Wolfgang has just appeared at my room. He is staying in the hotel opposite. He says that he is not going to let me marry you and he is going to take me back to Germany with him. What am I to do?"

I was in Court that day – I doubt if I did the case very well – but in Chambers that afternoon I confided the whole matter to Bill. I think it was the first time that I had discussed a personal problem with him, though he had so often given me good advice on legal matters. He listened gravely and intently, and after some minutes he pronounced judgment: "Eric," he said. "He's not a gentleman."

So, by the somewhat ungentlemanly tactic of causing my fiancée to disappear, I succeeded in marrying her four days later, and the following day we set off in my wonderful 1948 Austin 6 on a honeymoon which was to take in France, Lausanne, Verona, Venice, my beloved Trieste, Velden, Vienna, Hann-Münden, Bruges, Ghent – and Canterbury. Shortly before we departed it arrived: a brief in the Court of Appeal in a most complicated copyright case from one of London's leading firms of solicitors,

Theodore Goddard. I was prepared to postpone my wedding, so important was this case to me, although with Wolfgang lurking in London I was not very enthusiastic about such deferment. But Roy was reassuring: "Don't you worry, sir. The Clerk in the Court of Appeal is a personal friend of mine. In the same squadron with me he was. I'll slip over and see him and on my say-so he'll stand the case out until you come back. You go off and enjoy yourself." I hesitated to remind Roy of a previous occasion when he had sent me to the wrong Court, as a result of which I had had to go before the formidable Lord Chief Justice Goddard in sackcloth and ashes: Roy was very convincing that there was nothing to worry about, and so Elke and I went off for three blissfully happy weeks on the Continent, with a car that covered over 1,000 miles with no breakdown. (How sad we were when it disappeared without trace not long after our return.)

About 10'clock on the Monday morning following the end of our honeymoon I descended from the bus in Fleet Street to go to my Chambers in the Temple. Several friends greeted me, making odd remarks like: "Sorry for you, old man. It really wasn't your fault"; "I think they were a bit hard on you;" and so on. "Come on;" I said, "What's this all about?" Eventually someone took me into Inner Temple Library where I read the only Law Report of the *Times* the previous Friday. It was headed:
"WARNING TO BRIDEGROOM"
and began:-

"The Court of Appeal, when this appeal came on for hearing, acceded, with reluctance, to an application by Counsel (Mr John Clark) to stand out of the list an appeal set down for hearing in today's cause list on the ground that Counsel, who had been briefed for the appellant (Mr Eric Crowther) had married at Easter, was now on his honeymoon, and would not be back in England until the following day.

"LORD EVERSHED, the Master of the Rolls, said that it was most annoying, for the Court had a heavy list of cases . . . . If people found that they could not do a case they should not wait until the day it came on to ask for it to be stood out. The bridegroom should be warned that it must not happen again.

"The Court rose (at 10.45)."

I sat contemplating how to handle the situation. Roy was never wrong, that I had learned, so there was no point in trying to indicate the error of his ways. Furious as I was that he had done nothing, I decided to wait for him to speak first. In fairness to him, he did seem a bit subdued. After asking a few polite questions about the honeymoon, Roy came to the point: "I'm afraid there was a bit of a mix-up over the road about your Court of Appeal case. I had to send Mr. Clark over to get it stood out." It was interesting to see him awaiting my reaction. I decided to use one of Roy's pet phrases when things went wrong. "Well, never mind, Roy. I expect it was just one of those things." Roy brightened instantly. "Yes sir. Exactly what I was going to say. Just one of those things. Sit you down, sir. You must have been buzzing about these last three weeks like a . . . ."

The case was re-listed a few weeks later, and I must say that Lord Evershed was incredibly nasty – and I lost. The crushing blow came however when the representative of Theodore Goddard said to me as we left the Court: "And don't imagine you'll ever get another brief from our firm after the mess you've got us into."

Some years later, when I had moved Chambers, and was doing a return of Richard Du Cann, I refrained from reminding the same solicitor of our earlier encounter . . . . .

But it was not the honeymoon case that caused me to decide to leave those Chambers, but a combination of three other factors that occurred in swift succession. I mentioned earlier the solicitor schoolfriend who sent me about one brief a year. His supply dried up, and I chanced to meet him at a School dinner. "Sorry I can't send you my work any more" he said, "but your clerk says you don't want it."

Next morning I challenged Roy about this. "No sir, you don't want work from people like him. He's a snob."

"Whatever do you mean?"

"Well, he doesn't treat me with proper respect. You don't want work from people like that. It'll give you a bad name."

A little later Roy confided in me: "I never let any of my men earn more than £3000 a year. I always find that when members of the Bar earn more than £3000 a year they get upp-ish."

I was getting near the "upp-ish" limit and felt that now that I had a wife I ought to go, dedicated as I was to every other member of Chambers, especially Bill. (There had also been a bit of a contretemps when Roy said that he wanted to be Godfather to our first child, and I invited Tony Buck instead. Roy thought then that I was shewing signs of "uppishness" (if not downright snobbery.)

But where to go, that was the question. Oddly enough Roy himself provided the answer. I was briefed to defend at the Old Bailey a rich man accused of a rather ingenious fraud. Roy agreed an overall fee for the trial, which lasted six weeks, of £25 (less than £1 a day). The client could readily have paid more, but I was getting near the "uppish limit" of earnings. My opponent was that extraordinarily able advocate, Richard Du Cann. It was an awful trial, with Dick Du Cann quarrelling with me every day, a not very competent instructing solicitor, a lay client who was constantly asking me to do dishonest and improper things and not understanding why, if I had his best interests at heart, I was refusing, and Judge Maude making his usual fatuous jokes throughout. At last, just before Christmas the rambling summing-up was completed and the jury went out to consider their verdict (which was to involve convicting the defendant of nearly every count in the indictment) and Dick Du Cann came over to me, smiling for the first time during that long trial. "Have you ever thought of doing exclusively criminal work?" he asked. "Quite often", I replied wistfully. "Then why don't you pop round to see Robert this evening?" "Robert?", I queried. "Who is Robert?" Dick mocked: "My, you are green, aren't you? Robert's our clerk in Q.E.B. of course. I've mentioned you to him. He's expecting you this evening."

That night my life was to change, thanks to Dick's wonderful Christmas present. There had been a crisis in Queen Elizabeth Building, and as a result, for the very first time, two people from outside "the factory" (i.e. persons who had not been pupils there) were invited to join the Chambers, Ronnie Bartle and myself. My "interview" with Robert was not so very different, in its way, from that with Roy eleven years earlier, in that each clerk talked about his obsession, the only difference being that Robert's obsession was the disaster which had just befallen his Chambers whilst Roy's had been his life in the R.A.F. Fortunately I said the right thing about the crisis, and so I was in. "Will you start with us on January 1st?" Robert invited. "The better the day, the better the deed" (He was always full of wise saws and modern instances.) At that time New Year's Day was not a public holiday and so, having celebrated New Year's Eve more modestly than usual, I arrived at London Sessions to do four cases there on my first day in the new Chambers. I do not now remember the figures, but I should be surprised if in my first year with Robert I did not earn three times as much as in my last year with Roy – yet I was the same person. It was Roy and Robert who were so different. Roy welcomed my being away from Chambers for long periods every year teaching English as a Foreign Language in that most unusual school on the Suffolk Coast, because I was not worrying Roy about work. When I had been in my new Chambers a few days Robert asked me: "Will you be taking a holiday this year, Mr Crowther?" "Yes, Robert" I replied. "I'm going on a lecture tour of the United States for six weeks."

Robert frowned sternly: "Mr Crowther, everyone in these Chambers takes a week. Mr Burge has a week, Mr Jeremy has a week, Mr Du Cann has a week" – he was dazzling me with the great names in Chambers – "even I have only a week. Which week are you taking?"

Now I like my holidays, and resolved to fight for them, with as much natural cunning as I could muster.

"Robert," I asked rather suavely. "Is this an honourable set of Chambers?"

"Certainly it is," came the fiercely indignant reply. "Have you ever heard anything to the contrary?"

"No, but do not men of honour always keep their promises?"

"Of course they do," Robert was getting cross.

"You see, I have entered into a commitment to lecture in the States this summer. Coming from honourable Chambers ought I not to keep that promise?"

There was a long pause, during which Robert's customarily red face became positively florid. Then he gave judgment. "You'd better go there this year, Mr Crowther. But make sure it never happens again. Cut along now. I've got work to do."

That was not the end of the matter. I had to be punished for my ill-advised journey. During the six months preceding my departure for the New World I had become, under Robert's aegis, extremely busy. My desk was always covered with briefs both civil and criminal. Mistakenly, as I now think, I clung on to my civil practice after moving into criminal Chambers. I managed to clear away all the paper work before departing, but fully expected on my return to see that self-same desk covered with new sets of papers. (It is a fact of life at the Bar that you are always either too quiet and therefore impecunious and worried – or too busy, in which case you have no time for domestic or social life and then you are overburdened and –

worried. I had only one short period at the Bar when the work load seemed about right: that was during my last year with Roy.) But no – on my return the cupboard (or rather the table) was bare. So at half-past five I queued up outside Robert's little office with the junior members of Chambers (I was by now of eleven years' call) and the pupils to see what bounty would be put my way.

Robert left me until last. Then he looked up at me and enquired with apparent innocence: "Mr Crowther. Do you know what a judgment summons is?"

"Yes, Robert," I replied, "in fact the first case I ever did was a judgment summons."

"I wasn't asking you to go into legal history." Robert interrupted tartly. "I just want to be sure you know what it is."

"Well, it occurs when a person has had a judgment given against him and hasn't paid up and is brought before the Court for cross-examination as to his means."

"Good," said Robert with satisfaction. "You're doing one tomorrow – at Uxbridge. There you are. It's marked two guineas. Cut along now" (John Mortimer's amusing books suggest that the ultimate martyrdom is – or was –to be briefed in the Uxbridge Magistrates' Court. This at least was the County Court.)

Robert often used that rather public school monitor expression "Cut along now" when he was in a bad mood. One cold December afternoon Robert made one of his rare visits to my room, which was in Garden Court, an annexe to Queen Elizabeth Building. He was fuming. "Mr Crowther. You really must keep that young whipper-snapper of a pupil of yours in order. We've just received a telephone call for him from some girl-friend in France – right at the busiest period of the afternoon, too. Tell him this is a busy set of Chambers – not a matrimonial agency."

The pupil concerned was out at tea and I felt the need to defend my own. "I don't see how he could prevent her ringing up." I remarked mildly.

"He didn't have to give her the Chambers telephone number, did he?" Robert observed triumphantly, as he stormed back to the little office.

The pupil concerned was very upset. He had had great hopes of being asked to stay on in the Chambers after the end of his pupillage, and he judged, correctly, that his chances were fading. Christmas was approaching and he resolved to give Robert a present, as a peace offering. Whisky was decided upon, and the question was whether it should be a half-bottle or a full bottle. The pupil was somewhat impoverished at that time (though not now) and his finances suggested a half-bottle; yet could his sin be atoned for with less than a full one? Ultimately he decided on the full bottle, and I was commissioned to find out Robert's favourite brand. (One of the most nauseating features of life at the Bar is this custom of giving Christmas presents to the – usually very rich – senior clerk. We all tried to find out what the others were giving so as not to fall behind in the race for favours. One member of Q.E.B. always gave Robert an enormous hamper from Harrods. In fact Robert was so dedicated to the advancement of Chambers per se that what we gave him probably made not the slightest difference on the subsequent distribution of work in the New Year, but I am sure that it does in other Chambers. It is a practice that savours of bribery and corruption and ought to cease, as should also the habit of some work-hungry barristers of taking their more alcohol-thirsty chief clerks out for drinks in the evening – an undignified and lamentable practice.)

Anyway, a couple of days before Christmas my pupil went along shyly to the clerk's room with his peace offering: – "Robert. I've brought you a little present for Christmas," he said gently.

Without looking up, Robert said: "All right. Put it on the pile over there, and then cut along."

Another of my pupils had romantic inclinations on a much grander scale. I took him to a party somewhere in Essex on the basis that I could stay the night in his nearby home as I had cases to do in Ipswich next day. He soon attached himself to a statuesque blonde girl whose name was Joan Goddard and whose father was a solicitor, so it sounded as if there were good legal connections. All evening he danced with her, getting closer and closer as the lights got dimmer and dimmer. Periodically, from 1.00 a.m. onwards I would interrupt to ask when he would be driving me to his home, but he would brush me aside with phrases like: "Eric, can you not recognise true love when you see it? Just give us five minutes more." Eventually, after 3.00 a.m. thinking of my unfortunate clients the next day I put my foot down (on the dance floor) and said that we had to go. "All right, darling," he said tenderly (to Miss Goddard), "I'll see you tomorrow, on the steps of Ipswich Town Hall."

"What was all that about?" I enquired

"Well, I've invited her to lunch during the adjournment. Can you think of anywhere nice I can take her?"

"Not really," I replied, for Ipswich in those days was hardly the gastronomic centre of Europe, "but there is an Italian restaurant called "La Gondola." The only trouble is that it's so dark inside that you can't tell what you're eating."

"La Gondola" he replied ecstatically, "the very place. The name is so romantic."

My pupil had a busy morning. First he had to drive a very weary pupil master to Ipswich, then he drove in the opposite direction to defend himself on a parking summons at Chelmsford. He was clearly guilty of the offence but wanted to have a little practice in advocacy: he had never spoken in the forensic setting until then. I expressed my doubts about the ethical propriety of his defending himself when he knew very well that he was guilty – but it was only a parking summons, and he was convicted. Then he dashed into his wonderful 1927 Bentley and no doubt committed many other traffic offences in his struggle to reach Ipswich Town Hall by 1 o'clock. In fact he arrived twenty minutes late, left the Bentley in a space marked "Reserved for the Judge" and whisked the waiting girl off the steps and into the Gondola. He was not there to help me at all that afternoon but came to the robing room when my day's work was over at about 4.30.

"Eric, do you remember this beautiful young lady?" he enquired. smilingly.

"No," I replied, "that's not the girl you were dancing with last night. That's not Joan Goddard."

"Aren't you?" my pupil asked in amazement.

"No. I'm Linda," she answered demurely.

"But weren't you the girl I was dancing with at the party last night?"

"No, I've never seen you before in my life."

"I think I'd better take you both for a cup of tea and try to solve the mystery," I said; adding, practically: "We won't go to the Gondola. Let's go somewhere where the lighting is good."

Over tea the mystery was unravelled. That morning Linda had received a telephone call from a television producer who was wanting to do a programme on girls who had been educated at public schools. Linda was such a girl and he had asked her to meet him on the steps of Ipswich Town Hall. She had arrived a little late, but not as late as my pupil .... She had been surprised that during their three hour lunch no mention had been made of television, but she had thought this was just the "softening-up" process of the television interviewer. We never discovered what had happened to Joan Goddard and the original television producer: perhaps they are happily married by now!

By the time tea was over it was clear that Linda and my pupil were inextricably attached to each other, so, recognising the inevitable, I took the train back to London.

But this pupil quickly tired of his girls, and Linda was no exception. When my pupil ceased to telephone her, she started to come to London, and could frequently be found in an armchair in my room, quietly sobbing. Robert got to hear about it and said that I must get rid of her. "What would our influential solicitors think, Mr Crowther, if I brought them across for a conference and they found a woman weeping in your chair?" I saw the point of this and told the saddened Linda that she had to go. Thereafter for several weeks she sat waiting and weeping on the edge of Charles Lamb's fountain. Robert did not approve of this either. "It's not good for the image of Chambers, Mr Crowther, to have that woman weeping every afternoon just by your window." This time I stood up to my clerk: "Robert," I said "she's not my woman, and if she's got to weep somewhere I can't think of a better place than into the fountain" Fortunately the supply of tears dried up after a few weeks and my pupil felt able to reappear in Chambers at tea-time.

The main difference between Robert and Roy was that Robert was concerned for the image of Chambers, while Roy was concerned for the image of Roy. Roy's "governors" – the inept term that all clerk use when speaking of their charges – were in my opinion generally more able and more worried about upholding the finest traditions of the Bar than some of the "middle men" in my second set of Chambers whose main preoccupation was unashamedly making money and showing off with it. The difference in the incomes of the two sets of Chambers could be attributed entirely to the difference in outlook of the two clerks. Roy had an able junior who was never allowed to take responsibility (but is now the senior clerk in a very good set) while Robert had three juniors earning small salaries, but dividing the enormous volume of work most efficiently between them. Ronald was the "boy" when I went there ("He can look after your civil practice, Mr Crowther, if you insist on keeping it up. I don't know anything about civil work, and I'm too old to learn") Ronald had the most phenomenal memory of anybody I have ever met. Doubtless it stands him in good stead now that he has replaced Robert as the senior clerk in "Q.E.B."

Except on such occasions as when a newcomer to Chambers had to be taught a lesson about the length of holidays from Chambers, Robert was a generous man. I was very proud one day when he invited me to tea. "Let's go to the Howard, Mr Crowther. I always think the tea's nice there, don't you?" "I don't know Robert," I replied (thinking nostalgically of Mick's Cafe) "I've never been able to afford to go there before." "Oh, Mr Crowther, the things you say. You will have your little joke."

I was angered when, in my first few months in my new Chambers, I met old solicitor friends and clients who said: "Why, Mr Crowther, Roy told us you'd given up the Bar." I contemplated seeking an injunction against Roy to stop these lies, but Robert was against it. "Why do you worry, Mr Crowther? You're going to do so well from now on that you don't need to bother about his petty spite" And when eventually Roy was compelled to leave my former Chambers and found himself out of work, it fell to Robert and his other faithful junior James to get Roy a job as a clerk at London Sessions.

But there is something wrong with the system when good men can be hampered and mediocre advocates advanced by the whims or dedication of their clerks – technically and legally their servants. And yet, as I criticise the system, I cannot think of a better one. I certainly do not like the idea of the barrister arguing, as I heard Bholan doing, that he was "worth seventy-five."

I have told three stories about Robert which might seem to be against him. They are not intended to be, although deservedly, he had the reputation of a martinet, especially among the younger barristers. Now compare this account of a clerk doing his job with Roy's sending me to the wrong Court (which I had to explain to Lord Goddard) or failing to get my first Court of Appeal case stood out of the list while I was on my honeymoon.

Within a few years of joining "Q.E.B." I was in the big work. One day I was briefed to defend a very famous film producer who was charged with causing death by dangerous (now reckless) driving to two elderly women. The evidence against him was thin, and I decided to make a submission of no case to answer to the magistrates, three lady justices. When I rose to do so the Chairman said that she hoped I would not be long as it was now 12.45 p.m. and she had a hair-dressing appointment at 2 o'clock and wanted to have lunch first. I decided to humour her, and suggested that it might be better if I made my submission on another day, to which she readily agreed, and a Friday morning was fixed, about four weeks hence. The lay client was most upset and asked to have a further conference with me in Chambers. I could see no reason for this, but, as he was insistent, I agreed. When he came to see me in Chambers he said: "I can't stand any more of this. I've hardly slept since this accident. Now you've had it put over for a further month. I warn you, if your submission fails you won't see me at the Old Bailey I'll be alongside those two old ladies I killed" I could see from his hollow eyes and grim expression that he meant what he was saying. I had to be there for the submission – and it had to succeed.

In my days at the Bar there was a disgusting old doctor who depended for his livelihood almost entirely on his income as a part-time police surgeon: indeed he even wrote a book about his experiences, mentioning how he would extract confessions from recalcitrant accused persons by holding a large hypodermic syringe near their bared buttocks. It was my misfortune to come across this caricature of a medical practitioner frequently in my work in Court. Robust judges got wise to him. "Has there ever in all your long experience been a case in which the police have arrested a man on a drink-drive charge and you have failed to certify him unfit?" I asked him once.

"Yeah, I think there was, once," he claimed proudly.

"What had he had – a wine gum?" asked Judge Frank Cassels.

Shortly after the film producer's case was adjourned I was defending the chauffeur to a prominent surgeon on a drink-drive charge and, as was so often the case, we had this particular doctor. There had been a serious car accident in which the chauffeur had been injured, and, so anxious was the doctor to find that the driver's misfortunes were due to drink that he failed to diagnose the fact, borne out by considerable truly independent medical evidence, that the unfortunate man had a broken neck, from which he took many weeks to recover.

When the case came on at Middlesex Sessions the omens were not good. Of the "twelve good men and true" picked to decide the case eleven were women! Now I had always taken the view that women jurors were bad for the defendant in driving cases, and especially in cases of drinking and driving, and my practice had been to challenge them off the jury. In those days each defendant was allowed seven challenges, but more than half the jurors in waiting were ladies, and if I exercised the right of challenge to the full I was in danger of still finishing with a jury more than half female – and hostile, too – so I decided to leave not very well alone. Worse than that the Judge was well known for being a non-motorist, and a tee-totaller. In a very skilful passage in his summing-up he sought to defend the monstrous medical man. "This humble doctor, perhaps not very successful throughout his life, has been strongly criticised for failing to observe an admittedly important feature of the defendant's medical condition. May it be, perhaps, members of the jury, that he overlooked it because he was so appalled at the defendant's obviously drunken condition that this really over-powered his judgment? It is of course, a matter for you, member of the jury." (Judges often summed-up like that in those days). The trial lasted two days and the jury could not agree. At 6.30 p.m. the Judge discharged them and said that the case would have to be re-listed. (There were no majority verdicts in those days.)

That night I received a telephone call at home. "Is that Mr Crowther, the barrister?" a female voice asked. I admitted my identity.

"Well," she went on. "I'm ringing up on behalf of the jury in the trial you were in for the last couple of days – or rather eleven of us. We eleven women all wanted to acquit your client, but that silly little squirt of a man said that the Judge obviously thought he was guilty, and he wasn't prepared to disagree with the Judge. The women all want to apologise to you."

I never challenged a woman juror again.

So the case was re-listed before a new Judge on the Monday of the week in which I had to return to the Magistrates' Court for my film producer on the Friday. This seemed safe enough: cases usually move more speedily on a re-trial. Both counsel recognise the deadwood and avoid it. But we had reckoned without the Judge! He was a "new" Judge in every sense of the term, and quite the slowest judicial officer I have ever come across. The re-hearing got off to a bad start with the Judge arriving three quarters of an hour late. Apparently he had got to Westminster Underground Station and then telephoned the Court asking for an "official car" to be sent for him to complete the remaining two hundred yards of his journey. The person who took the message, who knew more about the ways of the Lord Chancellor's Office than this newly appointed Judge, treated the call as a joke and ignored it, and the Judge who had waited vainly (in every sense of the term) outside the Underground, arrived in a fuming rage. He soon calmed down though and said that he would need a lot of assistance from both counsel as this was to be the first case that he had ever tried. For reasons that were not at all clear to me he became involved in a lengthy discussion about racing cars during prosecuting counsel's opening address – and no racing car had been involved in the accident. The Judge constantly interrupted the proceedings to ask his own questions, and insisted on writing all the answers down very slowly in long hand.

By Wednesday afternoon not only was it clear that we should not finish this two-day case that week (and in fact it lasted twelve working days) but the likelihood was that the dreadful doctor would be giving his evidence-in-chief on Thursday afternoon and be ripe for cross-examination on the Friday morning: and clearly I, who had conducted the defence in the previous abortive trial, had to be the advocate to carry out this piece of surgery. But if I did, my film producer was liable to die .....

In company with my opponent I went to see the Judge on the Wednesday evening, and explained the position. He was kind and sympathetic, and agreed not to sit on the Friday morning. First thing on the Thursday he announced this to the jury. A little later I saw the very earnest Clerk of the Peace come in and and hand the Judge a piece of paper. Soon after this the Judge rose and after about half an hour, he sent for my opponent and me: "I'm very sorry, Crowther," he said "the Clerk of the Peace says I've got to sit on Friday morning. I already arrived late on Monday and he says he'll report me to the Lord Chancellor if the Court isn't sitting. I really am sorry."

I went to see the Clerk of the Peace. He was adamant. "These Courts are not run for the convenience of counsel," he fulminated. "You've got to be here. Get someone else to go to your silly little Magistrates' Court."

I returned to the trial very depressed. What was to be done? At lunchtime there came to me the only possible solution. Send for Robert! I telephoned my senior clerk and explained the predicament. "Where is he?" he demanded. "Where is that Clerk of the Peace?" "He's in his room" I replied. "Tell him he's to stay there. Tell him I'm on my way down," Robert ordered.

It was rare for Robert to come out of his own little office, rarer still for him to leave the Temple during the day-time, and the Clerk of the Peace looked suitably impressed and slightly nervous when I imparted the news to him, and he did as he was bidden and stayed put. I decided to await developments, and took a seat outside the Clerk of the Peace's room. About a quarter of an hour later a fiery Robert entered the Court building. Never had I seen his legs moving so rapidly, his arms swinging so fiercely, his complexion so florid.

"Where is he?" he demanded. "Let me get at him."

I could not hear what was said during the next twenty minutes, although the voices saying it were very loud. Eventually Robert emerged, a slightly triumphant smile on his lips.

"This Court will not be sitting on Friday morning, Mr Crowther," he announced quietly, and made to return to the Temple.

I followed him a little way and asked "Robert. The Judge couldn't persuade him, and I couldn't persuade him. Tell me, how did you manage it?"

He paused for a moment and I shall never forget his reply. It sounds so silly, so childish, but it isn't. It is part of the machinery on which the wheels of Justice turn – mutual understanding of the mutual necessity of the clerks of the Courts and the clerks in the Chambers working in harmony. "I told him," said Robert. "that if he made you come here on Friday morning, I should never speak to him again."

Chapter 11

"There's a Man in a Mackintosh"

Different Kinds of Judges and Magistrates

"There's a man in a mackintosh addressing the Court. Remove that man, by force if necessary!" I was the inappropriately garbed man, the Judge (inevitably) was Judge MacMillan, and the command was addressed to the two burly ushers at Shoreditch County Court, both ex-police officers, who, together with the Associate, whose main job seemed to be to make a cup of tea every half hour and put it on the Bench before the Judge, seemed to comprise the entire staff in the Judge's Court at Shoreditch.

I suppose it was my fault really. The advocate should arrive at Court at least half an hour early and that morning I did not arrive until 10.20. The ushers, despite their rather fearsome size, were both kindly, helpful men, and that day one of them was awaiting my arrival to do a Toynbee case. He told me that the solicitor on the other side in my case wanted me to telephone him, urgently; so I did. It took a few minutes to get through to the correct partner in the firm who said: "Look, I've just received your Defence in this landlord and tenant dispute and I think there may be something in it. I want to get counsel's opinion, but I think it will probably result in our withdrawing the claim, so that your client will be able to stay on as tenant. I don't want to waste costs by sending someone down so will you get the case adjourned sine die and I'll be in touch with you if by any chance we do decide to carry on?"

By now it was 10.30 and I went into Court to enquire where we were in the list. As I was going towards her, the Associate called out the name of the matter that I had been discussing. "Oh, I'm in the case!" I exclaimed in my flurry.

170

Little Mac, who was already sitting on the Bench, went ashen with rage. "There's a man in a mackintosh addressing the Court. Remove that man, by force if necessary," he ordered. The two ushers, who looked larger than usual that morning, moved towards me with reluctant menace. I reacted rather like Fagin when Bill Sykes was threatening Nancy. "No violence, please," I said. "There's no need for violence. I'm going anyway." I went out, removed the offending garment, and put on my wig and gown as quickly as I could and returned to the Court Room. Judge MacMillan had not taken any other case in the meantime, but was seated there, perched on the Bench, waiting to peck at me.

"Your Honour," I began, "I wish to apologise ...."

"Apologise!" the Judge exploded. "You think you can escape the consequences of such disgraceful conduct by a mere apology. Hum-m-ble people come to this Court, Mr Crowther, hum-m-ble people" (he managed to make them sound positively servile, which East Enders are not) "and they expect to see Justice dispensed with dignity and decorum" (he pointed to the public gallery where many impatient litigants were waiting to have their cases heard) "and you have displayed neither of those qualities here today." He then addressed me for at least a quarter of an hour, referring three or four more times to all these "hum-m-ble people." When at last the torrent of anger appeared to have spent itself, I remarked: "I am sorry, your Honour. Will you now accept my apology?"

"No, I will not," rejoined Little Mac. "Your conduct is far too serious to be remedied by a mealy-mouthed apology."

By now I was getting rather tired of this one-sided discussion, so I said: "Well, if you're not prepared to accept my apology, may we get on with the case? I am asking for an adjournment."

"It is refused," said the Judge firmly.

I considered the implication of the most decisive judgment that I had ever heard this Judge give, and then I remarked: "Oh, good."

"What do you mean – "Oh good"?" he demanded, apprehensively.

"Well, it is the first time that I have ever won a case in your Honour's Court, and I regard it as quite an achievement."

"What do you mean about winning the case? You asked for an adjournment and it's been refused."

"Your Honour, I am for the defendant, the tenant. As your Honour has refused an adjournment, the claim must be dismissed

171

and I am entitled to judgment.''

"On whose behalf were you seeking the adjournment?''

"The Plaintiff's, your Honour.''

There was a dreadful pause before the Judge began again: "I cannot believe my ears. This is the most shameful conduct by a member of the Bar of which I have ever heard – accepting instructions from both sides. Be under no mis-apprehension, Mr Crowther, Your Benchers shall hear of this." (To the best of my knowledge they have not done so, up to now.) "Who instructed you to make this misconceived and mischievous application for an adjournment?''

"The Plaintiff's solicitor, your Honour.''

"Tell him to come here immediately to explain his misconduct. I regard him as in the grossest contempt of Court. I cannot continue with my list now. I am far too upset. Associate, bring me a cup of tea to my room:" and he swept off the Bench.

Back on the telephone to the unfortunate solicitor I advised him: "I think you'd better come. The Judge is proving a little difficult," – which was perhaps the best example of litotes in which I have ever indulged.

It was around noon when the elderly solicitor arrived, wearing a tattered gown which looked as if it had spent a long time in mothballs. No other cases had been taken in the interim, the Associate explaining that the Judge was still "upset", and I advised the solicitor to make his own application to adjourn the case, as I had not been conspicuously successful.

The Judge returned to the Court and the solicitor began to make his application in a rather matter-of-fact manner. He had not uttered many words when the Judge interrupted him: "Just a minute, Mr Weepers." (I forget the solicitor's real name: we were not to meet again.) "Hum-m-ble people come to this Court expecting to see Justice dispensed with dignity and decorum." The earlier homily was repeated, almost word for word, for the benefit of the late arrival. The Judge concluded, addressing the astonished solicitor: "I find your conduct every bit as disgraceful as that of Mr Crowther – perhaps even more so. I shall consider reporting you to the Law Society. Your application for an adjournment is refused. This action is dismissed, with costs. What are the costs, Mr Crowther?''

"Two guineas, Your Honour, and I am prepared in the circumstances to waive them.''

The Judge looked anxious, probably suspecting even more collusion between the bewildered solicitor and me, and at about 12.30 we withdrew to allow the Judge to continue with the petitions of all those "hum-m-ble people" who had had to watch this charade for the best part of two hours.

"Well," remarked the solicitor, as in the robing room he removed his wing-collar and mopped his brow, "it's twenty years since I last appeared in a County Court, and I can assure you it will be twenty years before I appear in one again."

I think it would not be unfair, on the basis of my many experiences of him, to describe Judge MacMillan as a difficult Judge, but really he was not unkind or cruel. Some Judges and magistrates of those days were. They all seemed to be intellectual giants, and extremely gifted lawyers, but some were not very humane. I think that the change to humanity being a necessary quality for appointment to judicial office came with the advent of Lord Gardiner as Lord Chancellor, and although I think that some (but not many) Judges and magistrates now are hard and occasionally difficult, I cannot think of any who are cruel or inhumane.

But it was not always thus. The younger generation of barristers and solicitors knows of Glenn Craske, for example, only as a legend. I am not sure if he or Humphrey Wightwick would merit the prize for the most bad-tempered stipendiary of the fifties. "Humph" shouted so much at everybody that he eventually had to have a throat operation which rendered him speechless and forced him to retire. Glenn Craske for some reason that I have never been able to discover was known universally as "Uncle", but there was nothing avuncular in his manner. My first encounter with him was when Cambridge House briefed me in a matrimonial case on a Friday afternoon at the doctor's house in Balham High Road which served at that time as the Magistrates' Court for South-West London. It was a difficult matter, with the wife (for whom I appeared) alleging desertion, although she and her husband remained living under the same roof, a situation on which there was a lot of legal authority; so, on my journey on the 155 bus that afternoon I was accompanied by at least a dozen Law Reports.

"Stop," said Uncle, as I entered the Court, interrupting his current case; and, pointing to the authorities held in straps in both my hands, he demanded: "What's all that?"

"Law Reports," I replied, reciting the obvious.

"And you don't imagine that I'm, going through those on a Friday afternoon, do you?" he enquired in his customarily sepulchral tones.

This was my first encounter with Uncle, but fortunately I had been forewarned about him, and told that you had to stand up to him.

"I did not bring them all the way down here to strengthen the muscles in my arms," I replied.

"That's very rude," pronounced Uncle fiercely. "Who are your Benchers?"

"I belong to Lincoln's Inn," I answered. "Who are yours?"

Uncle's tone softened a little: "Aren't we getting a bit heated?" he enquired.

"You may be, sir, but I am not" I replied.

His tone became almost conciliatory as he climbed down: "What do you want?" he asked miserably.

"I want a fair trial," I said, "and I don't think I'm going to get it in this Court. I ask for the case to be tried by another magistrate."

"Put it in the list before Sir John," Uncle announced. A couple of weeks later it was tried by Sir John Cameron, the other magistrate at that Court, also a bachelor, but how different from Uncle – always fair, courteous and patient.

Yes, you had to stand up to Uncle. I once saw Mick McElligott appearing before Uncle. Early on in his case his face became bright red and he addressed Uncle in these terms: "In this Court this morning I have seen you be rude to a young police officer, to several witnesses, to a solicitor and to all the defendants and" – his voice rising to a crescendo – "you are *not* going to be rude to me!" Uncle kept quiet thereafter. Mick himself was to become a London stipendiary and, as "the Squire of Old Street," earned himself a reputation for not suffering fools gladly, but there was a rough justice about Mick that one could not fail to admire.

I, too, never suffered rudeness from Uncle after that first encounter, but he remained difficult. I was instructed one Saturday to defend a man who was denying a charge of being drunk and disorderly. The whole case lasted only a total of about forty minutes but, to cause the maximum inconvenience to everybody, Uncle insisted on trying it piecemeal; he adjourned it three times, so that it took place on four successive Saturday mornings. He had put over my closing address to the final Saturday, and, when I had completed it, he gave his judgment:

"This case will be dismissed, not for any of the reasons given by Mr Crowther in his far too lengthy speech, but because I've had a look at the charge sheet and I see that a doctor was called to examine the defendant. Well, he hasn't been called before me and so I infer that he did not find that the defendant was inebriated. For that reason, which I discovered myself, the defendant will be acquitted."

That was the trouble with Uncle. He always came to the right conclusion, whether as to verdict or sentence; it was the way that he went about it that was so objectionable. On one occasion he nearly found himself as a defendant in his own Court. After the move from the doctor's house to the first of the new Palais de Justice at Clapham Junction in the early 1960s the Court Inspector made an application to Sir John Cameron.

"Your Worship, may I apply for a summons for assault?"

"Well, Inspector" interjected Sir John, "as you know, applications are normally made at 10.30 am in Court No 1. Why are you making this application at 2 pm in Court No 2 ?"

"Because, your Worship, the assault took place after 10.30 am and it was committed in Court No 1."

"Tell me more, Inspector."

"Your Worship, at about 11 am this morning your colleague in Court No 1 threw an inkwell at me which hit me, although it caused me no injury. I therefore wish to summon Mr Craske for common assault."

Sir John decided to adjourn the application to the next morning, when he would be sitting in Court 1. One can only imagine the meeting that must have taken place that afternoon between the three of them that resulted in the application not being proceeded with next day. Later I was to become one of Sir John's colleagues at South Western and all that he would tell me of that meeting was that "good sense and diplomacy prevailed," and Sir John had both those qualities. Stipendiary magistrates in London normally sit only a four day week, but are "on call" the remaining two working days. It is with sadness that I remember that the first time that I was called upon to do an extra day; the reason was that Sir John had died during the night.

Although Glenn Craske was a bully, at least his bullying was indiscriminate, as his encounters with Mick McElligott, then a very senior junior, and the Court Inspector, shewed. And likewise his quality of being awkward was bestowed on all comers, without fear or favour.

South-Western Court had a tradition of an annual dinner, held in the dining rooms of Arding and Hobbs, and in my latter days at the Bar I used to be invited. On one occasion the guest of honour was Dr Keith Simpson, the famous pathologist. He concluded his after dinner speech in something like these terms:–

"I have only once appeared at the South-Western Magistrates' Court as a witness. At all other Courts that I have attended the magistrates have acknowledged that I am quite a busy person and allowed me to give my evidence first, its usually being quite formal in character, relating to the apparent cause of the death of the victim. On the one occasion that I appeared at your Court counsel for the prosecution in the case – it was one of murder – made the usual application for me to go first, reinforcing it by saying that I had to get away urgently to attend another autopsy. The magistrate said: "Death usually marks the end, and as this witness deals only with the death of the deceased I shall take his evidence at the end of the case," so I was still there five and a half hours later at four o'clock."

Looking in the direction of the Chairman of the dinner, Dr Simpson added: "I cannot remember the name of the magistrate concerned, but I understand that he had a nickname which seemed to be connected with some sort of relationship. I can't remember what that relationship was, but it was certainly not paternal, as this magistrate clearly never had a father."

During the thunderous applause that followed, Uncle simply sat and glowered.

As against London magistrates like Humph and Uncle (and a few others) there were some who were charming and before whom it was a delight to appear: Sir Frank Milton, just appointed Chief Magistrate, dignified, witty, erudite, urbane and fair, and very conscious of "the image of the magistracy", which he did more than anyone else has done in recent times to uphold and enhance; Hal Maddocks, at Tower Bridge, an immensely humane man who seemed to understand the spirit of Bermondsey and the London docks as well as Bob Mellish, the local Member of Parliament, and far better than Sybil Campbell. (Frank once asked me, much later on: "Who of those who have been sitting recently as deputies do you think should be the next of our colleagues?" and I named a name. "And why?" asked Frank. "Because I think he'd prove to be like Hal Maddocks," I replied. "That is praise indeed" commented Frank, but it was not praise enough to get my nominee the appointment); and perhaps the most delightful of all, Wally Frampton at Marylebone. How fortunate I was to appear before Wally when I represented Elizabeth on a plea of guilty to travelling on the London Underground without paying the proper fare and with intent to avoid payment thereof. At the end of my address the magistrate said: "In view of the mitigation so ably advanced by learned counsel on your behalf, I shall award you an absolute discharge," and then, to my surprise, he asked: "May I see your brief, Mr Crowther?" and then when he had looked at it, asked: "Would you mind coming to see me in my room after I have completed my list? I don't think it will take very long."

I wondered what I had done wrong this time – at least I was not wearing a mackintosh. The brief was a Toynbee one (I still retain it as an affectionate souvenir) and it was marked, unusually for a Legal Advice Centre case – for most of them attracted a fee of two guineas – "No Fee." But at least I was complying with the rules, and had instructions from a solicitor.

When I got to Wally's room he offered me a cup of tea and asked: "Was that your girlfriend you were defending?" "Why, yes," I replied, "but how did you know?" "Well, you've appeared before me on many occasions, but it's the first time that I've seen your hands trembling as you held your papers. She looks a nice girl – she's very beautiful – but tell her that you won't marry her if she does it again; it doesn't do to have a dishonest wife in our profession."

Elizabeth was waiting for me and I did tell her not to do it again, and so far as I know she never did; neither did she marry me. But how lucky I was to have Walter Frampton that day and not his colleague at the same Court, Geoffrey Raphael.

It was before Geoffrey Raphael that I had my worst experience ever in a Magistrates' Court. I had returned from London Sessions earlier than expected: the jury had stopped the case and acquitted my defendant at the end of the prosecution case. I don't know why I called in at Chambers at about 1.15 instead of going for lunch, but I wish that I had not done so.

"Oh, it's good that you're here, Mr Crowther," murmured Robert gratefully. "Just slip up to Marylebone and do this little threatening words."

"I was just going to lunch, Robert."

"Buy a sandwich on the way, Mr Crowther, and you can read the brief on the bus. There's nothing in it."

My sense of horror and dismay was to increase as the afternoon wore on. The seventeen year old defendant was a member of Colin Jordan's mob,, and had been arrested whilst selling their fascist newpaper outside Notting Hill Underground Station. He had been shouting out the banner headline from the paper. It read: "Kill all the Jews." Some people objected, and he was arrested.

Normally this type of case is last in a list after about a hundred motoring summonses. Ours was the only case at 2pm in Court No. 1. The magistrate opened the proceedings by saying: "I think that I should tell you that I am one of the leaders of the Jewish community in this country. Have you any objection to my trying this case?" I replied that I had not. If the magistrate made that declaration, it seemed to me that he would go out of his way to be fair throughout the case. I could not have been more mistaken! When I was cross-examining witnesses and obtaining admissions that they were not put in fear by the defendant's shouts, he would interrupt with: "No, but you felt threatened, didn't you? You must have felt threatened." When the defendant got into the witness-box Raphael interrupted him at an early stage with: "Do you realise that ten million Jews were sent to their deaths in the gas chambers of Nazi Germany by the likes of you?"

My closing address was not made easier by the magistrate's interruptions, but the thrust of it was that the defendant's behaviour was no more threatening than would have been the cries of a newsvendor calling out "Death to Nasser" in the Anglo-Egyptian war of a few years before. (Had the case been heard a couple of decades later I could have quoted the notorious headline in the *The Sun* newpaper: "Up the Argies, Maggie.") The magistrate sat in raging impatience waiting to convict, and then passed, without pausing for my mitigation, to sentence this young man: "Unfortunately the maximum sentence allowed by law for such loathsome conduct is three months imprisonment" (there were no fetters in those days on magistrates' passing a sentence of imprisonment on a defendant under the age of twenty-one and of previous good character) "and that sentence I . . . . ."

"One moment, sir" I interrupted. "Do you really feel that it is a good idea to make a martyr of this extremely stupid and ignorant young man for his one mistake?"

There was a terrible silence before Raphael turned back to the defendant, and glaring at him through his monocle, declared: "I'm not going to make a martyr of you, because that's just what you want, isn't it? You will be bound over for a year to be of good behaviour in the sum of £100."

I left the Court exhausted, and relieved that it was all over. But it was not. Obviously the young defendant's leaders were not satisfied about the conviction, for a few weeks later I received a well-paid brief to appear at London Sessions on the appeal before another rather terrifying judicial figure, "Ossy" McLeay. But from an early stage Ossy took an entirely different view of the matter, and laughed it out of Court as soon as the prosecution had completed its case, asking me what figure I was claiming for costs "here and below." As I left that Court three things happened.

Colin Jordan, whom I recognised from newspaper photographs, approached me with outstretched hand, which I ignored; a tall and beautiful woman came and kissed me: "Who are you, and why did you do that?" I enquired; "I am Colin's wife, and you were magnifique," she replied with the appropriate accent; "In that case don't ever do that again," I said, spurning beauty perhaps for the only time in my life; and my oldest friend at the Bar, oldest in the sense that we had been in the same form together at University College School, had met again as Bar students, and had always been friends, sternly rebuked me by saying "Eric, I shall never speak to you again. You did that case far too enthusiastically. How could you ever have appeared for those monsters?"

But my Jewish friend was wrong. In appearing for Jordan's henchman, and doing my best for him – an easier task before "Ossy" than before Geoffrey Raphael – I was doing the duty of every barrister as laid down by Lord Simon, the Lord Chancellor, in a speech to the Canadian Bar Association in 1943.

"There is an honourable tradition at the English Bar that even a man who may be busy with many different cases, if he is called upon to defend the meanest criminal, charged with the most despicable crime, is bound to give his own personal attention to that work, however odious and unremunerative it may be, to the exclusion of all other business coming his way. And in what spirit should it be discharged? It is, I venture to say, essential to the cause of Justice in dealing with any charge that the services of a man professionally trained should be available to defend those who are accused .... to make sure that the most is made of every flaw and of every gap in the net which seems to be closing around the unhappy man; and thus you may secure that all shall be said on the accused's behalf."

If it were otherwise, how could those who espouse unpopular minority causes be represented at all? And who would speak for the Krays (who had something to say on this subject, as I will reveal later), Charlie Richardson, the Yorkshire Ripper or the killer of P C Blakelock? This was realized later on by my old school mate, and we are now good friends again, I am glad to say.

I was to be briefed again in another matter arising from the activities of Colin Jordan and his gang. On that occasion, the day before the hearing, I received a telephone call at my home late at night and an aristocratic voice addressed me: "This is Sir Oswald Mosley speaking from Paris. You're representing one of my men tomorrow and I want to discuss tactics." It gave me some pleasure to reply:– "I take my instructions from solicitors in London, not from politicians in Paris. Goodnight, Sir Oswald." That, too, I believe accorded with the traditions of the Bar.

In the fifties and sixties not all those who appeared higher up the judicial scale than Craske, Wightwick and Raphael could be relied upon to behave better than they. Mr Justice Hallett was asked to resign because he could not refrain from interrupting during the hearing of cases, and Mr Justice Roxburgh, a senior Judge of the Chancery Division, was another Judge who suffered from Hallett-osis. I well remember my first appearance before him: he started to talk before he reached his seat on the Bench:– "That clock's wrong again. How many times must I complain before it's put right?" Then, glaring round the Court his eye lighted on me and he said: "Ah, I spy strangers! What case are you in young man?" I told him and he replied, smiling blandly: "Well, I'll put it last in the list. You're from the Common Law Bar I believe. We mustn't hurry you, must we? We all know you common lawyers like to talk a lot."

Even worse than the fate of being a young Common Lawyer appearing before Roxburgh J was to be a woman. On one occasion when a newly Called girl barrister appeared before him on a Monday morning in the crowded Companies Court the Judge teased her so mercilessly that she burst into tears. Then, changing to what looked like a gracious smile, he said, with mock sympathy: "If you're not strong enough for the rigours of a man's profession, my dear, why don't you do something else? There are plenty of easy jobs for barristers in the Civil Service ...." At that point all the many Chancery barristers in Court got up to a man – and they were all men – leaving the Judge alone in Court; the ultimate rebuke for his ill-mannered cruelty.

But to me cruelty to witnesses and defendants – especially defendants – is far worse than barrister-baiting; Roxburgh was right in a way: you do have to be pretty tough to be a barrister. By the end I had appeared in thousands of cases: I remember only two in which the unfeeling attitude of the Judge really upset me. Judge Mervyn-Griffith Jones, the Common Serjeant of London, had a habit of going over to the Court thermometer and looking at it before taking his place before the jury on the Bench. The temperature was rarely above freezing-point in his Court: it was possibly a little lower in that occupied by Mr Justice Thesiger.

Thesiger J. gave the impression of enjoying torturing defendants. Before passing his sentences (usually harsh ones) he would deliver lengthy homilies saying how he had to balance the interest of the defendant against that of the general public, and he almost invariably came down on what he regarded as the side of the general public. The Suffolk Assizes held at Bury St.Edmunds were always enjoyable occasions, except when Mr Justice Thesiger was there. Once, when he was doing his "balancing act," the Mayor of Ipswich, a down-to-earth woman of Cockney origins, walked off the Bench (where ex-officio she sat beside him) in protest. "I could not sit any longer in that torture chamber," she explained afterwards. On another occasion that remarkable and courageous advocate Ernlé Money (the local Member of Parliament) was appearing before Gerald Thesiger. He began his plea in mitigation: "Now I know that your Lordship will say that on the one hand I have to consider the defendant's interest and on the other I have to consider the interest of the general public." The voice employed was a remarkably good imitation of Thesiger, whose steely blue eyes became positively icy as he listened to this mimicry.

My client was charged with causing death by dangerous driving. He had fallen asleep at the wheel of a lorry that he drove in the course of his employment, gone on to the pavement, and killed two people. There was no more – and no less – to it than that, except that his employers had been forcing him to work such long hours, for rather poor wages, that his falling asleep was understandable. At the outset I thought that he should plead Not Guilty, but Michael Havers, later the Lord Chancellor, who has very kindly written the foreword to this book and who was prosecuting shewed me an authority to the effect that if you continue driving when you realize that you are liable to be overcome by sleep that is dangerous, and so I asked for the defendant to be allowed to change his plea. Thesiger agreed, but said that as he had originally pleaded Not Guilty he would put the case back to the end of the Assize and allow him bail only on condition that he arrived at the Assize Court no later than 9.30 each morning until then. I pointed out to him that the Court sat only at 10.30, that the only reasonable train (which all the London Bar took) arrived at 9.51, and that the defendant lived in Bromley in Kent. "There is a milk train at 4.30 from Liverpool Street," announced Thesiger icily. "He has the choice between that, or remaining in custody. If he is a minute late on any morning, he will lose his liberty."

So, for over a week, this poor man had to use the train in the middle of the night to get to Ipswich to listen to Thesiger conducting other trials, and so have the fear of God – no, not of God, surely – put into him. When I returned (on the train that arrived at 9.51) to represent him late the following week he was a tired, nervous wreck. We were the second (and last) case in the list. The other was also a case of causing death by dangerous driving. The defendant was a former High Sheriff of the County. Although only one person had been killed, the case was in many respects worse than ours: the driving had been atrocious, and drink was involved. But the former High Sheriff's advocate had been wiser than I. He changed his plea to Guilty only on the day of the hearing. Thesiger did his famous balancing act and ultimately decided that "in view of the defendant's good character and his outstanding service to the community it is possible to deal with this case by means of a fine and a three year disqualification." The fine was a modest one, and I felt encouraged.

My client was in his mid-thirties, a married man with two children. As an adolescent he had had a bad criminal record, culminating in sentences of Borstal training and imprisonment, terminating a little more than ten years previously, when he had met his wife, whom soon thereafter he married. Since then he had worked hard – too hard on the day in question – and kept out of trouble.

"In this case," the high glacial voice pronounced: "I have to balance your interests against the interests of the community," and he pontificated on this theme for over half an hour, the defendant standing before him in the dock; there was plenty of time to do this, as a Not Guilty plea had originally been entered in the High Sheriff's case, and it was still morning. "I also must have regard to the necessity for consistency in sentencing, and I have in mind that the last defendant, on a somewhat similar charge, was not sent to prison. However, he was a man of good character, upon whom a sentence of imprisonment would have inflicted great suffering. You are no stranger to prison, and will not suffer much there. The sentence of the Court is that you be imprisoned for twenty-one months, and be disqualified from holding or obtaining a driving licence for five years."

I did not go to see him in the cells until I had drafted the Notice of Appeal. "Sign this," I said. "That was vicious." His head was in his hands, but he looked up and asked me: "Can they increase sentence on appeal?" "Yes," I said, "but they won't in this case." "But they can. Another question. Does that Judge ever sit in the Court of Appeal?" "Yes," I replied. "But he won't on this one."

"Listen," he said. "I'm not appealing. I've worked out my release date. With one third remission it's Christmas Eve next year. I wanted to spend this Christmas with my wife and kids. It's clear I can't. I'm not prepared to risk missing the next Christmas with them. I'm not appealing if they have Judges like that in the Court of Appeal;" and there was no way that I could persuade him to the contrary.

Soon afterwards the power of the Court of Appeal to increase sentence was abolished. Now there are strong pressures to restore it, and even to increase sentence at the instance of the prosecution. When I am asked my opinion on this matter, I always think back to the man who worked so hard to make a good life for his "wife and kids" that he fell asleep at the wheel of his lorry . . . . .

At Christmas, the following year, on his release from prison, he received a cheque from me for the amount that I had received from the Legal Aid Fund for my two appearances in his case. I did not feel, in all conscience, that I could keep any of the money after such a disastrous result, and I had thought often during those fourteen months of him languishing in prison away from "the wife and kids."

I still treasure the letter that I got in reply: "I know you tried hard for me, but I never thought that a barrister would care so much."

When I had come up from the cells there had been a Court official bearing a note from the Judge:–

> "Dear Crowther,
>
> I was most impressed by your efforts on behalf of that villain. I shall be pleased if you will join us for lunch.
>
> Gerald Thesiger."

"Tell the Judge that I cannot come on account of a previous engagement," I said. I would prefer to have said, like Oscar Wilde, "on account of a subsequent engagement," but I lacked the courage.

I recently saw on television an advertisement for British Airways shares. I saw it by accident because I usually go out of the room to get tea or something stronger when the "commercials" come on, but this one was quite imaginative. It went back about forty years to a time when Heathrow was just a village on the edge of London and one man was talking about it as the world airport of the future while his more conservative mates were decrying his vision with shouts of "Nah". As Heathrow was conceived and born and grew, so numerous ancillary services were attracted. So was the criminal element, with such a large representation in the baggage handling department that the new airport quickly gained the international name of "Thiefrow". And inevitably the big criminals turned their attention to this massive new industry. For Charlie Richardson the most interesting part was the facility for car parking, run under a concession by the Airport's Authority. He moved his men in there. But some of the car park attendants were elderly, decent, honest men, who had to be silenced. One of these was William Charles Jeffries, a man who had worked hard and well all his life. The approach made to him was: "Would you prefer to carry on your job, "earning" a lot more, or would you like your wife and family to suffer?" He was given to understand that their suffering would not simply be the result of his falling unemployed in his mid-sixties. But the price to be paid for his silence, as a large part of the car parking fees found its way into the hands of the gang, would be quite generous: I forget now whether it was £50 or £100 a week – a lot of money a quarter of a century ago – and he and another dear old attendant, who was to be represented at the trial at the Old Bailey by Neil McKinnon QC (himself shortly afterwards to be a Judge at that same Court) succumbed to the temptation, and, as Judge Mervyn Griffith-Jones, the Common Serjeant, put it in his summing-up, "agreed to join in the existing conspiracy by remaining silent when men of any moral fibre would have spoken out." They did not know what to do with so much money. The conspiracy carried on for years and all the cash that Jeffries had got from it was found by the police in a suitcase under his bed – no Swiss bank account for him. The British Airports Authority got a High Court injunction from Mr Justice Willis freezing his assets, and Jeffries, who never went on a holiday in those years, got nothing at all out of it except worry, illness and misery.

It was not a joy to appear before Judge Griffith-Jones, who had spent most if not all of his professional life prosecuting in a manner that shewed little understanding of ordinary people and of common humanity. My own feeling is that his stupidity was responsible for the flood of pornography that appeared on the bookstalls after his unsuccessful prosecution of "Lady Chatterley's Lover," during a long trial throughout which the dock at that Old Bailey Court was occupied simply by the Penguin edition of that book. In his peroration Mervyn held up another copy of D.H. Lawrence's famous or notorious novel and asked the working-class London jury: "Members of the jury, is this a book that you would allow your servant girl to read?" Just imagine the fun that that great advocate (now a great life peer), Jeremy Hutchinson Q C, had with that question in *his* closing address! The prosecutor was a man remote from reality, who seldom spoke to other members of the Bar. All that he ever said to me, in the many cases that I did against him (all successfully, I seem to recall) was: "You're occupying my place. Get out of it." Almost his only friend at the Bar was Sam Morton, who was, I believe, his brother-in-law, who also became a Crown Court Judge, and this bit of doggerel floated around the robing room at one time:

> "Oh let me go back to the Bailey
> Before I leave this sod;
> Where Sam speaks only to Mervyn
> And Mervyn speaks only to God."

I support many of the traditions of the Bar: I think that most of them operate to the public good. One that did not was the tradition of appointing Treasury criminal counsel, who had done nothing but prosecute at the Central Criminal Court, as Old Bailey Judges.

Being a prosecutor does not necessarily make one a good Judge: indeed the best criminal Judges, for obvious reasons, are those who formerly prosecuted and defended in about equal measure. Furthermore, this somewhat incestuous system of appointment turned the Old Bailey into some kind of exclusive club in which you were either accepted or not accepted. It was much to the credit of Lord Havers that, when Attorney-General, he was instrumental in putting a stop to this form of pernicious patronage.

However, the two Treasury counsel prosecuting in the Airparks conspiracy case were Edward Cussen and John Leonard. Both became Old Bailey Judges for a short time, in accordance with the tradition, Edward Cussen being robbed by death of a longer period of office, and John Leonard quickly being appointed to the High Court Bench. Despite the general observations that I have made, both were scrupulously fair, both as prosecutors and as Judges. There were, I think, seven defendants in the Airparks conspiracy case, five of whom were villains, the remaining two – Neil McKinnon's client and Jeffries – being nice old men who had been inveigled inadvertently into something that they could not control. This seemed to be recognized by Cussen and Leonard, who cross-examined the real criminals vigorously and fiercely, but were gentle with the two car park attendants. Indeed so gentle and gentlemanly was Edward Cussen's cross-examination of Mr Jeffries that, in other circumstances, one might have thought that he was interviewing the defendant for a job as his personal valet and questioning him about his previous employment. "Any re-examination, Mr Crowther?" asked Mervyn coldly, when Cussen had completed his task, courteously and skilfully. "I would prefer to wait until after your Lordship's cross-examination," I replied with conscious irony, having seen how Mervyn, reverting to his role as Crown prosecutor, had mauled the other defendants. Mervyn chose to ignore that challenge and began his supplemental cross-examination in the same manner as with the other defendants: "Just see if you can help me, Mr Jeffries . . . . ."

Our defence, if we had one, was duress, and I say unashamedly that that very able and delightful advocate Richard Beckett (who appeared with me for Mr Jeffries) and I were going for a sympathy verdict. Jeffries was a sick man and we called his doctor to say that he had been seriously ill for a very long time. Mervyn would have none of this. In what passed for his summing-up but was more like a final speech for the prosecution he used a phrase for which I shall never forgive him: "And you have the defendant Jeffries, suffering from some illness, real or imagined . . . . ." Mervyn got his way and all the defendants were duly convicted. While the sentences of five to seven years that he passed on the main conspirators were fully justified, those of two and half years on the two elderly car park attendants, both men of excellent character with fine records of war service (in the ranks) were surely not. Jeffries was dying: his doctor knew it, his wife knew it, his solicitor knew it, and Richard and I knew it; but the Judge did not realize the fact or, if he did, was not prepared to allow it to make any difference. I wanted Mr Jeffries to die with dignity in his own home.

The trouble was that in those days bail was hardly every granted pending appeal against a long sentence, so I had to resort to the ruse of appealing against conviction, but it must be admitted that the defence of duress is a difficult one to establish. The application for bail pending appeal was heard by Mr Justice Cantley, a tough Judge, in Chambers. He was disinclined to grant it, saying that the case against Jeffries seemed overwhelming and that the summing-up had been no stronger than was customary in those days. I emphasized the tragic state of Jeffries' health, but the Judge did not seem impressed. "I've never granted bail pending appeal," he said, "unless I've felt sure the appeal would succeed, and I certainly don't in this case. I think this appeal against conviction has just been lodged for the purpose of getting bail." He was right, of course, and I felt once again that I was losing for poor old Jeffries. But then help came from an unexpected quarter. John Leonard, who was there to oppose my application, and had recited the facts leading to the conviction firmly but fairly, said quietly: "My Lord, I was present throughout this six week trial and it was obvious to me and indeed to almost everyone else in Court that Mr Jeffries was a very sick man at the beginning of the trial, and much more ill by the end of it. Although I am not of course a doctor, I support Mr Crowther's prediction that Mr Jeffries has not many weeks to live."

Cantley J. relented and granted bail. This was in mid-December and Mr Jeffries was able to spend that last Christmas with his loving wife and to die peacefully in his own home early in January, thanks to John Leonard, briefed to prosecute him. How glad I was when that kindly, fair and extremely able barrister was in his turn appointed Common Serjeant at the Old Bailey, and, later on became a fine High Court Judge.

Jeffries was one of those old-fashioned English people who believed in paying his way in life. His small house at Heston was being purchased on mortgage. He had savings, and from these he paid my fees and those of Richard Beckett – quite substantial sums, as these had been negotiated by Robert, who had his "governor's" best interests at heart. Jeffries was not the type to apply for and obtain legal aid by concealing the fact of his savings, as I fear most defendants do now. I find it somewhat nauseating how magistrates' courts, including my own, lavish legal aid on drug pushers and long term fraudsmen who pretend that they have no assets, when probably their financial position is better than that of the lawyers who represent them and the Judges who try them. But Jeffries was of the old school that believed in working and paying for what you get. I waited until after his funeral before returning all the fees that I had received to Mrs Jeffries. B A A certainly sought their pounds of flesh from all the defendants in civil proceedings, and they pursued Jeffries even beyond the grave, forcing Mrs Jeffries to sell up the house in which she and her husband had lived for so long. It was several months before I received a letter of thanks from her, and, when I did, I realized from the content and the caligraphy how completely shattered this elderly respectable woman, who had loyally attended the trial every day, had been by what had happened to her little world. "What do I do now, Mr Crowther?" she asked me, after the sentence of two and a half years had been passed on her husband. What possible answer could there be to such a question? Mr and Mrs Jeffries were truly "humble people coming to Court" – to paraphrase Judge MacMillan's famous words – who were entitled to expect to be treated with consideration and mercy; they received neither at the hands of Judge Mervyn Griffith-Jones. Practice at the Criminal Bar is not all fun: it sometimes leads to tragedy, and for me the case of Jeffries was the saddest case of all.

As if the sentence of thirty months were not enough, Judge Mervyn Griffith-Jones had added an order that Jeffries should pay £1,300 costs which, after his death, could only fall to be borne by his widow, Anne, who was his sole executrix and residuary legatee, an added reason why the former matrimonial home would have to be sold. Richard and I tried to spare her this by applying to the Court of Appeal for leave to continue Jeffries' appeal notwithstanding his death, but this application was refused, as was leave to appeal to the House of Lords, Lord Justice Widgery saying that it was "open to the personal representatives to petition the Secretary of State for relief" so that the Home Secretary could, if "so minded, seek the opinion of this Court." Whether or not this tortuous procedure was ever adopted I know not. The Court of Appeal gave its reserved judgment on 17th July *(R v Jeffries 1968 3 All E R 238)* and two weeks later I was a magistrate, so Jeffries was one of my last cases at the Bar. (I had also been briefed on the appeal against sentence of seven years of one of the main Airparks conspirators, though I had not appeared for him at the trial. This far less meritorious appeal also failed; the Airparks conspiracy was not one of my great successes.)

I should not like it to be thought that the Judges and magistrates that I have criticised in this chapter were typical of those holding judicial office in the fifties and sixties. They were not, although I do believe that the Judges and magistrates of today are much gentler and kinder, and that the types I have described no longer exist. Possibly not all Judges today are such good lawyers and such intellectual giants as those that I had to encounter, but, quite simply, to use a word that I was told at school never to use, but which I think is nice, they are much "nicer" people. It is true that I do not appear before them but only among them, but I meet a lot of practising lawyers – both solicitors and barristers – and have my ear pretty close to the ground, and this is the general opinion.

However, to balance the image of the judiciary of my days at the Bar, I should mention some Judges appearing before whom was always an enjoyable experience. One was Sir Carl Aarvold, the Recorder of London during most of my time as an advocate. A fine rugger and tennis player in his day, he was a sport in every sense of the term. His brief summings-up, delivered with a delightful lilt and a beautiful sense of gentle irony (he would often use the word "alas," when reviewing the defendant's evidence) were a joy to the ear of all who appreciate the effective use of language – if not always to the ear of the defendant. But the atmosphere was warm in his Court, and there were no histrionics. Sir Carl was one of the few Recorders of London who did not have a Treasury counsel or even a London practice background, and he was certainly the best of the three Recorders before whom I had to appear.

To many of my contemporaries it will come as a surprise to learn that one of my favourite Judges of those days was the Honourable Ewen Montague, the Chairman of Middlesex Sessions. I admire patience in Judges, and this was a quality that Ewen did not possess in great measure – or, indeed, in any measure. He did not suffer fools gladly; he did not believe that the police brought prosecutions without good reason; and he almost invariably convinced the jury that there were just thirteen intelligent people in Court: the twelve of them and himself, with the occasional possible addition of prosecuting counsel, if the last named were strong enough. I lost every defended case that I ever did before Ewen except one; but I always won when I was prosecuting. He was indeed "prosecution minded", but when it came to sentencing he was very shrewd and just. Only once did I feel that he went "over the top", and I was prosecuting that time – a young American who had pleaded not guilty to an insurance fraud but got nine months for it.

But most counsel quailed when they had to defend in a contested case before Ewen. In my first case before him he interrupted my cross-examination with: "To what issue in this case could that question possibly be directed, Mr Crowther? I see to my surprise that you have two briefs in front of you. Perhaps you read the wrong one before coming into Court." And he had a disconcerting habit of sinking his head in his hands and sighing (and occasionally murmuring "Oh, God!") during defending counsel's questioning or his closing speech. Different counsel of differing experience had different ways of dealing with this distraction. Sir Harold Cassel, later a Crown Court Judge, and one of the most amusing men at the Bar or on the Bench, used to look up solicitously and enquire: "Is your Lordship indisposed? I would be quite happy for this case to be transferred to another Judge if it is proving too burdensome for your Lordship." (It is said that the ushers used to charge half a crown admission fee to the public gallery when Sir Harold was due to appear before the Honourable Ewen, "the Man Who Never Was.")

The sighs from the Bench were particularly disturbing as they did not find their way on to the shorthand note, and Ewen, for all his testy interventions, was seldom successfully appealed. Over the week-end in a part-heard contested case I decided how I would deal with them. When Ewen on the Monday morning made a further lengthy groan ("O-o-o-h!") I responded with an even longer one ("A-a-a-a-h!") and the jury laughed. Ewen looked up, but stopped himself in time from saying anything that could be recorded by the short-hand writer, and I got through that case without further judicial interruptions; and that was the case I won.

But for all that, I liked and admired Ewen. He was highly

intelligent, quite just in his own way, and bore no malice. When the time came for his retirement, I was called upon to make the farewell speech in his honour in the Middle Temple Hall. I spoke of the terrors we all had in defending before him, and said how the defending advocate, briefed to appear at Middlesex Sessions, would try to put on a brave front by adapting some words from "Romeo and Juliet":–

"What's Montague? It is not voice, nor frown
Nor scowl, nor sigh, nor any other part
Belonging to the man. Oh! Be some other Judge!"

But Ewen took it all in good part and we became firm friends. A couple of years ago he wrote to me: "I am dying, Eric. I have cancer of the liver. They tell me it is always fatal, but it is a painless death. I have nothing to complain of. I have had a long, full, interesting life with many good friends, so do not grieve for me." But I find that I do.

In the County Court my favourite was, of course, John Barrington, but Judge Wingate-Saul was another Judge who always seemed to come to the right decision (even when he found against me!) as did also Judge Ruttle, who in his judgments could keep the litigants in suspense until the end, in a manner worthy of Agatha Christie; while it was inevitably a stimulating intellectual experience to appear before Harry Leon, who used to describe himself as "the difficult Judge at Willesden" but who, in reality, was much kinder than he chose to appear.

The trouble with Judge Leon, however, was that on the Bench he was too much the author Henry Cecil, seeking to create situations for his books. I remember once waiting to come on in the Willesden County Court and there was, in a case before mine, a very senior and rather pompous landlord and tenant expert appearing for a property company. Now Leon was always the champion of the under-dog, and the tenant in this case certainly fell into that category, being a rather dishevelled old age pensioner living alone in furnished property not protected under the Rent Acts. Counsel opened the case on the basis that there was no defence to the action, and it was clear that he was right. But Leon was not going to let it go through that easily.

"What about the Notice to Quit?" he asked. "How are you going to prove that?"

"Your Honour", replied Counsel "the Defendant has put in no

defence and I am expecting him to admit it".

"Oh, I don't suppose he will", said Leon. "I expect if you can't prove it strictly he'll be making a submission of no case to answer and standing on it"; and turning to the old man, he said: "That's what you'll be doing, won't you?"

"Standing on what, your Honour?" the tenant asked, incredulously.

"Yes, I thought you would be", the Judge encouraged.

"Now, Mr. Bagshot, I think you are in difficulties. How are you going to prove service of this Notice to Quit?"

"Well, your Honour, I have with me the senior partner in the firm of my instructing solicitors whom I propose to call as my first witness".

"Really Mr. Bagshot, you're not going to convince me that the senior partner in a big City firm goes out and posts all the letters. That's the job of the office boy. Call the office boy." (Leon had first satisfied himself that no-one who could possibly answer that description was in Court).

"Your Honour I am instructed that the office boy left the employ of my instructing solicitors some weeks ago."

"Well, Mr. Bagshot, I can only say that this case has been abominably badly prepared. I imagine you were not asked to advise on evidence. I see no alternative but to dismiss this claim – with costs".

"Would Your Honour kindly grant an adjournment?" pleaded Bagshot.

"Yes, but only until 2 p.m. If by then you haven't got your tackle in order, I shall dismiss the case". Then, turning to the bewildered tenant, he asked: "Have you suffered any financial loss as a result of the poor preparation of this case?"

"Er – no, not really", said the honest old boy.

Leon was obviously disappointed, but then an idea came to his fertile mind. "What about your lunch? You'll have to have lunch out to-day, and it's all the fault of the lawyers on the other side. I shall make it a condition of the adjournment that Mr. Bagshot personally takes you out to lunch."

"Well, really, Your Honour, I must protest," expostulated the now very red-faced Bagshot, as he contemplated his unkempt luncheon companion.

"Oh well, if you are not prepared to be reasonable I'll dismiss your claim straight away" threatened the Judge.

"No, Your Honour, I accept the condition of the adjournment", murmured Bagshot, wearily.

At 2 o'clock I was still waiting to come on, but was also eager to observe the outcome of this affair. By some miracle the solicitor had found the office boy – or an office boy – who was there, ready to give evidence of the posting of the letter containing the Notice to Quit. But Leon seemed to have lost interest in the case itself. "Tell me", he said to the tenant: "Did Mr. Bagshot buy you a good lunch?"

"Well, Your Honour", ruminated the old boy, as he licked his lips, "to tell you the truth he gave me 'alf a crown, so I added sixpence to it and I'ad a couple of Guinnesses".

For a defended divorce my favourite Judge was the ever courteous and patient Mr Justice Hewson, who had one distracting habit: he used to get up and walk about during the hearing, even when giving judgment! At the time I regarded this as a gross if pardonable eccentricity, but having myself in later years been afflicted both by backache and vein trouble I now think that he was probably gallantly trying to combat one of those complaints.

Another nice High Court Judge before whom to appear – although I doubt if the late Stephen Ward would agree with me – was Mr. Justice Marshall. He was a strong Methodist, and full of Christian compassion – except for sexual deviation of the kind displayed by Stephen Ward, the rather prim – I thought – Christine Keeler (with whom I had lunch in a private room at the Old Bailey during that sensational trial) and the far jollier Mandy Rice-Davies. Mr Justice Lyell was a Judge before whom I appeared in the Court of Criminal Appeal on an appeal against sentence. I did not know him at all, but afterwards he wrote to ask me if I would represent the son of a friend of his on another appeal to a (differently constituted) Court of Appeal. This boy, who had recently lost his father, had pleaded guilty to a charge of burglary. It was his first offence, and he had received a custodial sentence, Borstal training, which was usual for a first burglary in those days. Nowadays, under pressure from the Home Office, you have to commit about five burglaries before you get a custodial sentence and –surprise, surprise! – there are about five times as many burglaries. My efforts resulted in the young man being placed on probation instead of in Borstal, and his mother, who was a sculptress, sent me a beautiful carved head which I treasured until recently when it was stolen during a skilful burglary of my flat. Even more do I treasure the gracious letter that I received from the generous Mr Justice Lyell, saying how much happiness I had brought to the recently widowed lady. Unfortunately my efforts do not seem to have been so greatly appreciated by the boy himself, who a couple of months later committed another burglary. I represented him again and this time he received – Borstal Training. He was a young criminal in advance of his time.

But my favourite of all High Court Judges of those days was Mr Justice Barry, by nature so warm, so generous, so kind. Anne Curnow was prosecuting me once before him in a plea in a case at Kingston Assizes of causing death by dangerous driving and she said to me before the case: "Eric, I've sent out for a packet of paper handkerchiefs. I know you. With this Judge you'll have everybody in Court in tears, especially the Judge – and possibly even me!" We finished up with a £5 fine and the minimum disqualification. Why didn't I have him instead of Thesiger in my more meritorious case at Suffolk? But Barry J did appear as the Assize Judge at Bury later on, and I was in the middle of cross-examination of the main prosecution witness when the luncheon adjournment came, accompanied by an invitation from the Judge to join him for lunch. This time I was pleased to accept, and found myself seated next to the wife of the High Sheriff – not the same High Sheriff who had appeared before Thesiger J a year or two before. Service was slow, in accordance with the custom of the people of Suffolk, and the lunch was rather languid, and so I got worried about getting back to the Court – a walk of more than a quarter of an hour – in time to see my client before resuming my cross-examination, and I became restive. "You must have the sweet," insisted the High Sheriff's wife. "It's my own personal recipe. I'll never forgive you if you go without sampling it. Don't worry, I'll see that you get back in time."

When I had finished this delicacy, and was even more anxious as an hour's luncheon had now extended extended to an hour and a half – but at least the Judge was still there, sipping coffee – the wife of the High Sheriff instructed me: "Go out of the building, turn right, and you'll find a black Daimler, our car. Tell the driver that the High Sheriff says that he is to drive you immediately to the Court."

I did as I was bidden. "What about the Judge?" asked the driver. "Don't worry about him," I replied, "these are the High Sheriff's orders."

"Well, I hope it's all right," commented the driver nervously, as we set off and got stuck in the worst traffic jam that I have ever seen in Suffolk.

Later – much later – Mr Justice Barry resumed his seat on the Bench (I think it was about three o'clock!) "I really must apologise to everybody for my late return from lunch," he announced, "but I am afraid that some unauthorised person borrowed my car. I should like to apologise in particular to you, Mr Crowther. I remember from my own days at the Bar how nerve-wracking it is not to be able to carry on with one's cross-examination just when one is expecting to do so."

In my mind I had a vague vision of a second black Daimler lying behind the one that I had taken, but it all seemed too complicated to explain, and in this moment of crisis an expression from the past – an expression of Roy – (which I now confess that I am ashamed to have uttered to such a wonderful Judge) came back to me, and I said:

"It's quite all right, Your Lordship. It's just one of those things."

Chapter 12

Odd Ways of Getting Work

Survival was the name of the game for the young barristers of the fifties. To pay the rent of Chambers and of the council flat in which I lived with my invalid sister and "Ug", our cat, required an enormous amount of effort, ingenuity and variety. The most lucrative work available was the factory work that I did just before Christmas, packing Christmas hampers; the least, attempting to sell brushes from door to door; but I found myself lecturing in various Victorian evening institutes all over London on almost every subject, legal and non-legal, under what passes in England for the Sun. A regular job (which V found for me) was teaching English each Monday morning during term-time at Dulwich College to a group of Siamese students who had somehow alighted there. Dulwich is a long way from Hendon by bus. The officials of the Council of Legal Education were always very kind to me – from 1955 until the present day I have been their Lecturer on Advocacy – and they introduced me to groups of Africans who required extra tuition in Bar subjects and who used to come to my flat every Saturday morning. (When I gave private lessons to a very rich and beautiful Turkish-Cypriot lady, I had to do this at her flat in Knightsbridge.) Ardo, Bello and Nasir, the first Northern Nigerians ever to study for the English Bar, were really very bright and a delight to teach, and all did very well back at home, Bello, whom I was to meet at a law conference in Malaysia in 1975, becoming Chief Justice of his region. The same epithets could not be applied to a student who came on a similar basis from Buganda. He was unbelievably dim and my Saturdays with him were desperately dreary. When I mentioned to the Secretary of the Council of Legal Education that my new pupil seemed to understand nothing, so that the whole exercise seemed to be a waste of the British taxpayer's money Mr Harvatt replied that the lessons must continue as a matter of politics and religion. I must have looked uncomprehending, for he went on to explain that the Bugandan authorities had complained that all previous law students from that country had been protestants from British missionary schools, and the catholics were up in arms about it (not literally) so they had been invited to send their brightest student on a scholarship – and this was he! So we struggled forlornly on, my trying to drum into him the elements of the Law of Contract from that eminently readable text-book, Cheshire and Fifoot (both fine lecturers at the C.L.E. during my student days.) Yet nothing seemed to get through. However, one Saturday he arrived with a smile on his face, the first I had seen. He had found and bought a book on Contract that he understood, he said. Needless to say, he had forgotten to bring it with him, but he assured me that he was studying it hard and understanding every word. He told me the author, a name that I did not recognise. "Well please bring it next Saturday," I asked. "I really want to see this wonderful book you're using." He did. It was "The American Re-Statement of the Law of Contract." I suppose that I ought to have been relieved – it might, after all have been a book on Contract Bridge – but I had had enough and got him transferred to Gibson and Weldon. It did not seem appropriate to move him to the other "crammers", the Rapid Results College! He took, and failed, the Bar exams eleven times. I think that he must have been the cause of the introduction of the "Four Attempts Rule" in the examinations.

Bill Kee was very kind as always: he transferred to me a weekly lecture that he did in Fulham at an evening institute. The subject was Company Law. Is there any more tedious subject in any discipline? And each year the Building Societies Institute came up with some rather lucrative lectures on Real Property of which I also knew almost nothing, the connection there being my work before I took up law for a few months at the headquarters of the Abbey National Building Society (at Sherlock Holmes's premises). But, lecture-wise, the barristers to whom I owed most in the struggle for survival were my dear friend Michael Scott, who introduced me to Kennington and Holborn Colleges, where he had lectured for a while before moving to France, and Brian Calwell. Brian, who had an in-built survival kit (he had an impossible clerk and attended Cambridge House and Mary Ward legal advice centres in the hope of finding work) had inherited the secretaryship of some legal

lecturing society founded originally by Lord Birkett – it seems that
even Sir Norman had a struggle at the beginning of his career (he had
also attended Toynbee Hall as a legal advisor) – and Brian really was
the director of lecturers par excellence in those days (and a very
good lecturer himself.) Brian even had me lecturing on Local
Government, which I had never even studied!

Toynbee Hall opened up new vistas. During the weekly session of
the legal advice centre we used to adjourn for dinner there, which
was another good reason for attending Toynbee every week. The
Warden at that time was a man called Mallon, who very kindly tried
to involve me more in the activities of the East End. He used to
arrange on behalf of the local dockers "Brains Trusts" of which the
members would usually be himself, the very outspoken Bishop of
Stepney, Bob Mellish, the local Socialist Member of Parliament and
one of the most caring Members I have ever met – he is now a Social
Democrat Member of the House of Lords – and myself. As a result I
sometimes found myself (through Toynbee) being briefed to appear
for dockers. The difficulty about these cases was that they usually
came before Sybil Campbell, who simply did not understand the
doctrine of dockers' "perks" and used to send them all to prison for
pilfering from ships in the docks. This, however, resulted normally
in two briefs, and the appeal was usually successful, the Judges at
Quarter Sessions generally replacing the term of imprisonment by a
fine which the other dockers clubbed together to pay. Through
these "Brains Trusts", I got to know a lot of dockers and generally I
liked them very much. I think that it is a tragedy that they allowed
their leaders, by their exorbitant wage demands backed up by
strikes, to price the London docks out of the market and render the
British docker an endangered species. It saddens my heart to
compare the deserted docks of London with the bustle of Hamburg
or Rotterdam.

But then Dr Mallon came to me with another proposition. "East
End people" he generalised "know nothing about the law except
that they distrust it. I would like you to try to rectify the position.
We will provide a room, if you will give a series of lectures on "Law
for the Masses.""

I did not like the title "Law for the Masses" – I was not sure that I
could cope with the masses, anyway – so I changed it to "Leading
Cases Make the Law." The idea was that each week we should look
at the facts of a well-known case and try to see its impact on the life

of the ordinary citizen. We started with *Donoghue v Stevenson 1932 AC 562*, the case of the snail in the ginger beer bottle, in which Lord Atkin examined for the first time since Christ had done so, the concept of "Who is my neighbour?"

I had never lectured to a "general" audience before, and on the first occasion they seemed a rather odd, even formidable group of people. There was the local roadsweeper, who sported a communist party badge and also the rather inappropriate name of King, and who every few minutes interrupted with: "What about the workers?" But he proved a regular attendant and I became quite fond of him, as I was also of Mr Stuart, a perpetual student with a long white beard who I felt was probably a contemporary of Socrates, and who used to interrupt much more gently with: "Yes, but what does it all *mean?*" There was a highly intelligent and delightful Jewish couple: at least I thought they were intelligent and delightful until they told me some months later that they were leaving the class because they had heard that I had become engaged to a German girl. But I had brightened when I saw one very pretty girl sitting in the front row. My joy was short-lived, however, for about half-way through my lucid exposition of the House of Lords' decision in *Donoghue v Stevenson* she rose up and asked in a pronounced Cockney accent: "Oh, this ain't the art class, then?" and marched out, never to be seen again.

There was an elderly Pole, who spoke no English, but the only one I really disliked was a sleek, smooth, lean young man, who would ask awkward questions like: "But hasn't there been a recent Divisional Court decision the other way?" or "How do you reconcile what you have just told us with the Interpretation Act?" I had had enough of this impudent young puppy, trying to trespass on my beneficent simplifications, I decided, and I would teach him a lesson. I had a short homily prepared, beginning with: "A little knowledge is a dangerous thing." Fortunately I never got round to uttering it – probably I did not have the courage – for on the evening for which it was planned he came up to me after the class and asked: "Do you practise in the Divorce Division?" "A little." I replied, fairly truthfully, having at that time prosecuted one undefended suit (possibly Lawrence's). "That's good," he commented. "I'll be sending some papers down to you in the morning."

"You'll be doing what?" I demanded, open-mouthed.

"I'm a solicitor. I've opened up an office in the Mile End Road and I'm looking for a barrister to do my work. Are you game?"

"Why, yes." I said gratefully, and next day the papers in Cave v
Cave, an extremely difficult defended divorce case, which I was to
lose, arrived. Indeed, nearly all Anthony's cases were very difficult –
he was a solicitor who liked to sail rather close to the wind – and I
lost nearly all of them; most of them were before Judge MacMillan.
However, he remained loyal to me, and was a guest at our wedding:
he was also Jewish, but did not seem to mind my marrying a German
girl; indeed he gave us a beautiful coffee percolator as a wedding
present, which we still treasure. So I was sorry rather than surprised
to read a few years ago that Anthony had been imprisoned for four
years for fraud.

Yet he briefed me loyally, although I lost so many of his cases: I
even lost an undefended divorce of his (before MacMillan, of
course, sitting in the High Court as a Special Commissioner). After
one of his cases in the Shoreditch County Court, which I had lost
before my least favourite Judge, my opponent came up to me and
said: "You ought to have won that. You put up a good fight but you
had a more difficult opponent in Judge MacMillan than in me. I'd
like to brief you in future. Where are your Chambers?" So I started
to get work from that solicitor, Mr Bowling, and after he died his
son continued to brief me until I left the Bar, and I seemed usually to
win their cases, even those that looked like losers. So good came out
of evil, but I am sure that Judge MacMillan would not be pleased to
know that he acquired a client for me! But it bears out my
contention that as a barrister you impress solicitors far more when
you lose cases than when you win them.

But perhaps my most unjust acquisition – or rather retention – of
a client arose from eavesdropping and taking advantage of the
brilliance of my opponent In the early part of the war my family
lived on the ground floor of a shared house in Hendon from which
we were evicted one snowy February night by the Luftwaffe, which
inconsiderately dropped a bomb in our front garden. This killed my
grandmother and deafened my mother and put my sister and me in
hospital for some weeks. Three months later, on the night after we
had moved into our next abode (also in Hendon) the Luftwaffe did
the same thing again but this time the only casualty was George, my
goldfish (who had survived the earlier bombing). My mother, who
had a horror of debt, insisted on the rent of our flat being paid
promptly, and every Saturday I was despatched with 32/6d to the

estate agent, M E Neal. There I often met Mr Neal's son, John, who was a little younger than I, but also went to University College School. Somehow he remembered me in later years and when a Scrooge-like client of his called Feldman, who lived in Ipswich but owned a lot of property in North-West London, had a case in Court and his Ipswich solicitor asked John Neal (who had now taken over his father's agency) if he wanted to recommend any particular barrister, John suggested me.

The case was related to business premises and was brought under the Landlord and Tenant Act 1949 before Judge Leon in the Willesden County Court. Mr Feldman must have held the title of the most greedy and unscrupulous landlord in London until Rachman came on the scene. I cannot remember the amounts, but let us say that the tenant was paying £400 per annum under his expiring lease and for a new one, in the days before inflation. Mr Feldman was demanding £1000, and this figure he had to justify. The unfortunate tenant – and I use that epithet advisedly – was represented by an elderly Welsh barrister called Jones. His cross-examination of the landlord was a masterpiece. At the end of it Feldman emerged, mopping his brow, as a miserly landlord of Dickensian or Shavian dimensions. Shylock looked generous by comparison. So many shady deals had been revealed in this rigorous and relentless questioning that Judge Leon, who loved a bit of drama, was suggesting that the Plaintiff's activities might have to be reported to the Director of Public Prosecutions. Feldman was trembling as, his ordeal completed, he emerged from the witness box just before 1 o'clock, the Court having adjourned for lunch. But as I moved towards the robing room I happened to hear the tenant say to his solicitor: "You must settle this case. Give him whatever he wants. I'm not going in that witness box to suffer like Mr Feldman. I tell you, I will not give evidence."

When I had removed my wig and gown, an ashen-faced Mr Feldman was standing there with the representative of his Ipswich solicitor and Feldman said to me: "Settle it, my dear, settle it. I can't stand any more of this. Let him have it for what he wants to pay: £400, if you like. But let's get away from here."

"Go and have some lunch, Mr Feldman" I said. "and leave it to me."

I did not go to lunch with them, partly because I did not like Mr Feldman, but mainly because I wanted to be available when Jones

201

approached me: and he did, at about a quarter to two. "Well, we've had our fun." he commented.

"What's the least you're going to make us pay."

"Mr Feldman has been claiming £1000," I replied accurately.

"Yes, but what's the best you can do for us? Don't be too hard, will you?"

"£950." I announced.

"And is that as low as you'll go?"

I felt that I had gone pretty low, but not in the sense that Jones intended.

"Yes, that's our limit," I announced. "£950, and" – remembering the matter closest to all solicitors' hearts – "and our costs."

"You're a hard man," said Jones, which coming from him, I took as a compliment.

"So, at two o'clock, the settlement was announced. Judge Leon (better known as the author Henry Cecil), shewed signs of astonishment: "Well, both parties are represented by counsel and are sui generis and appear to be of sound mind – or at least they did until a moment ago – so I suppose that I have no choice but to sanction this extraordinary settlement."

A few weeks later the next brief from Ipswich came, an action for damages for assault in the Cambridge County Court, in which I was briefed to represent the very disreputable defendant. I might have lost one of my best clients that day, for I went up to someone sitting outside the Court and asked: "Are you Mr Widdikins? I think I'm representing you in this case." "No" came the stern reply, "my name is Skippon and I'm a partner in Messrs Fison, your instructing solicitors in this case." But fortunately he did not take offence, and Ben and I became great friends, and from then on I was always briefed by him in all his cases, which were many, at the Suffolk Assizes and the Ipswich and Norwich Quarter Sessions. By going there I broke into something of a monopoly, because until then most of the work in East Anglia had been the prerogative of those two very able protagonists, Leslie Boreham and Michael Havers (who were to meet as Judge and Attorney-General in the Yorkshire Ripper Case) but I must say that they entertained my intrusion helpfully and without apparent resentment.

Ben was a fine solicitor. The amount of work that he put into the Rainbow Murder Case, described in more detail in "Advocacy for the Advocate" at pages 82 to 85, was phenomenal. And it was Ben who gave me that first murder case . . . .

"Why did you start briefing me in the first place?" I asked him, when we were celebrating "Terry" Thomas's acquittal.

"Well, you did so marvellously for that old villain Feldman. He said you were absolutely brilliant."

"Did he say anything about Mr Jones?" I enquired hesitantly.

Bill's Company Law lectures which I took over were from 8 to 9.30. At about 7.00 I was alone in Chambers reading the next few sections of the Companies Act 1948 so as to be a few steps ahead of those students who would remain awake that night. Suddenly Sidney burst in. Sidney was the clerk in the Chambers above Roy's, clerk to, inter alios, Lord Hailsham (Quintin Hogg in those days) Lord Diplock and Brian Calwell. Sidney's little weakness was ladies of the theatre, for whom his "governors" frequently had to appear for nothing. On one occasion Sidney entered Brian's room and announced: "Miss Diana Dors to see you, sir" and, to quote Brian: "in did come the strangest figure."

Sidney's entrance to my room that night was equally dramatic, if less glamorous. "Oh, thank God, you're here sir. This brief got overlooked, and it's for a new firm of solicitors, A R Drummond of Epsom, and it's at Kingston tomorrow. You will do it for us won't you, sir? Mr Hogg will be so pleased if you'll save the situation. (In fact Lord Hailsham has never expressed his gratitude, and I doubt if he was ever informed of how I became his Chambers' saviour.)

So next day I repaired to Kingston Quarter Sessions. It had not been inconvenient for me to accept the brief, as it was the first that I had had for over a month, but I suspect that my Company Law lecture was more imaginative than usual that night. The Chairman of Quarter Sessions was that extraordinarily kindly Judge, Tudor Rees, and he listened very patiently to what was probably an inordinately lengthy plea in mitigation, and the defendant, a young man with a bad record, pleading guilty to a number of serious offences, was put on probation.

"That was a marvellous result," said the representative of the solicitors, who had been present throughout the case. "Please give me your Chambers address and phone number. I'm Jim Parker, junior partner in A R Drummond of Epsom. You'll be hearing from us again."

I didn't, of course. As every barrister knows, you never do in these circumstances. Then Elke returned to England just before Christmas 1957, and I was invited by a lady I knew to a New Year Party, so I took Elke along in the middle of the night, after the celebrations at the British Council, which I had been running, had finished. Only when we reached Epsom, and the district of the party, did I realize that I had not brought with me the address. I remembered the name of the road, however, and said: "Never mind. We'll walk along here until we hear the sounds of merriment coming from a house, and that's where the party will be." The street was not a long one but was remarkably quiet for the early hours of the 1st January, until we came to the last house, whence emanated the most tremendous hullabaloo. "This will be the place," I announced reassuringly as we walked up the path and I rang the bell.

"I don't remember inviting you," said a rather drunken Jim Parker, "but you're the barrister who did that case for us so well. How long ago was it?"

"Four years," I volunteered.

"Well, never mind. Come in. You're very welcome, both of you."

So we stayed the night, met Jim's fiancée Janet and his partner Keith and Keith's secretary Doreen, and we had a wonderful time, and from then onwards I was constantly briefed by the firm of A R Drummond – even in the Divisional Court. Jim and Janet attended our wedding, and we theirs a few weeks later. Sadly that union resulted in a divorce, and Jim died, a disillusioned man, not long after the break-up of his marriage. Even more tragic was what happened to his partner Keith. Shortly after he married his secretary "D" – and what a wonderful couple they were – while on the way to visit his mother in the North of England somehow he got on the wrong side of the motorway and was involved in a terrible head-on collision with a lorry. He spent several weeks in hospital, where Elke and I visited him once, and, just as he seemed at last to be recovering, he relapsed and died. So, of the quartet that we met that New Year's night, now only D remains as our friend.

Solicitors can be fickle, but lay clients are often loyal. One of my earliest jury cases was that of R v Corper and Rogers, a charge of burglary heard in Court No 2 at London Sessions by dear, mild old Henry Elam. It was a Toynbee brief. The prosecutrix however was neither dear nor mild: a humourless vixen who afterwards became a

Judge. "Why are you wasting time over this case?" she demanded. "It's as plain as a pikestaff that they're guilty. If you carry on this charade, I warn you, I'll put the boot in." I looked unlingeringly at her legs and seemed to see at the bottom of them a pair of jackboots.

I could, however, see the point of her remarks, even if they might have been more kindly expressed, but William Corper was a man who on principle never pleaded guilty. The case as opened to the jury did appear rather formidable. Two policemen in the East End of London had witnessed the two defendants coming out of a block of flats (with which they had no legitimate connection) in the middle of the night carrying in their arms a number of trophies: radios, clocks and the like. The police ran after them, the defendants discarded their loot (afterwards recovered and found to bear the fingerprints of the two defendants), and a lengthy chase ensued, ending when they finished up locked in two lavatories on the staircase of another block of flats with which they had no connection. Each was alleged to have said, when dragged from his retreat: "It's a fair cop, guv"; and so it seemed.

The defendants' story was as follows: they were walking home after spending the evening in some East End hostelry when suddenly Rogers felt an irresistable urge to go to the lavatory. Being too much of a gentleman to urinate in the street, he set off at a rapid trot in the direction of a block of flats nearly a mile away where he knew that there were communal lavatories on the staircase. Corper, not wanting to be separated from his friend, trotted along beside him: their pace increased as Rogers' need became more urgent. They had not been in the first block of flats, had not touched the radios or the clocks, and the presence of their finger-prints on those objects could only be described as a freak – a double freak.

Corper was an ugly little man who looked like a burglar (which he was) and he had a pronounced stutter. When cross-examined by the prosecutrix as to why he had found it necessary to run into a lavatory and lock the door he replied: "Well, it's a s-s-sort of a s-s-sympathetic urge you g-get, you know." But what I felt was never satisfactorily explained was the fact that Corper was found in the ground floor lavatory whereas Rogers, whose need had been so great, was locked in the one on the fifth floor.

So my closing speech was very short: I could not think of much to say, except to burble on about the burden of proof and remind the jury that scientists could be wrong; after all, at one time they believed the earth was flat.

Henry Elam summed up fairly, as was his wont, and managed to keep a straight face as he briefly put the defence before inviting the jury to retire. They were out less than two minutes before returning verdicts of Not Guilty for both defendants.

I defended Rogers once more, this time on a shoplifting charge; and he was acquitted of that as well. But I was Corper's "brief" from that moment on, although I never succeeded for him again. He did more for me, after legal aid came in, by always going to different solicitors "just to help you in your career, Mr Crowther." He was a careless criminal, and always left his finger-prints. On one "job" he wore a mask, but he never wore gloves. The victim in that case was an elderly Pole. Corper had pleaded Not Guilty, as usual, and we were awaiting the jury's verdict after a rather strong summing-up from Frank Cassels. In the cell, making conversation, I said: "That Polish chap put himself forward as a bit of a hero, didn't he?"

"He was quite b-brave, actually," replied the "innocent" Mr Corper.

"I didn't hear that," I remarked: it was too late to do anything about it now, I felt.

"No." said Corper. "I mustn't imp-p-pugn your p-p-professional integrity."

After my defences of him Corper got sentences of eighteen months, two years, three years and five years (five for the time he wore the mask): and once Henry Elam put him on probation. But whatever happened, he remained loyal.

Not long after my appointment to the Bench, I was drafted to Thames Court, scene of my former battles with Colonel Batt. During my first week there, glancing down the register, I noticed the entry:-

Name of Defendant	Charge
William Corper	Burglary

But the age was wrong. It could have nothing to do with my erstwhile client. However, when the defendant emerged from the cells there was no doubt about it: the same stocky build, close-cropped hair, broken nose and cauliflower ear; only thirty years younger. "I knew your father," I informed him.

"Yes, Dad said I might see you 'ere." he replied cheerily. "'e sends you 'is best wishes and says congratulations on your hellivation."

"How is your father?" I asked, rather forgetting myself, and entering too much into the family spirit.

"Oh Dad's retired now," replied the defendant. "'e got too old for the job."

"And you've taken over the family business?"

"Well, in a manner of speakin', yes" replied William Corper Junior, with a wry smile.

But this story, too, has a sad ending. Many years later William Corper Junior appeared before me at Bow Street, charged with two burglaries of chemists' shops in London's West End. Forsaking the family tradition he pleaded guilty to both offences and the gaoler told me: "His parents are here, sir, and his father wants to speak on his behalf."

So frail old William Corper senior tottered forward with the aid of a stick. "Mr Crowther, you've got to 'elp me b-boy. Me wife's here" – he pointed out a rather nondescript elderly lady in the public gallery –"and she knows what I'm going to s-say. 'E's dyin', Mr Crowther, and we want you to save 'im. You're the only one 'oo can. Please, please give 'im the m-maximum p-possible. It's the only way to k-keep 'im from the d-dealers. It's the only way to s-s-save 'is life. Do it, Mr Crowther for old times' sake."

I knew as a matter of law that one should not give defendants custodial sentences so that they could receive treatment, or be kept away from drugs. The Court, we are often reminded, is not a welfare agency. But my wicked old friend's appeal was so moving that I gave way – perhaps "for old times' sake." Turning to the young Corper I said: "I sentence you to a year's imprisonment, after which I hope you will be fit to return to your loving parents and give them some comfort in their old age. I wish you and your family all the best."

In happier times when William Corper senior was convicted – and justly convicted – of his burglaries, I used to say, just before he was led away, that I was sorry not to have got a better result, and he would realise my disappointment and comfort me by saying: "Never mind, Mr Crowther, you can't win 'em all, and I'll never f-f-forget that f-f-first time when you got us such a m-marvellous result." I, for my part, have often wondered how it came about. Was it the nasty sarcasm of my opponent? I would like to think so, but frankly I believe it was my own inexperience and incompetence. I suspect that what really happened was that when they got into the jury room one dominant member of the jury demanded challengingly: "Them two never had a chance with that brief defending them, did they?" Chorus: "No."

"But we're going to give 'em a chance, aren't we?"

"Yes."

I can't think of anything else that could have been said in those two minutes that would have produced that "m-marvellous result."

Bar students and young barristers often put to me this conundrum: "Solicitors won't brief barristers without experience, but how can we get experience if they won't brief us? How can anyone make a success of the Bar?"

Sometimes, in my more sardonic moments, I reply: "Eavesdrop accidentally when your opponent is taking last minute instructions, gate-crash a solicitor's party, and do a jury trial incredibly badly. That's the way to succeed at the Bar."

Chapter 13

"The Sword of Honour"

"You are not a name-dropper. You're a place-dropper," a friend once said to me, and I took it as a compliment. I would not like to be thought a name-dropper, and I hope will not be stigmatised as one after completing this autobiography, although I think that the only great name with which I could claim close personal friendship is Lord Denning, who, during my years at the British Council, did so much for me on behalf of overseas students, especially Commonwealth students, for he really loved young people. For a long time he was their judicial hero, and I found it sad that they turned against him: I think because of his decision in the Court of Appeal in the "fares fair" case brought by the London Borough of Bromley (Kent) against the Greater London Council over London Transport. But Bromley had only one London Transport bus route, the 47, running very infrequently (if at all) through its borough to Liverpool Street. Why, then, should the burghers of Bromley have to subsidise those of Bow, with fifteen routes running through their patch? If Bromley ratepayers had to pay part of Londoners' fares, why should not those of Birmingham or Bradford also be called upon to do so? But the result of Lord Denning's utterly fair decision, upheld in the House of Lords, of whose speeches I have heard no criticism, was to make Denning, against whom some elements of the Press conducted a campaign of vilification, an enemy of the student populace, while Ken Livingstone, the then Leader of the Greater London Council, became a kind of young people's folk hero. Ken Livingstone has no doubt many admirable qualities, but in fairness, altruism and generosity he is not to be compared with Lord Denning.

I speak from experience. Lord Denning has been very kind to me. But his is the only great name with which I will claim affinity in this book, for I dislike "name-dropping," just as much as I disliked the "possession-dropping" habit of two members of Queen Elizabeth Building of boasting of their houses, their farms, their cars and their antiques – "genuine antiques," they were careful to point out; not the kind to be found in Elke's shop.

But "place-dropping;" now that is a very different matter, and to that offence I plead guilty. Since I began to be able to afford to travel, shortly after the move from Roy to Robert, I have visited about three-quarters of the countries of the world, usually staying with former members of the British Council Students' Centre; and my ambition is to visit the other twenty five per cent. Yes, I love travelling, and as a barrister I very much wanted to go to Germany to defend in Courts-Martial there. Of course, one could not tout or advertise, but one could ask one's clerk to put one's name on the list, so this I did, but I was never briefed to conduct any of these cases abroad. "Why is it," I asked Roy once, "that Brian Calwell gets asked to go to Germany once a month and I never get briefed to go there?"

Roy was equal to any challenge from his "men." "Well sir," he explained patiently, "they have a peculiar system in that office. They divide the work between the various initial letters, but then they give it all to those early on in the alphabet. Mr Calwell's second letter is "a", but yours being "r" you're a bit unfortunate." I thought of changing my name by Deed Pool to "Carter", but decided against it.

When I moved to QEB I asked Robert to investigate why I was getting none of this type of work and he found out that it was because Roy had not got round to putting my name on the list. But Robert advised against my joining it now, as work at home was so much more lucrative, and I was prepared to take his advice, although it meant that I was never to appear in the British zone of Germany, where I could have stayed with Elke's parents.

I suppose the place names that I drop most frequently are Gibraltar and Trieste. "Gib," to which the Navy transported me in 1943, was the first foreign territory on which I had ever set foot, and so it made a deep impression, even if Main Street was a bit basic. I was to revisit the Rock again more than forty years on and found that it had not changed much, except that most of the shops were now selling electronic equipment instead of bananas. After "Gib", I was sailing about in the Mediterranean for a bit, had a spell in Malta where the Naval Barracks comprised an old prison, rejected by the International Red Cross as being unsuitable for a prisoner-of-war camp, and then spent some time on a captured Italian cruiser, Il Duca d'Aosta, travelling mainly between Valetta and Taranto, before being transferred to a small tank landing craft with a crew of only twelve on which I made my leisurely way up the coast of Italy via Bari, Brindisi and Ancona to – Trieste. With Trieste, it was to be a case of love at first sight as, from a calm azure sea, I saw this fine white city rising up against a tri-coloured background: the green fields of Opicina, the brown hills beyond, and the black mountains of the hinterland. Viewed from the sea, Trieste is truly one of the most beautiful cities in the world; and I was lucky enough to observe it for the first time from the sea. There I was to spend twenty-one very happy months.

In both Gibraltar and Trieste I was to have first hand experience of service trials. In "Gib" I became friendly with a much older man called Alan. While I was there General Franco opened the border for the first time since the commencement of World War Two, and Naval servicemen were allowed to go across to Spain for day trips. Alan went, and recommended it to me, so we decided to go together. When we reached the frontier I discovered that I had forgotten my visa, and I had to go back for it. "Never mind," said Alan, "there's a pub just across the border on the edge of La Linea called "Las Siete Estrellas" ("The Seven Stars"): I'll be there, waiting for you."

An hour or so later I crossed the frontier in search of Las Siete Estrellas. I did not find it, but a little man kept following me, offering his help. There was something about him that I did not like, so I told him in a mixture of English, Spanish and Naval-ese to go away. He did not follow my instruction, but continued to hang around, so I said: "Take me to Las Siete Estrellas."

"You look for friend," he replied perceptively. "Your friend no there: I take you to friend."

"You don't know my friend, so please leave me alone."

"Si, I know your friend. He is Senor Calvo – Mr No Hair. I know your friend. I take you him."

This puzzled me, for Alan was indeed bald. He was nearly forty – which to me at eighteen seemed extremely old – and had been on Gibraltar since the outbreak of war. Some others in the same position who had never got away were beginning to resemble the upper inhabitants of the Rock. But clearly my first Spanish friend knew Alan and I felt that I had no alternative but to follow him. We passed Las Siete Estrellas and went through many dark alleys and "callejuelas", with me nervously looking round and hoping to find my way back, until eventually we came upon a square in what passed for the centre of that dreary town and we entered a house. There, to my surprise, I saw Alan, surrounded by young women, one of whom was firmly ensconced on his knee. Both she and he had glasses in their hands and Alan appeared exceedingly inebriated.

"Sientete," said a rather buxom, older woman, signalling me to be seated. "Which girl you like?"

"I don't think I like any of them," I answered. "I don't really know them."

At this point one of them landed on my lap. "Buy me a drink, carino," she ordered, and, before I had time to refuse, two glasses of colourless liquid arrived in our hands. Mine tasted awfully strong, but that of the girl looked different, so I took it from her and tasted it, and it had the unmistakeably insipid flavour of – water! I did not like this, so I announced: "Alan, I'm going. I'll wait outside for you for five minutes and if you're not there then I'm going on a tour of the town on my own." Almost exactly three hundred seconds later Alan emerged, looking sheepish – and drunk. He was followed by Madame (or should I say "La Senora"?) and all the girls, who were screaming at us in Spanish. I did not speak Spanish in those days, but I gathered that the gist of their complaint was that they had not been paid (or paid enough). Alan and I tried in vain to reason with them. A crowd developed. I do not know what Madame said to the crowd, but it had nothing to do with our all becoming members of the European Community, and the crowd became hostile, and started throwing stones and bricks at us. At that moment a bus went by and had to slow down at a junction. "Come on, Alan," I shouted, as I ran after it and mounted it, dragging him on board just as it was speeding off, leaving the angry crowd shaking their fists at us and uttering expressions which I think that even the "O" Level Spanish that I attained in 1985 would not have enabled me to understand. The bus was soon on the main road on its way to its first stop, Algericas, twenty miles or so away! When we enquired the time of the next bus back to the border town of La Linea we were told that it would go – "Mañana." So we were stuck in Algericas for the night, which, having almost no money, we slept in the enormous and impressive cathedral. On our return to Gibraltar next day we were immediately arrested for being absent without leave, and brought before the Captain. "You'd better do the talking, Eric," said Alan. "You're going to be a barrister. You've got the gift of the gab." So it was I who put forward the plea in mitigation on both our behalves, in much the same way that I have done in the preceding pages. The Captain listened quietly and courteously, and then gave his judgment:– "I don't believe a word of this," he announced "You're both of you a disgrace to the service. You will each of you be confined to ship for thirty days." This was my first experience of summary justice.

Within a few days of my arrival in Trieste I found myself in the clothing store ("slop room", in naval parlance) an old fashioned shop in Via Mazzini, which the Navy had commandeered, and where I worked and slept and where rats ran over my bed during the night. It abutted on to the street, from which my office was separated by an aperture covered only by bars – no glass. On the day on which my first rations of chocolate and cigarettes arrived, I put these in front of me on the desk at which I was trying to write, and almost immediately a crowd of children gathered around the opening shouting "Signor, cioccolate, per favore – PER FAVORE!," and making hand-to-mouth gestures that I have seen since only among the pathetic child beggars of India. I gave them some, believing that it would get rid of them. This was a mistake. Soon thereafter there was a much larger crowd outside, the original Trestini equivalents of the scunizzi having been augmented by all their friends and cousins.

The cinemas had just reopened in Trieste, but the only films available for shewing were the very old ones of Charlie Chaplin, Buster Keaton and Harold Lloyd. In those days, as now, I wore horn-rimmed glasses for reading and writing; in those days, unlike now, I was very thin. I sat trying to work on the accounts – at which I have never been any good, anyway – to the accompaniment of the now much louder and more strident supplications for "cioccolate, cioccolate." During a temporary lull in the chanting one little urchin, who had obviously recently seen one of the actors just mentioned, but could not properly pronounce his name, suddenly pointed at my gaunt bespectacled figure and shouted out: "Guardi, Carol Lloyd! Eccolo, Carol Lloyd!" From that moment onwards all my colleagues on the base started calling me Carol Lloyd, and to this day my five remaining close naval friends with whom I served in Trieste call me "Carol."

The cigarettes on my desk had a pleasanter outcome. I have never been a heavy smoker, and have not smoked at all since my thirtieth birthday. But on that first day, after the children had made off with their spoils, a very attractive Italian girl, ten years older than I, made her way into the office and, producing a quantity of lire, made me understand that she wished to buy some of the cigarettes that now stood alone on my desk. I was still very naive in those days, and knew nothing of the black market in which nearly all the other servicemen in Trieste were actively engaged, so I divided the cigarettes into two halves and charged the girl exactly what I had paid for her half, and they were indeed duty free, unlike those that one buys nowadays at airports.

Evalina was clearly impressed, because she was back in half an hour, and in some miraculous way – for she understood no English, I no Italian – made me understand that mamma had invited me to dinner, and that night, in their sparsely furnished flat just above our magazzino vestiario I had my first plate of true Italian spaghetti, washed down by a wonderful chianti. I was in charge not only of clothing, but also of mess traps (knives, forks, spoons, etc.) and of the distribution of that wonderful libation known as "Pusser's Rum", some of which I took with me on that first visit. Papa was very enthusiastic about it, and made me understand that he liked a little rum in his tea. (Later on I had the impression that he liked a little tea in his rum.) Papa seemed very old (men of sixty-five are very old when you are eighteen) but Mamma (who died last year) was much younger, and Evalina, the oldest of their children, had two sisters and two brothers. After dinner Evalina and I conversed in our only common language –Latin. Latin does not make for lively conversation, and I decided that I had to learn Italian, especially as I was working with twelve Italians, only two of whom spoke any English; and I did learn to speak that beautiful language quite fluently in the next twenty-one months.

The family had just escaped from Yugoslav persecution in Zara, where they had lived for many years. They had reached Trieste in a small boat with few belongings; all were unemployed and they seemed very poor, and, as they had become my friends, I felt under an obligation to help them. Some of my gifts had great durability. I think that when we visited the now much more affluent family on our honeymoon, Elke was rather shocked to observe that their cutlery bore the imprint "R N Base, Trieste". But they were worth helping, and almost every evening I would find myself in the delightful company of "my Italian family". Only Beppi, the younger brother, let me down a bit. I got him a job as a driver with my Commanding Officer, who used to comment bitterly on the difficulty that Beppi had in arriving in time for duty in the mornings. "If he weren't your brother-in-law, Carol Lloyd, I'd sack him right away," he complained.

So everybody called me Carol Lloyd, and I assumed a new personality. Up in the barracks my weekly rations were set out under the name "Carol Lloyd". Then my very good friend John Guyatt, who knew of my former identity, brought down a second lot. "I think these are yours too," he said. "They were left there under the name of Crowther, so I paid for them and brought them over." So every week those responsible for setting up the rations put out a set for Carol Lloyd and another for the mysterious and quiet individual named Crowther, who never seemed to appear to take them, always having them paid for and brought away by someone else, and for the whole of my time in Trieste I drew double rations, sharing the cigarettes with Evalina and the cioccolate with the screaming children. I suppose that I should have been Court-martialled for this regularly repeated crime, along with the misappropriation of the rum and the mess traps, but I was never caught. But Justice has an odd and sometimes perverse way of asserting herself, and right at the end of my naval service I did suffer the ignominy and the anxiety of a Court-martial for a matter in which I felt completely blameless.

It all arose from my farewell party, of which I still have an invitation card and the menu. This took place in the naval clothing store, which by now had moved to much larger premises in the Molo Bersaglieri on the seafront. Parties in the clothing store were quite usual, and generally gave rise to no problems, the sentries on the gate being friendly and understanding. So all our guests, service and civilian, arrived without any difficulty. "Tubby", the well-named Italian waiter from the delightful restaurant opposite, "Pepi Granzo", brought food and wine from that excellent establishment (how sad I was on my next visit to find the restaurant closed and that the owner had committed suicide) and he passed it through the window into the office, converted now into a dining room. (The window was about ten feet high, so we had to provide a chair for Tubby to stand on during his important errands, and we were surprised and relieved when this did not collapse.) Good food, fine wine, excellent company, plenty of rum, witty speeches with dancing to romantic Neapolitan music – what more excitement could one expect from one's farewell party after twenty-one months? Well, quite a lot more was to come ....

It so happened that, after the last of my guests had arrived, a large British cruiser drew alongside the Molo, on the opposite side to the clothing store. On board was a Commodore, an officer of higher rank than any that we had on the naval base. He was a vain man, and immediately took over command, relieving our sentries of their duties and replacing them by his own. Our sentries did not mind in the least, but, unfortunately, they made for the nearest bar without informing me of what had occurred. The new sentries, unaccustomed to the free and easy ways of HMS Oboe (the code name for R N Base, Trieste) were astonished at the mass exodus from the clothing store in the early hours of the morning. The report that reached the Commodore a few hours later stated: "Between 4 and 5 am large numbers of persons, both naval personnel and civilians, women as well as men, left the clothing store in varying degrees of intoxication, making their way noisily through the main gates into the town."

In the morning the Commodore made his way to the clothing store. Ignoring the sign which read "Closed for Stocktaking", he knocked angrily until I arose from my bed to afford him entrance. He seemed none too pleased by what he saw, and was unsympathetic to my fragile state of health. Having established that it was I who was responsible for running the store and the party, he announced: "You're on a charge, a charge of conduct prejudicial to good naval order and discipline." I had already volunteered to stay on in the Navy for an extra six months because I enjoyed so much the life in Trieste, and this decision extended my stay for two more worried weeks. (It would have probably been longer, had not the sojourn in Trieste of the cruiser, whence were to come the three prosecution witnesses, been limited to a fortnight.)

My Supply Commander was a remarkable man. His predecessor, who worked long hours trying to sort out the muddle caused by *his* predecessor, finished up, as did so many in Trieste, with being Court-martialled for fraud, while in fact if anyone deserved to be prosecuted it was the officer from whom he had taken over. This Commander would have none of that. His brilliant, incisive mind, enabled him to work only half of each day, devoting the remainder to a variety of enjoyable recreations. He looked exactly like Orson Welles, and behaved a bit like him in "Citizen Kane". He had attended the party with his mistress and had made a brilliant valedictory speech, and it was to him that I went for advice.

"Whom should I have as prisoner's friend?" I asked.

"Nobody," he replied. "You're going to defend yourself. You're going to be a barrister, aren't you? This will be your first case, and you're going to win it." (I refrained from telling him of the disastrous result of my real first case in Gibraltar.)

"How am I going to win it, sir? I mean, really, technically, I suppose I'm guilty, aren't I?"

"Rubbish," exploded the Commander. "I'll have none of that defeatist talk. I'll tell you how you're going to win it. You'll plead Not Guilty and then say absolutely nothing. Don't ask anybody any questions. None of them bears you any malice, so they will only be telling the truth anyway, and you'll only make it worse by asking questions. Leave them alone. The Court will be surprised, and waiting to hear your side of the case."

"Yes, that's what I'm afraid of," I opined.

"What nonsense," he exclaimed. "I'll be there, and ask permission to call me first. Say that I've got an urgent appointment or something. They'll agree. Then leave it to me, and stop worrying."

(I was to think of this advice twenty years later, when I had to defend Jean, the wife of the gangleader Charlie Richardson. It embodied good psychology and I would have made it work, if Charlie had not "sacked" me towards the end of the committal proceedings.)

The Court-Martial itself was quite short. It was held in Navy House, Trieste, and it finished in the morning. I did as I was bidden, and held my peace as the Commodore and the two sentries gave their evidence –rather convincingly, I thought. Shyly, I declined the offers to cross-examine. The "Judges" were all officers specially brought up from Malta, as all the officers on HMS Oboe and on the small ships (mainly minesweepers) that we served, knew me too well to try me. The Commodore had picked up in the store an invitation card to "Carol Lloyd's Farewell Party". The Presiding

217

Officer asked: "Who on earth is this Carol Lloyd?" It seemed too complicated to enlighten him.

Then my turn came, and I made my request for the Commander to give his evidence first and this was agreed. Following his instructions, I asked him just two questions:–

"Were you at the party?" and "What did you think of it?"

To the second he replied (I hope not accurately): "Dullest party I've ever been to. Never really got off the ground. Trouble was there wasn't enough to drink. I suppose poor old Crowther couldn't afford a proper supply on his pay as a Petty Officer."

I sat down in amazement, and the eager Lieutenant who had been deputed to prosecute me, rose to cross-examine:–

"What time did you leave the party, sir?" he enquired.

"About six in the morning," replied the Commander, truthfully this time.

A cunning glint came to the Lieutenant's eye: "Sir, if the party was as dull and as abstemious as you are suggesting, why did you remain there all night?"

"I'll tell you," replied the Commander. "I'd have dearly loved to have gone earlier, as I had much better things to do" (I thought of his mistress, whom I had met for the first time at my party) "but Crowther's a good chap and this little party meant a lot to him. He's worked hard and conscientiously in that store for the last twenty-one months and he's done a good job. I like him – he's a bit dull and unimaginative of course –but, frankly, I didn't want to hurt his feelings."

"No more questions," said the Lieutenant, rather desperately.

"I think we'd better retire," observed the President of the Tribunal, and, on his return a few minutes later, he announced:

"We don't want to waste any more time on this case. The charge is dismissed."

My relief and gratitude were intense. I do not think that I would have been given "jankers" (imprisonment) so near the end of my naval service, but, if found guilty, I should have at least been awarded a dishonourable discharge, which would have prevented my joining the Honourable Society of Lincoln's Inn, and becoming a barrister.

"Going to have another party before you leave?" the Commander asked me, on the way out. "The cruiser's leaving in a couple of days."

"No thank you, sir," I replied. "The last one was quite memorable enough for me."

But the incident had demonstrated rather forcefully an axiom that I was often to hear at the Bar: "A good witness is worth more than a good advocate."

This did not prove to be the case the only other time that I participated in a trial in Italy. Guido had started work with us as one of the twelve labourers who worked in the Clothing Store in Trieste, replacing twelve naval ratings (and I have to say that the Italians worked far more willingly and efficiently). Guido was so bright and keen that I promoted him to do the accounts, which for the first time were properly kept. (I had been doing them up to that time). Then one morning I learned that Guido had been arrested by the Venezia Giulia police for "collaboration with the enemy". The "enemy" meant the Germans, Italy's ally until two years before. Guido had been very friendly with a high-ranking German officer. When the partisans had come seeking that officer to exact the same sort of brutal vengeance upon him that they had meted out to their former leader Mussolini, Guido had hidden him in his home and enabled him to escape. (He would, pari passu, have done the same for me, I am sure.) The truth had come out, Guido admitted his terrible crime of saving the life of his friend, and I went along as a character witness.

Although by now I spoke fluent Italian, the Court insisted that I addressed it in English, which was "translated" by an interpreter, employed by the prosecution. I have put the word "translated" in inverted commas because what was produced was a watered down version of what I was saying. When I referred to Guido as being an excellent and reliable worker this became "a fairly reliable worker"; when I said that he was always punctual this became "usually punctual". It was clear that the Court was not to be allowed to hear anything markedly in Guido's favour and when, eventually, I protested and started to address the Court in Italian the prosecutor began to shout me down and the Presiding Judge ordered my removal from the Court. A few minutes later Guido's little wife left the Courtroom weeping, and told me that her husband had received a sentence of twenty years' imprisonment. We never heard of Guido again, but I suppose that he was released not long after in one of those amnesties by which the Italians clear their gaols, an unjust practice which I hope that we shall never follow, for Justice should never be expedient and capricious. I love and admire so many things about the Italians, but their system of Justice, which I do not think has improved much in the intervening years, is not one of these.

So, thanks to the Commander I was able to fulfil my ambition to practise at the English Bar, even if Roy did not enable me to appear as an advocate in Courts-Martial in Germany. But I did, under Robert's regime, appear in six Courts-Martial in England, two for each of the armed services, and I have to say that it was only those conducted by the Navy that impressed me favourably. The circumstances of one of these I will recite in detail.

The jury had stayed out a long time, and it was nearly seven when I returned to Chambers. "Thank God you're back, sir," said Robert. "You're doing this return of Mr Burge in Portsmouth Barracks tomorrow. Mr Burge is still in the Stephen Ward trial. I've fixed a conference for tonight at 9.30. Get on your way to Waterloo. Ronald's bought you the ticket ...."

To this day I maintain my naval connections. I am writing this at HMS Raleigh at Torpoint in Cornwall, where I come three times a year to lecture on Evidence – to Supply Officers.

James Burge was the head of Chambers at Queen Elizabeth Buildings (if one excludes Robert). He was a man of few words, most of them impolite, and extraordinarily mean. Generally speaking, the Bar is a generous profession, but two of my three heads of Chambers were among the stingiest men I have ever met. Burge had a huge practice, largely in licensing, a particularly lucrative field; he was really the king of licensing. One morning, at Willesden, I achieved a double victory. Burge was my opponent in a licensing matter and I won the case. It was just noon on a very hot day and, seeing him set off from the Court with a purposeful look, I followed. He had a great liking for his beer, so I knew where he was going. When, in the nearest local hostelry, he ordered a pint of bitter I sidled up and said quietly to the barmaid: "And the same for me. This gentleman is paying," and I winked at her and she winked back understandingly at me. Burge had put down a £1 note and there was very little change (there would be none now) so he complained: "Heh! Where's the rest of my money?" "There isn't any more," laughed the girl, "you're paying for your friend."

"Well I'll be ———," burbled Burge (I will leave the reader to insert the participle; "expletive deleted," as said ex-President

Nixon) "Of all the bloody cheek!" Back at QEB I was assured that I was the first member of the Bar who had ever got a drink out of our Head of Chambers!

Burge lived on the South Coast, and used to get away on the Brighton Belle as soon as possible. I therefore had no chance to talk to him about the case that I was to do for him next day which, as it turned out, was just as well. As I read my brief on the train that evening I realised that this was an important case: not a matter of life and death, perhaps, but one in which the immediate jewel of a man's soul, his good name, was in danger of being sullied. The defendant was a Lieutenant-Commander of over thirty years honourable service, due for retirement in a few months' time, and charged with indecent assault on four of the boys on the training ship of which he was currently in command. The conference took place in the hotel in Portsmouth where I was to spend the night, a rather sleepless one, for I was worried about my client. His defence was, quite simply, that the allegations were all lies: he was a strict disciplinarian and some of the modern intake into the Navy resented authoritarian discipline; this was their way of getting their own back. After the conference my instructing solicitor and I had dinner with him and his wife. I must say that I liked my client. His reputation, his pension, his whole life were at stake, but he made no attempt to "wring the withers".

I entered Portsmouth Barracks soon after eight next morning. It was my fourth visit to the most depressing place in which I have ever lived. The first time I went there it was for drafting, and I learned that I was to be sent to Trincomalee. During embarkation leave I fell ill with sinusitis, and I could not go there. A few years ago I did visit it, at the invitation of Krishnan Viknarasah (Vicky) who had been quite the most outstanding member of my British Council Debating Group, and I found it a most beautiful natural harbour. I would not have been able to admire its beauty in 1943, however, as the ship carrying my draft to Ceylon (as "the island of dusky trees" was named then) was sunk by a Japanese submarine and there were no survivors. My second visit took place a few weeks later, when I revisited "HMS Victory II", as the barracks were called, for redrafting, this time to Gibraltar – and La Linea .... (both of which I revisited last year for the first time in forty-four years: "Las Siete Estrellas" està siempre alli!); and the third was for the purpose of return to civilian life – being given a demob-suit, an identity card and a small gratuity.

But the fourth visit was to comprise the hardest day's work I had ever experienced. The Court-Martial sat at nine in the morning and began with the defendant being divested of his sword which lay before him throughout the proceedings, the handle facing him. If he were convicted on any charge, the sword would face the other way.

We had a half-hour break for lunch in the Officers' Mess and the Judge-Advocate finished his summing-up as the clock struck nine that night. At the beginning the Presiding Officer had said that the proceedings would have to be concluded that day as he was "operational" tomorrow, but thereafter no attempt was made to hurry the proceedings, which were conducted with great dignity and consideration. (May I comment in passing how much fairer is the Navy's system of opening the proceedings with the prosecution presenting its case by way of the "circumstantial letter", setting out in writing the main facts on which it relies, than is the system in ordinary jury trials of the proceedings being opened by counsel for the prosecution, most of whom present the case in a balanced and impartial way, whereas a few of them confuse a duty to prosecute with a licence to persecute?)

For a while the case seemed to be going well. The first three ratings to give evidence were nasty, vindictive youths and it required no great skill in cross-examination to shew them up for the pernicious little liars that they were. But with the fourth boy matters were quite different. He had an angelic appearance, and the longer he gave evidence the more convinced did everyone (including myself) become that he was telling the awful truth. I cross-examined him gently, but not for long, as I realized that I was losing ground all the time. I became very depressed as to the likely outcome.

My closing address was brief. I dilated for a little while on the defendant's excellent war record and his long loyal service without previous complaint (it is a matter of amazement to me how many advocates do not put in their client's good character, often his best asset, when this is available to them); on the improbability that a happily married man with children – I had called the wife to give evidence – would succumb to temptation in the way alleged when so near to retirement, thereby jeopardising both his fine reputation and his substantial pension rights. I went on something like this:–

"I appreciate that time is precious in this case, and that the hour is now late. I shall not waste time discussing the allegations made by the first three complainants. I would venture to suggest that there is no tribunal in the land which would convict on their lying testimonies. I cannot, alas, say the same of the fourth witness. I concede that he appeared to be a decent, honest lad and that I made no headway at all in my cross-examination of him. But when you come to consider your verdict, will you please take into account the fact that he is serving on the same small ship as the other three, living with them, day in, day out, at close quarters? Is there not just the chance, and therefore the real risk, that he has been influenced, even corrupted, by the other three?''

The summing-up of the Judge-Advocate was very fair – as fair as are most summings-up nowadays, when we have very independently-minded Judges in the Court of Appeal, not always seeing their prime duty as upholding the verdict of the Court below, and a good deal fairer than were most summings-up to juries of those days.

There is another difference between Courts-Martial and criminal proceedings in the civilian Courts, in that the Court-Martial remains in situ to reach its decision while the parties withdraw. The two hours we spent in the corridors outside the vast room used for the trial constituted an agonising experience for all of us, especially, of course, for the Lieutenant-Commander, and it was after eleven at night when we were invited back in. Imagine our relief to see the sword with the scabbard still facing towards the prisoner! He was allowed to retrieve it. He was still deemed to be a man of honour, an officer and a gentleman.

The last train to London had gone by now, but the Navy very kindly found me a bed in the Ward Room. On the way back next morning I started for the first time to think about the law in the case. The indictment, or its naval equivalent, might be considered oppressive, with four charges relating to separate incidents on different occasions and with different boys. I could have applied to the Judge-Advocate to have had the charges severed and heard separately by different tribunals if I had had time to think about it, on the ground that the prejudicial effect of all the evidence being heard together would outweigh its probative value. If I had done this, and my application had succeeded – as it should have done – the Lieutenant-Commander would have been acquitted of the first three charges and convicted of the fourth. Where ignorance is bliss ....

223

Burge blundered into my room late that afternoon. "Well, how did you get on with that case of mine?" he demanded.

"Rather well, I think," I replied, without undue modesty.

"Did you apply to have the indictment severed?"

"Er – no, I didn't."

"Then you're a bloody fool."

"But we won the case, James. He was acquitted of everything."

"You should have got the indictment severed. You're a bloody fool," he adjudged, as he stormed out of the room.

Chapter 14

The Princess and the Flat

"What a lovely little flat," my friends exclaim in envy when they visit me in Lincoln's Inn. "However did you manage to get it?" "Well actually," I reply modestly, "I got it through Princess Margaret." And I think the claim is not wholly false. The flat itself is not the most convenient in London. To reach it one clambers up fifty-six narrow stairs, assisted, when one has dined too well in the Inn, by wooden pegs inserted at intervals horizontally into the stanchions. The kitchen is the smallest in London (one has to stand in the tiny hall to cook), one has to be an acrobat to take a bath, and the head is liable to suffer against the sloping roof of the bedroom if one wakes up too suddenly. It was built in 1599 and is charming and quaint and has what the surveyors like to call "Scarcity Value."

Soon after I changed from having Roy as my clerk to having Robert in that capacity, I became extremely busy. Some of the cases in which I found myself defending were "long term frauds", often lasting several weeks, in which vast piles of papers had to be digested. Two precious hours of each day were wasted in travelling between home and the Old Bailey (or Chambers); the journey had to be made by car because the papers were usually too cumbersome to take on the underground and bus. I would come home, have dinner and then settle down to work far into the night. Except over dinner I seldom spoke to my children save to say: "Be quiet. Daddy's trying to work." The busy barrister is seldom the ideal father. How wonderful it would be to have a quiet flat in the peace of Lincoln's Inn, to which I could retire straight after Court, emerging only to have a quick, good, and relatively cheap dinner in the lovely New Hall there! So I applied several times, always unsuccessfully, being told: "These flats are given on seniority, and you are still very young." (I was forty by now!) And so my applications for flats went on being turned down until ....

One Tuesday afternoon Colonel Bridges, the Under-Treasurer of the Inn, phoned me in Chambers. "Eric," he said, "You know that Princess Margaret is our Treasurer this year. She's suddenly discovered that she is free next Monday evening and she wants "her" students to perform a mock trial for her. It's ridiculous, of course – less than a week's notice – and none of our barristers wants to do it, but it's a Royal Command. You're our last hope. What do you say?"

I could well understand the reluctance of the majority of the members of Lincoln's Inn, who belong to the Chancery Bar, out of whom one is lucky to get an opinion in a year, to take on such a rush job, but I was a criminal lawyer, accustomed to being given my cases the night before. To have six days for preparation was a luxury! So I replied: "Provided I can do it my way, and have the fullest co-operation from the Benchers, I'll take it on." These rather far-reaching conditions were accepted and I settled down to the job of writing the script of a murder trial. Her Royal Highness agreed to be foreman of the jury, which was to comprise Benchers and students in equal numbers. I cannot remember who was the Judge – possibly the pro-Treasurer, Mr Justice Buckley, a very friendly man. As usher I appointed an Old Bailey Judge, Edward Clarke QC, before and against whom I had often appeared, who had been an actor before coming to the Bar (there is a lot of affinity between the two professions) and he played the role of this crusty Court official to the manner born. Buckley J too had come from a background of the theatre. My own role was that of a kind of instructing solicitor to everybody. As the prosecutor I had Mohamed Ardo, one of my Nigerian spondees, who had stayed on to be my pupil, and as defence counsel – Rudy Narayan.

Rudy was, and is, a charismatic and flamboyant character. He has done many things since pleading before Princess Margaret. He has built up a busy practice in two cities, London and Birmingham. He is head of his set in London, which, unusually, operates outside the confines of the Inns of the Court, in a building which he has called "Justice Chambers". He has written a number of books, usually in a racy hurried style. His use of epithets is more abundant than that of any writer since Dickens, but the manner of his writing is in some wise reminiscent of James Joyce. He married a tall and beautiful Pakistani girl whom he met, I regret to say, at one of my parties. "I regret to say" because I had seen Naseem looking lost and lonely in the British Council Students' Centre and asked her over for a festivity that I was to give that Saturday, and Rudy was always a welcome guest at my parties in those days (as was I at his). Alas, their marriage was to end in a divorce, and brought misery to both of them and, doubtless also, to their two children. But if Rudy built up a good practice at the Bar, Naseem was to be at least equally successful in her practice as a doctor in South-West London, and derives much satisfaction from that. Rudy is reputed to have offered himself as a Parliamentary candidate to each of the main political parties: perhaps he should decide which he really wants, or which really wants him. He has flirted with Black Power and been instrumental in setting up a Society for Black Lawyers; but are black lawyers different from other lawyers? I think not. He often appears as the spokesman of the black community on radio and television. He spent two years in the British Army, serving in Cyprus, and returning with a sergeant's stripes. His "in-Court" rows with many Judges, some of whom think that he provokes quarrels with the Bench in order to gain the sympathy of the jury, have led to his being suspended from practice from the Bar more than once. On the most recent occasion when this was threatened I read in "The Times" that Rudy had written to Mr Gorbachov asking him to intervene .... Other Judges, including Lord Scarman, have praised Rudy's powerful and courageous advocacy, and on the few occasions on which he has appeared before me he has behaved impeccably. No one could possibly ever accuse Rudy of being inactive or lazy; he has the great merit of being a "character", and characters brighten the world, especially the legal world.

I first came across Rudy as a loyal, regular and able member of my British Council Debating Group. Once he won the competition that I organised at the British Council to find the best student speaker of the year. As a young man Rudy shewed promise, and I wanted to help him, and I felt that I could.

He would face the same problems over finding a pupillage and Chambers as I had endured, so I introduced him to Sir Antony Buck, who agreed to take him on as his pupil, and was so impressed with him that he strongly supported Rudy's candidature for a seat in those small, happy, respectable – if not highly successful – Chambers. Unfortunately Rudy who, like many of us, is undoubtedly his own worst enemy, queered his pitch in two ways:

having lost one of his early cases he wrote to the Judge concerned in the most vitriolic terms of abuse to complain of the Judge's conduct of the case. (I wrote to Judges to complain – in mildly reproachful terms – twice; both times to rather distinguished Judges but both times late on in my career; neither replied); and then, when a party took place in Chambers, and the Head of Chambers, Sir Arthur Irvine QC, then Solicitor-General, came over, glass in hand, to greet Rudy warmly with the words: "Well, how nice to see you again, my dear fellow," Rudy, outshining even Molière's "Misanthrope", replied: "What are you talking about? You've never seen me before in your life, you stupid old fool!" Even so, I think that Rudy resented and could not understand the fact that he was not offered a seat in those Chambers.

But Murder before Margaret took place long before that happened, while Rudy was still a student. He conducted the defence extremely well, and, if I recall correctly more than twenty years on, he won the case, and the whole evening was a pronounced success, all the Benchers being very sporty and in good spirits. Afterwards Her Royal Highness invited all the main participants into the Benchers' Room to join her for port. After we had been there for quite a long time I was surprised to realize that the Princess was beckoning me to go over to her. "You, I believe, were responsible for organising all this?" she demanded. I admitted that this was the case.

"How well do you know that fellow who played the part of the defence lawyer?" she asked next.

"I think, very well" I replied.

"Well, do you know, he's just asked me to a party," she went on. "What are his parties like?"

I drew a deep breath. "Well, if Your Royal Highness can imagine a basement room in Clapham, with a hundred people dancing together in a room that might comfortably hold thirty, the atmosphere filled with smoke which can't escape because the windows are closed and sealed on account of the frequent complaints of the neighbours of the noise coming from the record player – noise so loud that it precludes the possibility of any normal conversation as the guests dance cheek to cheek (and even closer) – and alcoholic refreshment being liberally served throughout from a large bowl into which all the offerings of those present have been indiscriminately poured on arrival – well, that's the general atmosphere of Rudy's parties."

Princess Margaret pondered a moment as she flicked the ash off her cigarette, and then she smiled seriously and announced her decision: "I think I'd better not go," she said pensively. Sorry, Rudy!

A few weeks later my little flat in the Inn was advertised as being to let. It was just what I wanted, a bijou pied-a-terre – or, more accurately – a pied-au-ciel, so I applied – and this time I was successful. That is why I always claim that I got it through Princess Margaret – by Royal Appointment ....

Chapter 15

Differing Attitudes to the Police:

The Kray Twins and the Richardson Gang

Just as there is no stereotype of the barrister, there is no common mould for the criminal. During the duller moments of a morning in Court I sometimes look around those waiting to come on, trying to guess who will be defendants and who are plain clothes police officers. On the whole the defendants are more smartly dressed, but otherwise it is very difficult to distinguish between the two groups.

There was nothing physically remarkable about the Krays when I met them. Perhaps it was because they were such celebrated clients that Robert said: "You've got a conference with the Kray Twins this afternoon, sir. I think you'd better use Mr Jeremy's room." (He always referred to Jeremy – now Lord – Hutchinson, QC, as "Mr Jeremy", an affectionate form of appellation not employed for any other member of QEB.) So I was ushered into the small room of one of the leading silks in the country, overlooking the verdant Temple lawns, where Ronald and Reginald Kray were waiting for me with my instructing solicitor.

The Krays complained they had been libelled. An article on the front page of the "Sunday Pictorial" had shown Lord Boothby sitting smiling between the two of them, all with glasses in their hands, and had asked: "What is one of Britain's leading peers doing with two of the country's most notorious criminals?" and it went on to hint at the possibility of a homosexual relationship. It was all quite untrue, of course. Lord Boothby had wanted to raise money for a charity and the Krays had their methods of raising funds (and indeed did a lot for charities) and they had just been celebrating a successful joint fund-raising effort. Lord Boothby, for whom I did not act, got huge damages in an out-of-Court settlement. The Kray

Twins, my clients, got only a brief and grudging apology and their costs. But I had to advise them to accept this, and they did.

They had been tried at the Old Bailey for serious offences of violence, but acquitted. Implicit in the newspaper's description of them was that the jurors' verdict was perverse, and that they should be behind bars. The jury or juries which had acquitted them had to be satisfied beyond reasonable doubt before registering a conviction; the newspaper, to succeed in its defence of justification, would have to prove only on the balance of probabilities that the jury's verdict was wrong, and all the old mud would be raked up again. It had to be said that they were in a very different category from Lord Boothby, and I could not be sure that they would win.

They accepted my advice with a good grace. They were easy clients; most professional criminals are, treating crime as a sport – a professional sport – in which not all the matches can be won. Yet for all their affability there was something sinister about them, and as they left the little room I did something that I never did before or since in any situation: I rushed to open the window and breathe the pure Temple air from outside. I felt an evil presence in the room and I had to expel it. The "evil spirits" of my Cambridge House Chinaman had entered into Mr Jeremy's room at QEB.

I did not defend the Krays before Mr Justice Melford-Stevenson in the protracted case which resulted in their receiving sentences of, I believe, twenty-five years each. I was in the case early on, but by the time it came for trial I was on the Bench. They were pleasant clients, though, and expressed gratitude that anyone would defend them, after what they were alleged – and ultimately found – to have done. In fact it was that veteran of the Left and most able advocate John Platts-Mills who defended them, on legal aid. The prosecution put forward their gang control of and gang warfare in the East End of London as a giant military operation, with one of the Krays – I think Reggie – as Commander-in-Chief. This was just a figment of fervent police imagination, according to the Krays. Yet while Platts-Mills was making his passionate final address on their behalf to the jury, in the face of some sardonic interventions from the ultra-Conservative Judge, he got a note from Reggie Kray which read something like this: "Well done, my boy. Keep it up. If you carry on like this you'll get promotion – the Colonel." It shewed, coming from a man about to receive a twenty-five year sentence, a good sense of humour.

There was nothing humorous about Charlie Richardson. In the

fifties and sixties the Krays ran the East End, while Charlie's sphere of influence with his protection rackets lay South of the River. (Another gang called the Tibbs Brothers, also jailed for long periods, were in charge of North London.) Although in the Richardson case I seemed to be receiving all my instructions from Charlie, in fact the person I was briefed to represent was his wife, Jean. She was a red-headed girl with a wild gypsy beauty, frightened and overwhelmed by her arrest and remand in custody. She was also completely innocent of participation in the serious conspiracy with which she was charged. When one read the enormously lengthy depositions, the only thing that Jean had done was that on one occasion one of Charlie's terrified "debtors" had 'phoned up asking if his "debt" could be deferred slightly, as he was in financial difficulties, and it was Jean who had called her husband to the telephone. On that basis she was arrested and kept in custody for about four and a half months. Why? the reader may ask. The answer, I suspect, is that the superintendent in charge of the case believed that if Jean were kept in prison, away from her and Charlie's children – I seem to remember that there were six of them – Charlie would crack and confess and spill the beans regarding himself and all his co-conspirators. If that were the case he seriously underestimated Charlie, a man who thought only of himself.

The weekly visit to the cells at Bow Street was a depressing experience. Every week I found Jean more haggard, more desperate, but I had to pass Charlie's cell on my way to see her, and he would purport to give me fresh instructions. On one occasion they went something like this: "Now Jean's the only one with a good character, so she's the only one who can afford to cross-examine the prosecution witnesses about their previous convictions under section 1(f)(ii) of the Criminal Evidence Act 1898, so these are the questions that I want you to ask."

"Look, Jean is my client, not you," I replied, "and if I ask no questions at all at any stage, the magistrate or at any rate the trial Judge is going eventually to ask: "What is the evidence against this woman?" and, when he finds that there is none, he will discharge her. If I start wading in with a lot of cross-examination on character he will think she is after all implicated and leave her to the mercy of the jury." (Perhaps I recalled my own Court-martial experience in Trieste, over twenty years earlier.)

"I'm paying for you," said Charlie earnestly, "and I don't pay people for doing nothing." (I was sure that was true.) There were other altercations of this kind and my relationship with him was not a happy one: indeed, he did not seem a happy man; I never saw him smile. Sometimes he would assail me on my way to see Jean with some such greeting as: "I've been reading paragraph 1825 of Archbold and I think it can be turned to our advantage." I found it strange that the literature in the prison library should include Archbold's "Criminal Pleading, Evidence and Practice" and indeed that Charlie should be allowed to bring it to Court with him. But his mastery of the law and the acuteness of his mind were such that, given other circumstances, he might have been a formidable criminal advocate.

The conduct of the police in the case was disgraceful. It seemed as though, in their enthusiasm to obtain convictions, they were prepared to descend to depths of cunning comparable to those of some of the defendants themselves. This was particularly true of the officer in charge of the case. Unfortunately I cannot remember his name with certainty, otherwise I would reveal it, but I suspect that he is a man who has gone on to higher things in the Metropolitan Police Force. Generally speaking as defence counsel one has a friendly working relationship with the police who prosecute. This was certainly not so with this officer. Every week I applied for bail for Jean: every week, without warning me, this officer would produce to the magistrate some unexpected and in my view spurious reason why bail should be refused. On one such occasion I found him just before the Court sat and asked: "Well, are you going to produce any more surprises for me today?" "No, I don't think so," he replied casually.

So once more I addressed Geraint Rees, a generally discerning stipendiary, who was to become an Old Bailey Judge, but a magistrate who clearly had little time for and shewed little patience with any of the defendants – including the only woman – in the dock; begging for this lady of good character to have bail to go and look after all her young children who were pining for her. I thought at last I was making some impression, until the superintendent rose up and said: "There is a grave doubt as to whether they are her children. I had a 'phone call from a lady in the North of England last night claiming that the children were hers. I was expecting her to be here to tell you that herself, but she hasn't arrived. I understand there is trouble on the railways."

"Bail is refused," snapped the magistrate, spurning my application to put the matter back until two to see if this lady who allegedly claimed such prolonged intimacy with Charlie would arrive. (This police officer certainly knew his magistrate.) I bought the evening paper and found nothing in it about difficulties on British Rail and no-one ever suggested again that Jean was not the mother of her children.

Making bail applications in the Richardson case before Geraint Rees was a hazardous occupation. It was on one such occasion that a young pupil startled us all, as recited in more detail in "Advocacy for the Advocate", by rising up and, when the magistrate asked if there had been any change of circumstances since last week, replied: "Yes, there have been seven," and, counting slowly on the fingers of both hands, he added: "Tuesday, Wednesday, Thursday, Friday, Saturday, Sunday, Monday." Full marks for courage, if not for tact!

The magistrate realized that the effect of the heavily guarded prison van with all its police motorcycle outriders being brought to Bow Street every week was to disrupt London's rush hour traffic, so eventually he arranged for the remands to take place to and on Saturday mornings. On the last occasion, after I had ignored Charlie and made yet another abortive application for bail on Jean's behalf, my instructing solicitor invited me to lunch. He was Raymond Davis, who was a young man then, and still seemed young nearly twenty years later when he appeared before me at West London on behalf of one of the Richardsons' sons, charged with offering for sale obscene magazines in a shop in Earls Court. (Charlie was still in prison at that time.)

Raymond bought me an exceptionally good lunch as a solace for the bad news that he was about to impart to me. "I'm afraid I'm going to have to ask you to withdraw from the case. Charlie doesn't like the way you're handling it, and he's paying the bill." I must have looked disappointed, for it was the biggest case that I had ever been involved in, for Raymond added, consolingly: "You'll probably be glad to be out of it in the end." This proved completely true, for in the next year I was to find myself involved in a great variety of interesting work, while the sordid Richardson case dragged on for many weary, unpleasant months at the Old Bailey.

I saw Raymond Davis recently and asked after Charlie. (Jean was to divorce him, shortly after the trial, to remarry and go to live in Australia.) Charlie had by now served his twenty-five year sentence, but Raymond said that he no longer acted for him. "Before Charlie was sentenced," he told me, "he entrusted me with his gold watch, gold lighter and gold cigarette case for safe keeping. I was single at the time, and living with my mother. Our home got burgled, and Charlie's gold items all disappeared. Unhappily we were not insured. When Charlie left prison I felt constrained to replace them at my own expense."

In due course the Richardson trial came on at the Old Bailey before probably the wisest and most experienced criminal Judge of his day, Fred Lawton. After a couple of weeks, and long before the close of the Crown's case, the Judge asked Kenneth Jones, who led for the prosecution, and who is now himself a High Court Judge: "What is the evidence against the woman?" "Your Lordship has already heard it," replied prosecuting counsel, for the evidence about the telephone call had by now been given. "I have heard none," said Fred decisively, "Let her be discharged." It had taken many months, and a strong Judge, for Jean to get Justice.

The conduct of the police superintendent, who had been instrumental in having that innocent woman arrested and kept in custody, was not untypical of some officers of those days.

Like most people of my generation, I had been brought up to respect and trust the police, so it came as something of a surprise to find officers of the Metropolitan Force giving perjured evidence in Court; even more of a shock to find juries unanimously believing them. It was certainly the case in the 1950s that where the only evidence against a defendant was an oral admission, strongly disputed by the defendant, a conviction would usually ensue, and many weak cases were bolstered by such "verbals". Although accepted by juries, they were not always believed by Judges. In a murder case at the Old Bailey the only evidence against my Irish client (one of six accused of the murder) was an alleged oral two-line admission to two Detective-Sergeants.

"Did he make this admission freely and voluntarily, or did you and your colleague force it out of him?" I asked in cross-examination.

"Oh, entirely free and voluntary," came the not unexpected reply.

"Then why didn't you put it in writing and get him to sign it in a matter of this importance?" I enquired.

The Judge stopped the case against the defendant, but there were those in the public gallery who did not agree with his decision. Outside the Courtroom this group of "heavies" closed in on the former defendant as I was in the process of congratulating him, and he sped down the steps of the Old Bailey hotly pursued by them, never to be seen by me again.

A case which caused me more anxiety was that of a middle-aged man of impeccable character accused of burglary. He had returned home late at night and heard a noise coming from the house of his neighbour, whom he knew to be on holiday, so he entered the garden and was looking through the window when the heavy hand of a policeman descended on his shoulder. "I was looking for something to steal" was the remark that the policeman attributed to him to justify his arrest. We had evidence available from the neighbour, who had asked him to keep an eye on the house, and had returned from his holiday the following day, that a cat had got in and, in its efforts to escape, had knocked over a piece of furniture, causing the noise that had attracted the defendant's attention.

I was worried when the case at London Sessions got transferred from Henry Elam to Ossy McLeay. The latter had the reputation of being very prosecution-minded, and was extremely harsh on sentence: all of those convicted of burglary before him got sent to prison. But he stopped the case at the end of the prosecution evidence, and awarded the defendant all his costs. It so happened that a few nights later I found myself sitting next to Ossy, whom I did not previously know socially, at a legal dinner. "What did you make of that burglary case that I did before you the other day?" I enquired. "The officer was a bloody liar," Ossy replied laconically, but accurately.

I am afraid that many Met. officers of those days were liars – and worse. Barristers would discover this sad fact early on in their careers, but the ordinary members of the public, sitting on the juries, continued to believe and trust the police. On to this scene of lying and degradation came Sir Robert Mark, a Commissioner of Metropolitan Police appointed from outside the Force (he came from the Midlands). He quickly sensed the atmosphere of dishonesty and corruption in which he found himself, and issued a stern warning to what he called "the rotten apples" to get out, or be prosecuted. Some were brought to trial, and the matters that were proved against them were truly horrifying. Long prison sentences often ensued. Sir Robert's attitude and activities did not make him popular except with those honest policemen determined to do a decent job, but he cleansed the Met, at the cost, however, of bad publicity for the Force. The result was a far higher standard of conduct on the part of London's police, with much less credibility on the part of the public. Other factors have also influenced this change of attitude. The media image of the "bobby" of the 1950s was Jack Warner's stolid portrayal of the reliable, heroic PC 49 of "Dixon of Dock Green". "The Sweeney" and American police programmes have changed him into a slick, cynical creature, adept at cutting corners and not averse to dishing out a punch or two. So I recall a case where a man with an appalling criminal record was charged with attempted hijacking of a lorry load of whisky. He had been caught by police sawing away at the Crooklok on the steering wheel; he had signed a full written confession to the crime. At Court he claimed that the evidence of the police of his being in the cab of the lorry was "all lies", and that his confession had been obtained under duress. He had simply been taking his dog for a walk when the non-animal loving officers had pounced on him. (Dogs are always a good ploy with British juries.) A close friend called to give evidence for him on some subsidiary issue seemed surprised that he had a dog. Yet he was unanimously acquitted by the jury. Perhaps it did not matter much, as a week or two later he was arrested again for a similar offence. It could be that his recent triumph had made him overconfident this time, for he forgot the gloves that he had been wearing on the warm evening of his previous escapade, and left his fingerprints in the cab of the lorry, and juries do usually accept fingerprint evidence. So he got five years.

Sir Robert Mark was a good man; even, I would say, a great man. In a comparatively short time he achieved wonders for the Metropolitan Police. It was comparatively short because he resigned on a matter of principle regarding the question of whether complaints against the police should be investigated within the police service or by an outside body; I happen to disagree with him on this point, but I must confess that I know less about it than he does. His problems as Commissioner are admirably set out in his book, "Policing a Perplexed Society", of which I am privileged to have a signed copy. A brilliant writer, he is also a fine speaker. I well remember hearing him address a large group of black people at a dinner in the House of Commons arranged by Rudy Narayan. In answer to the challenge: "Why are there so few black policemen?"

237

he replied: "Send me the best of your boys, and I will accept them." It is unfortunate that not many responded.

Most of those who remained with the Met. under Mark were good, honest, decent men, who had to live down the Force's previous reputation for perjury and corruption. How had this come about? So far as the corruption element is concerned the question can be answered in one word, the same word that is the reason for most crime: "Greed"; but why officers should try to convict innocent citizens is more difficult to fathom. I am sure that their superiors do not want this to happen; yet the officer who has no successful arrests may not be the prime candidate for promotion. But I think that the reason for the untruths lies deeper. I think that it is something basic in us all. We all like to win; we do not like to be shewn to be wrong. Somehow also we ally ourselves with causes and will stick with them through thick and thin. If we are in a bus or a taxi involved in an accident we will automatically be on the side of "our" driver, even if we have not observed the cause of the accident – unless he has treated us outrageously. The police officer who makes an arrest espouses a cause. Back at the station, perhaps the case does not seem quite as strong as it did outside the pub: he is tempted to gild the lily to shew that he is right; the unobtrusive verbal is the simplest way of achieving this. There are a few barristers who will go "all out" to win. I do not mind so much when they are defending, but I deplore counsel for the Crown who cannot distinguish between the verbs "to prosecute" and "to persecute".

Improving the evidence is a temptation strongly to be resisted, and, since the advent of Sir Robert I believe that for the most part it has been; there are those, I know, who would say that I joined "the Establishment" about this time and that this has influenced my views, but I don't believe this; I am not an "Establishment figure". It is ironical that when many police in London (I rarely found this phenomenon outside the capital) were lying, their evidence was almost invariably accepted by juries and by magistrates, while now, when the majority are usually telling the truth, they are usually disbelieved, by juries anyway; and I feel that it must be very discouraging for the honest police officer, who has made a proper arrest and presented his account of the matter decently and fairly, to have his credibility savaged by defence counsel and then find that twelve of his fellow citizens doubt his word. It is the price that Justice is paying for the misdeeds of the past and the misrepresentations of the media, but he must derive consolation from the fact that the person to whom we all turn first in time of trouble is – a policeman. If our civilised society is to be preserved we must trust our police – and they must be worthy of that trust.

Chapter 16

How Goya Would Have Helped the Pensioners

Charlie Richardson was the only client who ever dispensed with my services (and he was not really my client). Another client failed to appear following a conference. He was pleading guilty to the most appalling cruelty to animals and had asked me what he would get, and I had replied: "I don't know, but I'll tell you what I think you deserve as you've got a previous for this sort of thing – a long sentence of imprisonment." He did not turn up at Court. On the morning of the hearing he drowned himself in a lake in Epping Forest.

Raymond Davis was right, and ultimately I was grateful to Charlie for sacking me. Had he not done so I would not have appeared in one of the most interesting cases of that decade, the Goya case.

One night in the early part of the sixties Goya's portrait of the Duke of Wellington disappeared from the National Gallery. It was a very large painting, valued at £4¼ million, and the hue and cry that followed its disappearance produced no clues, until a few weeks later letters started appearing addressed to the editors of various newspapers. The import of these communications was that the writer had the portrait in his possession and was prepared to release it on his terms. These were that a trust fund should be set up, the trustees being people prominent in public life, and he gave names from which they could be selected (the inclusion of Lord Boothby was perhaps not very judicious when he wrote to the editor of the Sunday Pictorial's sister paper, the Daily Mirror) and the object of the trust was to be the provision of free television licences for old age pensioners. The sum that he required to set up the trust fund, to be invested for this laudable purpose, was, I believe, £2 million – at any rate about half the value of the picture. He must have been disappointed that none of these public-spirited individuals shewed any inclination to respond to this worthy cause, and there the matter rested for over four years, the poor Duke receding once more into forgotten history.

Then, suddenly, another letter was received, nearly half a decade later, indicating that the Duke was waiting at New Street Station in Birmingham, and there he was, in the left luggage office. This galvanised the police into action again, and some weeks later a man by the name of Kempton Bunton was arrested in connection with the matter. His name was not the only unusual feature about him. A hefty hulk of a man, aged 63, a lorry driver and a bluff Yorkshireman, he held strong views on many topics, one of which was the iniquity of the television licence fee. He felt so strongly about this that he had been to prison over it many times. The way he saw it was this: the licence fee goes to the BBC, an organisation that he did not admire, so he adapted his set so that it would receive only the independent channel. (I think there was but one in those days.) He received no benefit from the BBC; ergo, he should not pay for the licence. This view was not shared by the licensing authorities, or by the local magistrates, who constantly fined Mr Bunton for failing to pay the licence fee, and then imprisoned him for periods of thirty days at a time when he refused to pay the fines. He always served the term of imprisonment: he was a man of principle. (He had no other criminal convictions.) His second strongly held opinion was that old people were often lonely, disabled and housebound and that the television was their only source of pleasure; therefore it was pernicious of the Government to exact from them a tax for something that was virtually a necessity. His various submissions to the Post-Master General on this subject all being ignored, he had to do something about it. So the Duke of Wellington was held to ransom. If the police had realized that they were dealing with someone holding fanatical views about television and had investigated the records of those who go to prison rather than pay for their television licence, the Duke might have been back on view in the National Gallery much sooner.

Initially Mr Bunton appeared at Bow Street Magistrates' Court, where a system of distributing legal aid cases among solicitors on the list to those defendants who did not ask for a particular legal representative was operated fairly and in strict rotation. In one way this was not very beneficial to the defendant, as the solicitor who got the case was a "one man band", who, for the sake of his other clients, could not devote his full time to the Goya case, and had no staff to carry out investigations and to send off on missions. On the other hand, Hugh Courts was passionately interested in art, so in a way this made him a suitable solicitor, even if his lay client did not share his enthusiasm. Hugh and I used to play squash together every Sunday morning (he invariably winning) and so I got the brief.

The lack of supporting staff in the solicitor's office was compensated by my having a most keen and conscientious pupil. Surendra Popat was an Indian from Tanzania who wanted above all to be a barrister, despite the disability of being paralysed since birth from the waist down, necessitating his moving everywhere on crutches. This did not prevent his making many journeys to help Hugh Courts with the enquiries necessary in this case, including several visits to the Colindale newspaper library to go through all the papers which had written about the Goya at the time of its disappearance, and the almost total victory that we were ultimately to achieve was due in no small measure to Surendra's enthusiastic efforts. Indeed, Hugh recognised this and applied for, and obtained; an ex gratia amount for Surendra from the legal aid fund. It is good to know that Surendra now has a highly successful practice at the Bar, and does not need such payments.

The committal took place at Bow Street, and the superintendent in charge of this case, in contrast to the one I had encountered in Richardson, was fair and helpful and decent; but he was not dealing with a real villain, only an eccentric nuisance.

The Crown indicted Bunton on six charges at the Old Bailey – public mischief, three counts of blackmail, one of theft of the portrait valued at £4¼ million, and the last of theft of the frame, valued at £98.

Public mischief is a vague, unpopular charge, and it was not difficult to get the Recorder, Carl Aarvold, to throw it out at half time. (I use that expression rather than "at the end of the prosecution case", because it seems more fitting for a trial conducted by a Judge of his sporting attributes.) The word "blackmail" did not appear in the Larceny Act 1916 under which Bunton was charged, although it is now a specific offence under the Theft Act 1968. But the essence of the offence is that a reasonable person would be put in fear by the "menaces" of the blackmailer, and the jury rocked with laughter when they were asked: "Can you imagine the editor of the Daily Mirror sitting trembling in his chair in case he got another letter from the defendant threatening not to return the Goya unless the editor got round to organising the Kempton Bunton Trust? Do you think that the editor is a man of such delicacy and sophistication that he cares two hoots whether the Duke of Wellington is hanging in the National Gallery or reposing in Mr Bunton's bedroom?" It was not difficult to get a verdict of "Not Guilty" on these ridiculous charges of blackmail.

That left the two theft charges. It is the essence of a charge of theft that the defendant should have intended permanently to deprive the owner of the property. But Mr Bunton had caused the picture to be returned, albeit in a rather unorthodox way. How could it be said that he intended permanently to deprive the National Gallery of it when he had shewn by his action the completely contrary intention, even if rather belatedly? Edward Cussen was prosecuting, and he tried to get over this hurdle by asking this question:–

"I suggest that the reason you kept this picture for all these years was because you came to like it?"

"Laike it," replied the Yorkshireman, looking contemptuously at Goya's masterpiece which was standing now in Court No 3 at the Old Bailey. "I wouldn't 'ang it in my kitchen!"

As in the case of Jeffries, yet to come, one was conscious again of two charming old gentlemen having a sparring match, as Cussen cross examined Bunton. At one stage he asked the defendant: "I suppose you told your wife you'd got this four million pound picture hidden under your bed?"

"If I'd told 'er," replied Bunton, "all Yarkshire would have known."

There was a moment of drama of which the jury (and the Press) never knew. Bunton was a very rotund man and it was a mystery how he had got through the narrow security bars at the National Gallery, carrying this enormous portrait. After its return (or rather its transportation to New Street Station) the left luggage attendant there had given a description of the man who had handed in the parcel, which resulted in the police producing a photo-fit of the man concerned, a young, thin man with a moustache and dark hair.

The letters purporting to blackmail the newspaper editors had all been rather badly typewritten. Bunton told me that he had no typewriter in his home and did not know how to use one. "Let's call your wife on that point," I suggested. "Call 'er," he said derisively, "do you want to ruin everything?" "Well then, call another close relative to like effect," I essayed, and one day this close relative appeared. He fitted the photo-fit picture exactly, and his slim figure could have eased through those bars at the National Gallery four years before. "Get him out of here," I advised, as soon as I saw him, "unless you want him arrested, too." We managed to get acquittals on the blackmail charges without risking his involvement, and Bunton was also found Not Guilty of stealing the Goya.

The case had considerable repercussions, even worldwide. Museums all over the world felt insecure and under-insured, and the cost of insuring works of art rose enormously. It was indeed this that caused the Heath Government to try to introduce for the first time museum charges in Britain, but it never succeeded in getting this highly unpopular measure through. Moreover the law of theft was changed, so that section 6(1) of the Theft Act 1968 reads: "A person appropriating property belonging to another without meaning the other permanently to lose the thing itself is nevertheless to be regarded as having the intention of permanently depriving the other of it if his intention is to treat the thing as his own to dispose of regardless of the other's rights; and a borrowing or lending of it may amount to so treating it if, but only if, the borrowing or lending is for a period and in circumstances making it equivalent to an outright taking or disposal."

Kempton Bunton has made his mark!

There remained the count of theft of the frame. This was a cunning charge, but logically the separation of the picture from the frame could be justified, because Kempton Bunton said that he had separated the picture from the frame. The latter he found too bulky to carry about, so he had left it in a cheap lodging house near Kings Cross Station on the night of the Duke's transfer from the National Gallery to less salubrious surroundings. (How Mr Bunton managed to keep the picture undamaged during its travels around the country was little short of a miracle.) Realizing the difficulty that the absent frame might cause, for his abandonment of it might be regarded as the clearest possible evidence of an intention permanently to deprive the owner (the British public) of it, I used the opportunity given to the defendant to speak at the end of the Magistrates' Court proceedings to make a statement on Mr Bunton's behalf. "Take this down," said the magistrate, Geraint Rees, sternly to the clerk, as I began my passionate appeal to the landlady to dig it out of some dusty cupboard in which it might have been lying for over four years and restore it to the nation. But the plea went unheeded and the Duke stood unadorned in the Old Bailey. This, no doubt, was why the jury convicted on the count relating to the theft of the frame. It was disconcerting, after hearing five verdicts of Not Guilty in the case, to have a verdict of Guilty on the final count. Even more disappointing was the sentence passed by the Recorder, Carl Aarvold, normally a kindly and understanding Judge, of three months imprisonment. There was no such thing as a suspended sentence in those days; otherwise surely he would have had one of those. Kempton took his sentence stoically and philosophically: "Well, one thing, I'll get free television there," he said as he descended the stairs, and on the evening of the day of his release I arranged a party for one of the most interesting and idealistic clients I had ever had. For several years after the case he would send me signed picture postcards, some of which I have had framed. They are all of the Duke of Wellington ....

Financially, however, the Goya case was not very rewarding. Mr Bunton was represented on legal aid and the taxing officer at the Old Bailey was not generous (or he was careful with public funds, whichever way one prefers to look at it). He was called Mr Black-Adder: I never met him, but those who went to appeal to him for more funds said that he lived up to his name. But if he could be persuaded that there were an element of fraud in the case that had been tried, then the public purse would be opened wide, and extraordinarily large fees would be paid out by the Bailey on legal aid in such cases. They usually lasted a long time – though nothing like as long as now, when they may drag on for nearly a year – and a young barrister could make what seemed like a fortune if he were briefed to defend (or to prosecute) in a fraud at that Court. So, although generally speaking fraud is boring, for mercenary reasons most of us wanted to do it.

In the mid-sixties Ronald Bartle had an extra reason for wanting to "do a fraud". He was about to get married and he and his fiancee had agreed to buy an old rectory in the country and desperately needed the money for the deposit. Ronnie and I were called to the Bar at about the same time and had always been friends and we shared a room at (though not in) QEB, which we entered in January 1962, being the first outsiders (non-pupils) ever to be invited to those hallowed Chambers (known outside QEB as "the Factory"). Another occupant of the room, who arrived later, was Paddy Pakenham, son of Lord Longford. Paddy described himself as "boisterous" and it was a not inept epithet. On one occasion he was swinging around his robe-bag, which contained his wig enclosed in a metal case, and it hit my pupil Roger Barby on the knee, hurting him quite badly. On another Roger and I had persuaded Ronald that he ought to have a bowler hat, though neither of us wore one. Ronald was (and still is) a stickler for etiquette, so we told him: "You must have a hat now that you're becoming well-known so that you can raise it to any High Court Judges you may meet in Middle Temple Lane. You can hardly touch your forelock or salute." This argument convinced him, so he went out and bought a bowler for £15 – a lot of money in those days. But Roger and I had reckoned without Paddy.

When I said that our Chambers were at rather than in QEB I meant that we were in the annexe at Garden Court, fifty yards off, and away from Robert's watchful gaze, so there were opportunities for fun, which took various forms. As Ronald returned proudly wearing his newly acquired bowler, Paddy, who happened to be looking out of the window, observed his dignified descent of the steps from Charles Lamb's fountain, and shouted out rather disrespectfully: "Cor, look at Old Ron in that titfer," and, before we could stop him, he had rushed down our staircase to greet the newly adorned Ronald by sweeping the hat from his head, hurling it high into the air. From then onward it was like an old Charlie Chaplin or Harold Lloyd film, as with horror we watched the bowler falling rapidly towards the railing. "It won't!" we gasped, but it did! It became firmly impaled on one of the spikes.

Ronald seemed rather crushed as, a moment later, he fingered sadly the hole in his headgear. "Look what you've done to my nice new hat," he complained, but Paddy was quite unabashed: "It's improved it," he observed. "I've provided you with some ventilation."

"What about when it rains?" asked Ronald, practically.

"You can buy an umbrella," said Paddy. "I know where there are some going very cheap."

I suppose that it was because Ronald was so good-natured that we could afford to rag him so much. He was extremely happy when, shortly before his marriage, his Old Bailey legal aid fraud case arrived on his desk. It was just the sort of case that Ronald – and indeed most barristers – would like. There were six defendants, but his client was right on the fringe of the fraud. There were hundreds of pages of depositions and scores of witnesses, only one of whom affected Ron's client. He would sit in the Old Bailey for six weeks or more, have to cross-examine one witness for about twenty minutes, take his own client through his proof of evidence for about half an hour, and finally make a brief effective closing speech – something that Ron was good at – before leaving the Court several thousand pounds better off. It was little wonder that Ronald looked sublimely happy, and would come in after Court each day and open the voluminous papers, and stroke the brief, and purr contentedly: "I like my fraud."

None of the rest of us had frauds just at that time and we got rather tired of Ron's smugness, and decided to shake him out of his complacency. I was the main perpetrator of the outrage, but Paddy and my pupils at that time, Surendra, Roger and Tony Wilcken – now a very successful barrister – were all co-conspirators.

Late on the afternoon of the day prior to the commencement of Ron's trial, the junior of all the clerks, John, then about seventeen (now a respected senior clerk in other Chambers) entered our room at Garden Court carrying a brief comprising one sheet of paper folded down the middle and not even dignified by being bound with red tape. Ronald was gazing beatifically upon his fraud brief, not untied now, because he knew by heart all the parts of the papers that affected his client, and had thoroughly prepared the case weeks before. Deftly John removed the big fraud brief from under his nose and substituted the rather grubby piece of paper. To our intense disappointment there was no reaction from Ronald as John made his way slowly towards the door, bearing the larger brief, so that I had to distract John with some ridiculously facile question in order to retain him longer in the room. Suddenly Ronald woke up:

"Heh! John. That's my fraud, what are you doing with it?"

"Oh," replied John nonchalantly, "it's going to someone else. Mr Rusk particularly wants you to do this important case at Clerkenwell tomorrow – personal friend of his or something. That's why he's marked up the brief fee."

"Yes, but my fraud …. I've got it all prepared."

"Well Robert says there's nothing in it really and one of the pupils can do it, and Mr Rusk's a valued client of Chambers. I don't know if you want to argue it out with Robert."

John did know that none of us wished to argue things out with Robert, and Ronald sat looking disconsolately at his new brief as John removed the old one from our room.

Peter Rusk was the solicitor we all liked least to have as a client; his instructions were quite appalling, and indeed I had refused to accept work from him before all this happened. His briefs, if not on legal aid, were usually marked two guineas, and none of us could understand why Robert tolerated him. Surely it could not have been the presents he brought round at Christmas time: ties for the clerks and bars of Cadbury's chocolate for those barristers who would still accept his instructions. Ronald's new brief was exceptional: it was marked three guineas.

Five pairs of eyes watched expectantly as Ronald sadly read right through his new brief. The son of a clergyman, he is not given to oaths or calling on the name of the Lord His God in vain, so eventually he sighed heavily and said: "Good Heavens. Just listen to this boys, it's even worse than usual," and he proceeded to read from the brief:

"The Queen Against Ivor Botham"

"The defendant is charged with indecent exposure on the steppes of Kensington Palace ...." He interrupted the reading to say: "Just look at how he's spelt "steps": "s-t-e-p-p-e-s–he thinks he's back in Russia."

Then he continued:

".... on the steppes of Kensington Palace, which, as counsel knows, is the home of Princess Margaret, although it is the Queen who is bringing these proceedings, and counsel is asked to take this as a preliminary point to squash the indictment. The defendant is NOT GUILTY of the offence, as he is an old friend of Instructing Solicitor from Leningrad, and counsel must put his best feet forward and fight tooth and claw to obtain an acquittal. Counsel is asked to stress that the defendant is a man of good character, having only two minor convictions for rape and incest."

It is the measure of the quality of Peter Rusk's briefs that Ronald, a barrister of about twelve years standing, read the whole thing through without realising that it was a spoof. Later on, Rusk was to transfer from being a solicitor to become a barrister, in which capacity he appeared before me on many occasions, with such devastating effect that I took to carrying around with me a little notebook in which I recorded some of his more outrageous and outré remarks under the heading of "Ruskies". But those I will save and savour for another occasion.

Unfortunately when Ronald was reading the brief aloud to us and reached the part about Princess Margaret, Paddy could control his mirth no longer and burst into raucous laughter in which we all joined. Ronald looked accusingly at me: "This is your work, Crowther," he alleged accurately. "What's happened to my fraud?"

"You'll find it across the other side of the passage," I replied, and it was a joy to observe his relief as he happily retrieved his real brief for next day from the lavatory.

So fraud cases, as taxed by Black-Adder, were lucrative both for the prosecution and defence, but generally speaking they were tedious. Accounts (even false ones) lacked the human touch. I am not very interested in figures – well, not in ciphers, anyway. One exception to this was the case of the Queen v. Secluna. I think that Mr Secluna was the client who fascinated me most after Kempton Bunton. An Indian, he was very different from Bunton, a thin, ascetic man who reminded me in some ways of Mahatma Gandhi, although he always wore a suit. He neither drank alcohol nor smoked and he was a vegetarian who, to judge from his gaunt appearance, even ate very few vegetables. A man of few words and great dignity, he was ready to take his lawyers' advice on all matters; an easy client.

Mr Secluna was charged with seventeen counts of fraud on his former employer, for whom he had worked for many years as an (unqualified) accountant for the paltry wage of £15 a week. The employer was a rich man who spent little time at the business premises, preferring the race courses, where he gambled heavily, while Secluna beavered away in the office. As a result of Mr Secluna's falsification of the accounts, it was alleged, many thousands of pounds had gone missing. They could not be traced into his meagre bank account in England: the suggestion was that they had been sent to his family in India.

The case took place in the days when the police were still trusted, by juries and the public. So there was no written contemporaneous interview with each answer initialled, no signed confession under caution, but after a lengthy interview the police officer had simply gone away and made up his copious notes, not even bothering to get the defendant to read them through or sign them. Nowadays a signed interview, supported by a video recording, will be challenged, often successfully, on the basis of "tampering" or that the admissions were obtained by a threat to withhold bail. It was all different twenty years ago, and the reality was that this was a trustworthy officer: I had had him against me in fraud cases before, and had found him to be a man of his word, and this was worrying. His words came out very forcefully, as he had an extremely loud voice, which boomed forth like a twenty-one gun naval salute.

The officer's apparent integrity caused me much anxiety, because part of his evidence against Secluna was extremely damaging. During his long interview, Secluna had said that he had altered the figures under duress from his employer, who was always needing extra money to pay his gambling debts; and this was Secluna's case at his trial (denied, of course, by the employer). But then, towards the end of his statement, Secluna had stated that because of what his employer had been ordering him to do he realised how easy it was to commit fraud, and the last four false entries were for his own benefit, as he was very hard-pressed for money, and he agreed that he had purloined about £2000.

It would have been easy to have argued that under the strain of continuous questioning by the police officer the frail Secluna had given way, and briefly but wrongly admitted a small part of what was alleged in order to end his ordeal, and, after hearing the officer's booming voice, the jury might have accepted that contention. But that was not Mr Secluna's case: he had never admitted to those last four offences; he had never stolen a penny.

It was a strange trial, the only one that I ever had with an entirely female jury. The Judge was Bernard Gillis, QC, a man rather conscious of his own dignity – or, more fairly, perhaps, of the majesty of the law of which, as a regular Old Bailey Judge, he was an important instrument. A stickler for etiquette, he was rather prosecution-minded and quite severe: Secluna, although of previous good character, was likely to get at least three years if convicted of any part in this fraud on his employer. On the other hand Bernard Gillis was a courteous and patient Judge, with, I suspect, a kind heart beneath a strict visage.

The prosecutor I knew well. A decade earlier he had taught with me for two summers at Sizewell Hall, and we had had great fun opposing each other in the Fines Court there. At the Bar he was not such fun: he was a man who dearly loved to win, and, as he almost invariably prosecuted, this was not an attitude to be commended; I hope that he is fairer now that he is a Crown Court Judge.

At the beginning of the trial my opponent came and confided in me: "Eric, this is the first really big case that I've ever had from the Yard and I'm anxious not to lose it. You've got quite a reputation now for getting villains off." (I was flattered). "Can't you persuade your client to be sensible, and I'll put it mildly? Why won't he plead guilty?"

"Because he says he is not guilty," I replied simply.

"Well, what about pleading to those last four counts? He's admitted them to the officer."

"Yes that's the trouble," I sighed. "I'll go and have another word with him."

"I'll do whatever you say, Mr Crowther," said the defendant, "I know you have my best interests at heart, but I did not say that to the officer."

"Then you will plead Not Guilty to everything," I advised.

The main witness for the prosecution, the employer, did not cut a very pretty figure in the witness-box and, under cross-examination, it became apparent that he was as Secluna had described him, a profligate spendthrift, and I could tell that the ladies of the jury did not like him. But the police officer sailed deftly through my cross-examination like a battle-scarred destroyer steering through a poorly-laid minefield, and came into harbour unscathed. The Judge was riding against us, so it would all turn on my closing speech.

The trial, which lasted a week, had not been a very pleasant one, mainly on account of the antics of my opponent and the unfair methods that he was adopting to try to secure a conviction. I was constantly protesting, and my objections were usually upheld by the Judge. He was due for leave the following week, so he sent the jury out just before four o'clock on the Friday afternoon, urging them to try to reach a unanimous verdict. (There were no majority verdicts in those days). At nine o'clock he called them back into Court with a view to discharging them and ordering a re-trial. "Have you been unable to reach verdicts on any matters?" he asked, rather wearily.

"We have agreed on thirteen of the counts," replied the foreman (or forelady – I refuse to use the expression 'foreperson', which I think is silly). A peevish expression came to the face of my opponent who realized, as did I – and I am not an optimist by nature – that these must be verdicts of Not Guilty. When these had been duly delivered the ladies of the jury were invited to retire again, and I began to think out afresh my plea in mitigation in respect of only four matters now. At eleven at night the Judge recalled them, and I feared that he would tell them that as they had been unable to reach a verdict after so long he would discharge them and there would have to be a re-trial on another day. I dreaded the possibility. Re-trials are never easy for the defence. For one thing the prosecution knows what the defence is going to say; and in this case the four counts in respect of which Mr Secluna was alleged to have made admissions would be isolated from the rest. But Judge Bernard Gillis took a very unusual and, I thought, generous course. He ordered the jury to retire yet again, adding: "It is very desirable in the public interest that you should reach a verdict in this case tonight. You have not accepted the prosecution case on thirteen counts in this indictment. Perhaps this should influence your decision on the other four."

I found this the more remarkable because throughout the case he had demonstrated that he believed the defendant to be guilty. By 11.15 p.m. Mr Secluna had been acquitted of all charges.

The Associate then handed me a note asking me to go to see the Judge. I wondered in what way I had assailed the dignity of the Court this time, but the Judge was not wishing to rebuke me. Instead he said: "Crowther, I am, as you may know, rather fussy about the use of the English tongue, and I should like to say that your closing speech was couched in the language of Shakespeare and Milton, and pronounced with perfect diction. Congratulations. You deserved to win."

This was not the view of my opponent, who was just about to leave the robing room when I arrived there to change. He stamped his foot petulantly and said: "You've ruined everything. I knew you would!" And he stalked off, leaving me alone at the Old Bailey as midnight approached.

But I was bitterly disappointed. The defendant had left the dock rapidly after his final acquittal, for which he had waited more than seven hours in the cells. I had looked for him outside the Court room, both before and after seeing the Judge, but in vain. I had wanted to congratulate him and (I must confess) to be thanked for my, as I felt, not inconsiderable efforts on his behalf. But he was nowhere to be seen. It was a midsummer evening, but some lines from Shakespeare about the winter wind being not so unkind as man's ingratitude came to mind. So I was sad, lonely and weary as I descended the steps of the Old Bailey so late that night with only Archbold to accompany me. And there, at the bottom of them, stood Mr Secluna. He walked towards me and clasped my hand, and held it warmly in both his hands for about a minute, and he did not say a word, but by the lights of London I could see that there were tears in his eyes. And there were some in mine, too, as without a word having been spoken, we parted there, outside the most famous Court in the world, never to meet again.

Chapter 17

Walking the Tightrope:

The Transition from Barrister to Magistrate

The Indian student's question, designed to embarrass the Chief Magistrate, Sir Frank Milton, did me no harm. When we were free we used to go in a group from Chambers to have tea at the A.B.C. in Fleet Street, and I am such a heavy drinker (of tea) that I associate the closure of that branch shortly after my appointment as a magistrate with the withdrawal of my custom. On my return one Tuesday afternoon in April 1967 I asked James, our sixty year old 'junior' clerk: "Any 'phone calls while I was out?"

"No, not really," he replied.

Now you cannot practise for seventeen years at the Bar without recognising an equivocal answer when one is given, so I pursued the matter in cross-examination.

"Look James, either there was a 'phone call or there wasn't. Has there been a 'phone call for me?"

"No sir, nothing important." he answered.

"James, please allow me to judge what is important. Has anyone 'phoned me?"

"No, only some bloody stupid woman from the Lord Chancellor's Office. Wanted to know if you wanted to sit as a deputy stipendiary for the next two weeks. I told her that you'd got no time for that sort of bloody nonsense."

"But wait a moment, James. I'm booked to go on holiday for the next two weeks. If I sit as a stipe instead, how does it affect you?"

James withdrew his position slightly. "Well, Robert says you've been looking a bit pale lately and you need a holiday, so as to be fit for all the heavy cases he's got lined up for you when you get back."

I was touched by Robert's solicitude for my health, and pleased that I had won him over to the idea of my having more than one weeks holiday a year.

"James, will you please ring this lady at once and tell her that I'm available?"

"Probably too late now sir, she'll have got someone else. You shouldn't stay out so long at tea. Robert's mentioned that to you before."

"Well at least try ringing her at the Lord Chancellor's Office."

I saw him mis-dial several times, and realized two things: first that the clerks did not want to run the risk of losing me now that I was beginning to reap a profitable harvest for them (which I found rather flattering) and, second that there were no clerks' fees on sitting in temporary judicial office – although I understand that Ronald, Robert's successor, has now instituted such a system of commission.

Eventually I became impatient and told James to let me have the telephone and I rang Katie Lorimer, who is certainly not a "bloody stupid woman" but a charming, intelligent and helpful person, who was still working in the Lord Chancellor's Department more than twenty years later. Fortunately she had not got anybody else, and so it was agreed that I would receive a letter appointing me to sit as a deputy stipendiary magistrate at Clerkenwell Court for the next two weeks at a fee (or a salary) of, I think, £17 a day.

I was delighted; not so my family. We had planned a fortnight's holiday at the Bedruthen Steps Hotel in Cornwall. We finished up with a week-end on the Isle of Wight. That Tuesday night I wrote to the hotel explaining that I had had what was tantamount to a summons from the Queen to sit in judicial office for the period of our proposed holiday and that therefore my wife and I and our two children would not be able to come. The hotel management were not impressed: they sued me for the price of the holiday. I employed the services of a Cornish solicitor whom I had liked when we had been on opposite sides in a case in Redruth a few months before. He told me: "The Judge here is always on the side of the hoteliers. I advise you to pay into Court half of what they are claiming." I did, and it was accepted. My first two weeks as a metropolitan stipendiary magistrate were not very rewarding financially.

So we set off for the Isle of Wight in 'Fifi', my little Fiat Cinquecento. As the ferry left Portsmouth Harbour it started to rain, and it rained with ever growing intensity throughout the whole

255

of that extremely morbid week-end. So heavy and continuous was the rain that the only time I set foot out of our hotel was to cross the road to a sports shop which I had observed opposite to buy a yachting cap in order to convince Ronald and Paddy and my pupils that, come wind and rough weather, Crowther would be out there, braving the elements.

We returned home on the Sunday night, under conditions approximating Noah's flood, and, as the water rose above the floorboards, I started to wish that Fifi were amphibious. It was still raining next morning when I set off by bus and tube for Clerkenwell Magistrates' Court (I did not take Fifi, as I was not sure if parking spaces were provided for deputy stipendiary magistrates, and in any case the Court is quite near to Kings' Cross Underground). Not normally a particularly punctual person, I made a point of being very early that morning. I had heard somewhere that "punctuality is the politeness of princes" and I saw myself, rather pompously, as the representative of the Queen, and so I had to be on time. In fact, I was far too early. I arrived at 9.15. I was a little disappointed that there was no red carpet out to greet the new magistrate, but I put this down to the still falling rain.

The Court was closed. Imperiously I rang the bell. Nobody answered, either then or when I repeated my call. It seemed that all that I could do was to wait on the steps of the Victorian building that was to be my first seat of judgment. It was still raining. I was wearing my last pair of pussers' (naval) shoes and my last pussers' raincoat. Both had given me legion service, but had seen better days and were letting in the rain. A cascade of water fell onto my head from the awning above the narrow step. I felt utterly miserable on this, my day of triumph. Although it was the beginning of May it was still cold, so I put my hands into the pockets of my raincoat and, in one of them, to my comfort and relief, I found the yachting hat that I had acquired two days earlier. Fearing another overflow from the awning I put the cap on my head, returning my cold, wet hands to my pockets. And it was while I stood there, thus attired, that a little old man came up to me and said: "Good morning, guv'nor. What are you up for this morning?"

I dealt with the situation, I thought, with great dignity and diplomacy. "I'm not UP for anything as you put it." I replied coldly (in every sense of the term). "I'm here because I'm interested in the administration of justice."

"So am I guv'nor," he retorted. "They've got a new beak 'ere this morning, and I want to see 'ow 'e makes out."

I did not think that this conversation could profitably continue and so I withdrew for a cup of tea to the comparative comfort of a nearby workmen's cafe, from which I returned about three quarters of an hour later, when, to my relief, the Court was open. My first usher was a little surprised, I think, when he came for me, to find the new stipendiary with his shoes and socks off, drying his wet feet in front of the gas fire. Footwear restored, I entered Court Number Two of the Clerkenwell Magistrates' Court and bowed to the members of the British public who stood there in the gallery, looking like a sad collection of portraits by Hogarth. But one had rather more life in him, and I noticed that he was winking and waving at me. Then I recognised him as the man who had greeted me about an hour earlier on the steps. That was the first time that I had realized the significance of having "friends at Court".

Suddenly, as I settled down on the Bench, an awful realization came to me. I had the power to deprive a person of one of the most precious gifts that God has given us – liberty. All went well for a while with the simple offences of drunkenness, obstruction and prostitution with which Magistrates' Courts usually deal early on in the lists, but then the crunch came: a man of twenty pleaded guilty to stealing quite a substantial sum from his employer, and at the time he was on probation for having stolen from a previous employer, the second job having been found for him by the Probation Service. It was an obvious case of imprisonment in those days: it would not be now, but at the time there was no restriction on imprisoning people under twenty-one, and thefts in breach of trust almost always attracted custodial sentences. I tried to steel myself towards the inevitable, but then his mother came forward, a pathetic little woman, desperately worried: "Oh don't send my son to prison, sir," she begged. "He's a good boy at home. I've got another boy who's blind, and they're such good friends. He reads to my blind boy every night."

The tragedy of their impoverished lives came home to me, and I compromised with my conscience by sending the defendant to Quarter Sessions for possible Borstal training, but I did so on bail; I just could not send him away on my first day.

The previous Friday I had received a telephone call in Chambers from someone who said that he would be my clerk on my first day and would help me in every way he could. I could not quite place the accent: was it Welsh or Irish? When I arrived I found that I had the first black clerk that I had ever seen. Billy Strachan (whose son now often appears before me) was immensely kind. He invited me to a pub lunch over which he advised me: "You've got to make decisions, man, if you come into this job. That's what it's all about. You should have sent that young man to prison; and, as a matter of law it was wrong for you to put him on bail if you were committing for sentence."

He was right, of course, but he had not sought to embarrass me in Court by showing me up – unlike 'Sergeant Major' Mindham at Bow Street who delighted in such practices. On one of my sentences he commented, more to the general public than to me: "It's probably a very good idea and a pity that Parliament won't permit it." The Sergeant-Major and I did not get on well and when he saw me for the first time after my eventual appointment he greeted me with, "We-e-ll sir, you made it," and it was not difficult to read into his comment the unspoken words: "In spite of all my efforts."

But Billy, who afterwards became a Chief Clerk with his own Court (Hampstead) was good to me, as was his chief, the jolly, delightful and highly practical Mr Worthen. Billy was a very erudite man – possibly the clerk most learned in the law of all the clerks that I have ever met; he is in great demand as a writer in legal magazines. After sitting with him that first Monday I felt stronger and better equipped for my tasks and soon I had hardened my heart and was sending people to prison with the worst of them. Offenders were incarcerated far more readily twenty years ago than they are now, despite the rising crime rate. (Quaere: may not this more tolerant attitude be the cause of our having to tolerate more of it?) If I came into Clerkenwell with a whimper I went out with a bang, for on my second Saturday there appeared before me five defendants, including a woman, arrested for what was, I believe, Britain's first great bullion robbery. I remanded them all in custody: it was probably the wrong decision, as all were subsequently acquitted by the Old Bailey jury.

Thereafter I sat many times during the next three months at Bow Street, West London, Thames (my favourite of the London Courts) and Wells Street (my least favourite: it is like a computer centre; a sort of extension to the Fixed Penalty Office.) At West London I replaced Ronnie Guest, one of the most intelligent and intellectual

of the London stipendiaries, who was going blind: a particular
tragedy as his great passions were books and pictures. (He is, I
believe, still alive). I was asked to take his place on an evening
session in West London Court to give young police officers practice
in the presentation of evidence: this was great fun. I seemed to be
sitting more than any of my known rivals, so it caused me great
dismay, as already recorded, to read in "The Times" on my birthday
of that year of the appointment of Edgar Bradley, clerk to the Poole
Justices, as a London stipendiary; a job that he was to do supremely
well.

By now I had almost persuaded Robert of the need for long
holidays if one was working very hard, and I was booked in
September to go on a six week lecture tour of the United States.
Two days before Elke and I were due to sail from Rotterdam to New
York, James, the "junior" Clerk entered with a rather smug look on
his face. "That bloody woman from the Lord Chancellor's Office
has been on the 'phone again, sir. Wanted you to sit for six weeks at
Marylebone starting Monday. I told her you'd got more important
things to do."

"Get her on the phone, James." I said again, rather desperately.
"I want to talk to her."

Katie Lorimer was immensely kind. I explained to her that my
family and I had given up Cornwall for Clerkenwell, that these
lectures in the States were very important and I did not like letting
people down, and that I had had only one break this year, a wet
week-end in the Isle of Wight. "Miss Lorimer," I said finally. "I've
sat a lot as a deputy. I don't want to be always the bridesmaid and
never the bride. What do you advise me? Should it be America or
Marylebone?"

"My advice is that you should go to Marylebone," she replied
firmly, and the next day a good friend, an Admiralty barrister, was
on his way to Holland to pick up the S.S. Groote Beer to sail to New
York in my place, and for the second time that year Elke was
deprived of a holiday.

I remember those six weeks sitting at Marylebone as being among
the happiest of my professional life, despite the appalling building in
which one was forced to work. Marylebone Magistrates' Court was
– and is – an old swimming bath, and the magistrates and clerks are
always going off the deep end about the dreadful state of that
unsuitable edifice. But the staff were immensely helpful, and at the

259

end of my 'stint' I was invited as guest speaker at the Court's annual dinner at Lord's Pavilion. I began: "I intended this year to spend my six week summer holiday in America: instead I spent it at Marylebone." The speech went well. After it, Mr. Penfold, the very kindly Chief Clerk, remarked to me: "If you're looking for an appointment as a stipe, sir, I shouldn't worry too much." Up to then I had wondered who was watching my performance on behalf of the Lord Chancellor, unjustly suspecting several 'men in machintoshes' in the public gallery: now I felt that I knew.

Marylebone has always been a fascinating Court with a great variety of work affecting a large cross-section of society, with good defence advocates like Neville Coleman (the "Solicitor – General" of Marylebone), and Roger Sanders, now a Crown Court Judge, then a young barrister, just cutting his very promising teeth, appearing before me. It was a beautiful September and, Elke having decided to visit her native Germany, instead of going to America, most evenings were free to take my beloved Labrador for long evening walks in Richmond Park, a luxury not available to us when there was a brief to work on for the next day. The Court work was invariably interesting, and full of surprises. I shall never forget the last case that I tried there during those six weeks, on the final Saturday afternoon.

It was a contested case of wilful damage, now known as criminal damage, and the protagonists were two very respectable-looking, well-spoken middle-aged ladies, whom I will call Mrs. A. and Mrs. B. Both came to Court in very sober dark dresses, and each was wearing a large hat: they might have been going to church for a funeral rather than to Court for a trial, but in those days people used to dress up to come to Court. (Nowadays many of them dress down for the occasion.) Neither party was represented; neither had any witness. I invited the complainant to give her evidence, which she did in a dignified and composed manner.

Mrs. A. said that at about two o'clock one morning she was sleeping in her basement flat in Paddington when she was awakened by a screeching of brakes and a squealing of tyres and, by the light of a street-lamp, conveniently situated just outside her flat, she saw Mrs. B. (whom she knew) alight from a car, carrying a package, which she proceeded to unwrap, and, a moment later, Mrs. A. was to observe Mrs. B. throw the contents of that package, comprising two bricks, through her bedroom window, which, not surprisingly, broke. To reinforce her story she brought along two bricks, some broken glass and a damaged curtain.

Mrs. B. denied it. "It wasn't me," she said. (In fact she appeared so elegant and well-educated that she probably said: "It wasn't I.") And that was the whole case.

Well, one wants to try to show that one is taking a lively interest in what is going on, especially when the parties are unrepresented, and one way of doing this is to ask what one hopes sounds like an intelligent question. "Mrs. B.," I said ponderously. "You've seen Mrs. A. in the witness-box and you've heard the manner in which she has given her evidence." (I pause to stress again the appearance of matronly respectability of each of these two ladies). "Can you give me any reason why I shouldn't believe her?"

"Yes," Mrs. B. replied calmly. "I can give you four reasons why you shouldn't believe her."

"Go on," I encouraged.

"She's an abortionist, she's a brothel keeper, she's a prostitute and she's a police informer."

I was very surprised, but when I had recovered from the shock of this unexpected information I turned to see the reaction of Mrs. A., whose demeanour had changed completely. Her former quiet dignity had deserted her: her whole body was shaking with rage, her complexion kept changing between red and white, and the feather on her hat was quivering angrily.

"Madam," I asked nervously. "Would you like to ask her any questions about what she just said?"

"Yes," she shouted, pointing an accusing finger at the triumphant looking Mrs. B. " You – why the hell do you say that I'm a police informer?"

That afternoon I learned that the people of Paddington have their pride.

But, after Marylebone, there followed a fall-off in my sittings, my just being called on to do the occasional day at Wells Street when, presumably, the regular incumbents there were bored out of their minds. (I don't mind trying traffic cases relating to moving vehicles, but when they have all been standing still it is tedious beyond endurance.) Alongside this there was a diminution in my work at the Bar. The clerks had lost faith in me as a future investment and, save when solicitors insisted on my personal attendance to do cases for them, it was Yard prosecutions at Uxbridge and the like for me, and my income fell dramatically. Once again I found that I was 'neither flesh, nor fish, nor fowl', but walking a delicate tightrope between Bar and Bench.

It was after a few months of this that Robert ushered me again into 'Mr. Jeremy's room', where I had my first interview with him seven years before. For the first time he spoke to me of my partial desertion of him. "Mr. Crowther," he began softly, "why don't you give up this mad idea about being a stipendiary? It is the lowest form of judicial animal life and you're worthy of something better. I see you in silk, like Mr. Durand and Mr. Jeremy, and eventually on the High Court Bench. You never saw Marshall Hall, did you? No, he was before your time. The idol of the crowds he was. They used to come for miles to the old Bailey to hear him. You remind me of him in so many ways. I can see you there, like him, in the front row . . . . ." His eyes misted over with a mixture of nostalgia and prophecy: "Wouldn't you enjoy the adulation of the crowds, Mr. Crowther?"

"They've all got television," I pointed out. It had been a brilliant performance, but he had failed to convince me.

"Robert, if they'll have me, I'm going to be a stipe." I said.

"All right," he retorted sharply, "if you want to ruin your life, that's up to you," and he stamped angrily out of the room. It was clear at any rate that I had ruined my practice.

This being so, I sought an interview with the Secretary of Commissions to the Lord Chancellor, Sir Thomas Skyrme, to try to find out what my chances were. He, too, like Robert, seemed to be trying to discourage me from becoming a metropolitan magistrate.

"Have you thought of taking silk?" he asked.

"Or applying to be a County Court Judge?

Or a deputy chairman of Quarter Sessions?

Or a chairman of an industrial tribunal?

Or a provincial stipe?"

To all these questions I replied meekly but stubbornly: "No, I just want to be a metropolitan stipendiary magistrate, that's all."

Perhaps Tom Skyrme, shrewd man that he was, was just testing my resolve, for eventually he replied: "Well, there will be a vacancy at the end of July and I can't tell you more than that there are three likely candidates under consideration and you are one of them. The announcement will be made towards the end of July. If selected you would be sworn in by the Lord Chief Justice on July 30th and you would start to sit on July 31st. Would that suit you?"

Remembering, perhaps, how playing coy and hard to get had reaped such dividends with British Rail, I replied: "Not really. I'm due to sail with the Sail Training Association in the Tall Ships' Race as purser on either the 'Sir Winston Churchill' or the 'Malcolm Miller' during the last two weeks of July, and it's too good an opportunity to miss. We should be sailing into Gothenburg on 31st July, so I won't be available for the Lord Chief until after then."

Sir Tom's handsome face brightened: I had said the right thing. "I think the Lord Chief Justice might be prepared to sit specially early for you on 1st August, and we could cover 31st July; if you are selected by the Lord Chancellor, that is," he added, with typical bureaucratic caution. Then he went on:

"I sailed into Gothenburg Harbour on my own yacht many years ago. Wonderful sport, yachting," and the rest of the interview was devoted to what was obviously his main leisure interest in life – just as Roy had spoken continuously of his days in the R.A.F. sixteen years before, but there (apart from their good looks) the similarity between the two men ended, for Tom Skyrme was one of the most conscientious and industrious people that I have ever met. I came away feeling that I was likely to get the job that I had coveted since childhood.

But thereafter not all ran quite so smoothly. I was not sure who one of my two 'rivals' as revealed by Tom Skyrme was (possibly Christopher Lee, or Mark Romer, who were appointed soon after me, but who, although we knew each other well, were far too gentlemanly to raise such matters with me) but there was no doubt as to who was the other one.

Melvyn Carstairs was an elderly barrister whom I knew well as we had often been opponents. He had a vigorous, rather hectoring style in Court and I remember once hearing him rebuked by dear old Walter Raeburn when I was defending at the celebrated West Ham Quarter Sessions, where almost nobody was ever convicted, for hurrying through his cross-examination of the defendant in a bullying manner. "Kindly do not rush matters and confuse the defendant," said the Recorder – one of the kindest men that I was ever to meet – "a man's liberty may be at stake here" (he was under-estimating the West Ham jury once again) "and all of us need time to consider the matter."

Even so, I got on well with Melvyn, and so when he came to see me in my Chambers one evening I listened to him sympathetically.

He spoke to me in the same staccato style that he had used to cross-examine the defendant at West Ham, in his efforts to wear down my resistance.

"Listen Eric, I had a bad war. Captured and tortured by the Japs; made to work on the Siam railway; malaria and lost half my guts. Never been really fit since. You had a good war, didn't you? I came to the Bar with no money and no prospects. Always poor. Rotten clerk at first. Hell of a struggle, working like a dog now. I need a rest. I need this job as a stipe, and I've been sitting quite a lot as a deputy. I've been to see Tom Skyrme and he tells me I'm one of three in line for the next appointment. You're obviously my keenest rival. If you're appointed you'll be the youngest ever to get the job." (This was inaccurate, as both Ronnie Guest and Nina Lowry were younger than I when appointed).

"If I don't get it now, I'm finished. I'm nearly twenty years older than you. They won't want me any older than this. It's my last hope. You've got plenty more chances.

"You've always been a good friend of mine. Get in touch with Tom Skyrme and tell him you don't want it this time. Ask him to postpone it for a little while. I'll never forget it if you do. Why don't you write now?"

It was a moving performance, and I nearly did as he requested, but I remembered the words of Walter Raeburn (one of my referees, as a matter of fact) and I said: "Don't rush me. I need time to think. Give me a few days."

"All right," he said, "but don't take too long. The suspense of this is making me a nervous wreck, let me know soon. It's my only chance."

Thereafter he rang me daily, but each time I procrastinated. "I haven't made up my mind yet," I said.

About a week later I received a brief (a small brief, now, of course) to appear at Marylebone. When you spend a lot of time at a Court, either as a magistrate or as an advocate, you get to know the jailors well. It is wise to cultivate them. If, as an advocate, you are on good terms with them, your cases will come on early. If, as some young barristers do, you treat them arrogantly and offensively, they can give you hell. In my long time in the law I have come across only two whom I disliked. They were both bullies: one, many years later, I had removed from West London because of the way he treated defendants. All the rest I have thought to be doing their difficult job considerately and admirably. Those at Marylebone were particularly kind.

I was not before Carstairs on the morning in question, but when my little case was over the jailor took me to one side.

"Your colleague in the other Court, sir," he observed. "I don't think he's all there. He spends all his spare time with us asking us about you and what you did wrong when you were here and if we had any complaints about you. He says there's only you standing between him and a permanent appointment. He's got a fixation about it, sir, and it's not healthy. And we don't like the way he treats people in Court – young police officers and defendants. But if he goes on the way he's been carrying on, neither of you will get the job."

"I'll go and see for myself," I said, and so I sat in Carstairs' Court. I did not like what I saw. Carstairs was very brusque with everyone, a cross between Glenn Craske and Colonel Batt, thought not quite as offensive as either. Lists were (and still are) long at Marylebone. He had not finished his morning list at one o'clock when a young barrister rose to his feet:-

"I wonder, sir," he asked timorously and politely, "if you would be kind enough to hear my case before you rise. It is only a short plea lasting about five minutes and I have another case to do at South Western at two o'clock."

"Certainly not," snapped the deputy magistrate, "I want my lunch. You can return one of them." and he signalled to me to follow him to what had been my room.

"That's the way to treat 'em. Young whipper-snapper," he commented; then with a change of tone, he entreated; "What have you decided to do about the matter we discussed?"

"Nothing," I replied. "Just nothing."

"Why not?"

"From what I've just seen I don't think you'd make a very good magistrate. You haven't got the patience, and you've already forgotten what it's like to be at the Bar. I think you're suffering from 'magistritis'."

"Listen, Eric," he pleaded. "Let me take you for lunch."

"No thank you, Melvyn. I don't feel like any lunch." (I would liked to have said: "I have another brief at South-Western at two o'clock," but those days were over.)

"The matter we discussed is closed."

Melvyn did not get the next (or any) appointment; he was to appear before me, surly, resentful and rude, a few times, and within a year he was dead. It is a pity when a man's ambition becomes an all-consuming obsession. I have known, later on, a similar fate befall another man who would, in my view, have been a most admirable stipendiary, but was never appointed because of something unwise that he did off the Bench, and who reached an equally tragic end.

Robert and James raised no objections to my joining the Tall Ships Race in mid-July 1968 and I flew to Aberdeen to join the Malcolm Miller. The weather was tempestuous and, after making several vain attempts to land at Aberdeen Airport, the 'plane eventually finished up at Glasgow, whence we were ferried by bus through flood-like conditions to the city of the Northern Lights, which we reached at about four in the morning. I feared that the ship would have sailed without me, but the sea was far too rough for that, and in fact we stayed for two more nights in the docks of Aberdeen. This enabled me to get to know the ship's Captain, Glyn Griffiths, very well, and we found we had a lot of interests in common, perhaps because he had been for many years a probation officer. I had seen many fine captains in the Royal Navy, but Glyn was by far the best at instilling loyalty and enthusiasm into the boys under his command. One thing that made him interesting was that no one ever knew what to expect of him next. On the third wretched evening in Aberdeen he lined up his ship's company on the deck and he said: "I've just received the weather forecast. There's a Force 8 gale blowing and things aren't likely to improve here for the next three days. This is a fairly new ship and it's never been at sea under such bad conditions. On the other hand if we don't sail we'll miss the Race. It's a difficult decision. Our purser spent several years in the Royal Navy under wartime conditions, so I'm going to let him decide. Do we sail, Purser?"

I was taken completely by surprise, but was aware of about forty pairs of eyes watching me anxiously, and I was not quite sure of the nature of their anxiety: was it about risking their lives, or missing the race? I decided that what these young lads had all come for was adventure, so I raised my fore-finger, contemplated the prevailing hurricane pensively like an old sea-dog, and then said: "We sail!" There was a loud cheer, echoed many times thereafter by everyone aboard except the sixteen year-old boy who lost both his sets of false teeth overboard that first very rough night.

After twelve hours during which everyone aboard except Glyn and me was sea-sick – I have never been sea-sick, I am glad to say – we awoke to find ourselves encompassed by perfect sailing weather which prevailed for three days until we arrived in the little Danish harbour of Frederickshaven. It was a wonderful cruise. I had come to like and admire Glyn very much and had confided in him that my whole future was probably being determined at this very time that we were sailing across the North Sea. One of the watch officers had a similar, but more distressing, problem. A large American company had taken over his electronics firm and made him redundant, at the age of about fifty – a horrible situation. He had put a 'situations wanted' advertisement in many English newspapers and was waiting to get to Denmark to telephone his wife to see if anyone did want him. No one did.

I was sitting with Glyn in his cabin not long after we had reached Frederickshaven, but I had failed to notice that he had and was reading a copy of 'The Times'. Suddenly he looked up and said sympathetically and sincerely: "I'm awfully sorry, Eric, it's not you." I shuddered. "They've appointed a stipendiary magistrate but his name is Raymond. Funny he should have the same surname as you."

"Let me see that," I said, as I snatched the paper from him and read that "Raymond E.J.R. Crowther has been appointed a metropolitan stipendiary magistrate with effect from August 1st." My mother had many good qualities but decision making was not one of them. Having christened me Eric John Ronald, she decided that she did not like Eric and so she went back to the Registrar and persuaded him to add Raymond. Afterwards she changed her mind again and decided that Eric was preferable after all, to my great pleasure, because I detested the name Raymond. Somehow the Lord Chancellor's Office had got hold of the name that I had hoped had passed into dissuetude (from Lincoln's Inn, I suppose). Let Glyn take up the story from there:–

"Eric looked at the paper, whooped with joy, rushed onto the deck and took the dinghy ashore and when he returned several hours later he was nothing like as sober as a judge but nearer to being as drunk as a lord. He had with him in the dinghy four females whom he had found somewhere ashore, and enough champagne for everyone aboard."

The champagne, very expensive in Denmark, was welcome; the

267

girls were not. "Those girls are not coming on my ship," declared Glyn. "Not over my dead body. Take them back ashore immediately." It was the only time during the fortnight's sail that I saw him angry. Later on, girls (British-made ones) were permitted by the Sail Training Association to participate in the Tall Ships Race (and they usually won) but by then Glyn had retired to be a social worker in Hampshire.

Sir Thomas had been as good as his word and Lord Chief Justice Parker had been persuaded to sit specially at ten o'clock on August 1st with two other Judges of the Queen's Bench Division to swear me in, in the Lord Chief's very impressive Court. That ceremony over, Lord Parker, before whom I had appeared many times, indicated that he wished to shake hands with me (a custom not normally permitted between members of the Bar) and the usher placed a chair in position for the purpose. I was not and am not particularly slender, and, as the Lord Chief grasped my hand, I felt a chair leg give way beneath me. There was an embarrassing moment, but I got my hand free and jumped off the chair in time to avoid disaster.

Then I got into Fifi, my little Cinquecento, and drove all the way down the Wandsworth Road to South Western Magistrates Court, at exactly thirty miles per hour; after all, I was a magistrate now, and those who enforce the law should uphold the law. It was encouraging to realise as I drove along that so many other drivers obviously realised my triumph over Melvyn and my other unknown rival, for a lot of them hooted as they passed, and a few even gave me the Churchill 'Victory' sign.

Due to my keeping so strictly within the speed limit, it was 10.35 by the time that I got to Lavendar Hill, near Clapham Junction, where my first 'own Court' was situated. Outside on the pavement was Mr Hayward, the Chief Clerk, and I am afraid that I misinterpreted the up and down movements that he was making as being jumps for joy at my appointment. They were not, for his countenance, as he greeted me, was dark, and he said:

"Five minutes late on your first day! This isn't very good, is it, sir? I hope you'll try to do better in the future."

"I've been with the Lord Chief Justice," I explained.

"Now, sir," he went on, "don't try to make excuses ...."

This was my first lesson in the independence of the Judiciary. There were many more interesting lessons to be learned, and many more rewarding experiences to be enjoyed, and many fascinating cases to be tried in the years to come – more years even than the seventeen that I had spent at the Bar – but the relating of those must await my retirement, as I do not wish to end up in any kind of Pickles. I will not alter this decision, despite the advent as Lord Chancellor of Lord MacKay, who most welcomely has expressed himself in favour of a kind of "Judicial Glasnost".

Index